A Year in Acting Class:
Critical Thinking for the Actor

I have always loved rehearsal. I especially loved listening to the director's notes. Even the notes that weren't for me. Over time, I discovered that I learned and grew more from the notes given to the other actors than I did from the notes that were given to me.
I hope you have the same experience with this book.

Let me introduce you to the actors who will be in class most often:

Alejandro had studied with lots of teachers in Chicago before making his way to Southern California. Otherwise, he's new to acting. (about 3 classes each week)

Polly is new to acting. She's been in class about a year before this book starts. (Once a week)

Joe has been in this class for several years. The first class he ever attended was here at The Workhouse. Over the last two years, he has been a busy, working professional actor. (Once or twice a week)

Jen never acted before studying at The Workhouse. (About once a week)

Debra is a semi-pro actor with a lot of experience. (Once a week)

Shawn has not been an actor before. (About once a month)

Al is a semi-pro actor with a lot of experience. (Several sessions)

Ann has had a few acting jobs. (About once a week)

Talia joins the class in May and continues for the rest of the year. (Once a week)

There are also several other actors who drop in for a few sessions.

Welcome to class!

Duane

Let's get started…

January/February

I sometimes say that all human beings are qualified to act because we're playing human beings. If you're a human being, raise your hand. Okay, you're qualified.

Sarah, anything I can do to be helpful?
I don't think so. I think we've got a good premise of making it real.
Good.
Having the video playing in your head, which I've never heard before so that's pretty cool.
I think it's a concept that is unique to this study. In our technique the video is where the truth lives. Like if I asked you who your favorite high school teacher was in your real life, your answer is in your video. You're seeing your favorite teacher?
Right now I am, yeah.
If I ask "Who's your favorite teacher?" you wouldn't know what to say until you saw a picture.
Right.
I see a guy in a bow-tie and I say, "Oh yeah, Mr Peebles." If I say Mr. Peebles without seeing a guy in a bow-tie, something's off. That cannot be true. So the truth is always in the video. And that's central to everything we do here.

I don't think I had the video.
You know where you did? Your daughter's disability. Did you shoot a video of a very hyperactive little girl?
Yes.
I think in that moment, you did have video.
Okay. Okay.
I was really glad to see that. I can't read your mind but sometimes I think I can. And I think you saw your husband Tom a little better?
Yeah.
You have a better video of Tom, don't you?
Yeah.
What I'm watching for out here is if you tell the truth. And when you have video you have truth. That's what I want you to work on as we move forward. But you're seeing glimmers of how that might work, right?
Yeah.
At one point, you really saw something funny and then you said "It was funny." The more video you shoot, the more you have a reason to say that. Because your video made you say that.

When you first receive your dialogue, none of that video is there. That's what your job is. You have to provide that. And do it in all the details. Then make sure you use that video to propel the language. Don't let the language go unless the video makes it go. *Okay. Yeah.*

You're grasping all of these concepts well. Good work so far today.

Sarah, you've spent some time thinking about this.
It's what I want to do. I don't want to give it up.
No reason why you should. You seem like you're talented.
I hope you would tell me if I wasn't. You could be like, "Sarah, just stop." (laugh)
I'll be honest with you. I've never seen anybody that I wanted to say that to. Everybody can act. It's just how hard do you want to work and are you smart and can you take direction and are you flexible and driven and how thick is your skin, can you take rejection? Those are the questions but I don't think there's anyone who doesn't have the ability to do it. So I've never said "You shouldn't do this." Besides, I think it's a good thing to do. Whether we build careers or not, it's a good thing to do. It creates more love and beauty in the world.
Yeah.
Speaking of love and beauty, let's have Joe and Alejandro step to center stage.

Joe, how did that scene go for you?
I'm sure some things were different. I was taking a different approach. I was thinking about what you said about persona.
Joe. I really liked how you took that on. Who you decided this guy was. You were totally believable as a guy who has spent his life in boxing. And I liked the gusto with which you dove into this character. As you alluded to, you were concerned with creating a persona, and I think you succeeded in doing that. I'll have some adjustments for you but I really liked who you decided this guy was. And my notes might simply be, if this was stage, I think you're fine. I don't think I'd want to pull you back if this were a stage performance. But for camera, I don't want you to be quite so "good" at what you're doing. It felt a bit deliberate.
It was.
Right, we were working on persona. But the camera will catch you at that. So keep in mind, camera is a "fail" medium. We have to avoid the good way. But if this were stage, I'd be like, "Give that guy a callback. That looks to me like a boxing manager if ever there was one."
There are a number of good things happening. I like the habits and instincts that you're developing. Which include arrows from here to here and keeping the scene active and full of events, as opposed to predictable. And I've been mentioning for a while that your

rhythms are good in general. I think there might be times in this scene when you're prioritizing rhythm over video.

Correct, yes.

And I want you to watch out for that.

Going easy on myself, I think that's part of the developing process.

It is.

Natasha, how is it going?

It doesn't feel real.

Why do you think that is?

I'm not sure.

When we are acting, there are two brains at work. One is Actor Brain and that's you - that's who you really are. The other is Character Brain - this young woman you're playing who's father-in-law is visiting. So the more video you create for her, the more fully you can live in your Character Brain. In your Character Brain you're thinking about your daughter, you're thinking about your husband, how great your relationship is... and that makes you stop thinking in Actor Brain, thoughts like "How should I say this?" or "What should the line sound like?" Those are Actor Brain thoughts. The Character Brain is where we're going to find our truth. So the more we can submerge ourself in Character Brain, the better.

Okay.

When we do that, we can keep Actor Brain quiet, which is usually judging how good we're doing.

The more you shoot the character's video the more you'll start to care about what's happening, care about her, care about the details of her life.

One of the greatest things about being an actor is that you get to fight for people you've never met. And show what a beautiful human being they are despite their flaws and vulnerabilities. That's the great thing actors get to do. And this is just an everyday young woman, you know? She isn't a superhero. She's not the president. She's just a young woman with a kid and a husband trying to do the right thing. Those people are worth fighting for. We get to show the beauty in that. To show her struggles.

One of the phrases that has been coming up lately is "It's hard to be a person."

Yeah, it is.

It's hard to be a mom with a special needs child. It's hard to be in a relationship. That's hard work. That's part of the vulnerability of almost every character. A teacher, a mom, a parent, a student, "It's hard to be a person."

That's how the audience can care about you. When they see that you struggle like they struggle. We all struggle together. That's a bond you can create with your audience when you're letting the audience inside those thoughts. It's hard to be this person. She has a great family and a good relationship, but it's still hard.

That's a thing I find really compelling that we can bring to our work and fight for people we've never met before. People who are just trying to do the right thing. But it's hard to do the right thing. And if we represent that, we're developing characters that the audience can identify with and root for.

I like that.

Does that feel actionable as well?

Yes.

Here is a note about your eyeline. Sometimes your eyeline wanders a bit too much. That can be a way of us deflecting the audience's eye. So I'm going to ask you to take on the technique of "I dare you. "I dare you to knock me off my mountain. I'm right here. I'm going to stay here and give the audience access to my eyes." By using "I dare you," we can actually invite the audience's eye in. How does that sit with you? That "I dare you" idea with your eyeline.

It will take me a while. That makes a lot of sense. I know that I do that. I think that's really my Actor Brain.

Great. I agree with you on that. And when I ask you to play "I dare you," initially that will all be Actor Brain, but it's going to cause you to create a deeper well of Character Brain, because you're not letting Actor Brain get away with Actor Brain tricks. It's going to force you to now fill in the blanks more in Character Brain. Does that feel actionable?

Yes.

One thing I say to almost every student at some point but I don't think I've said this to you yet. There is a scientific study[1] - this is science, it's not me - which tested various professions, and the profession with the most testosterone is actors. They were tested against firefighters and football players, and actors have the most testosterone. Football players have more muscles, firefighters face greater dangers but actors have more testosterone.

So where that "I dare you" idea comes from is trying to get my testosterone in my belly pumping. Get my killer instinct, my "Try to knock me off my mountain…" more of that kind of energy flow.

I can see that.

Many studies suggest that one of the greatest fears known to man is public speaking, which is exactly what we do as actors. That's the greatest fear. So no wonder actors have the most testosterone, because what they do is the scariest thing there is.

That leads me to think that when it's time for me to act, it's time to get my testosterone pumping. It's time for me to get competitive, to get dominant over my environment, to take control. Those types of energies in Actor Brain are very welcome. Does that feel actionable?

---

[1] Heroes, Rogues and Lovers: Testosterone and Behavior - James McBride Dobbs, Mary Godwin Dobbs, Authors. (2000)

Yeah.

When we were talking about testosterone, did yours get going a bit? Did you feel that buzzing?

Yeah. (laugh)

Yeah, get that testosterone buzzing. We need that. Because acting is one of the scariest things ever. We need extra bravery.

Nature is on our side when we activate our testosterone. Obviously actors come in all shapes and sizes and genders so it's not about muscles. It's not about growing a beard or whatever. It's not about those things. Everyone has testosterone and so when it's time to act, it's time to bring mine. Does that feel actionable?

Yes.

You look a bit like you're already feeling more powerful.

Mm-hmm. Yeah.

Good. That's always welcome. Because the camera is intimidating, the scenes are intimidating, the lines, directors, casting directors, audiences, critics, that's all intimidating. So we need all the testosterone we can muster to neutralize all of that.

Natasha, how was that adjustment for you?

Good. I still think it needs work but it's going good.

Me too. Regarding the "I dare you" approach, I was glad to see you - I know it was a little bit in Actor Brain, I saw it pulling you out of Character Brain, and that's to be expected, it's a new note for you - but there were moments when I think you settled into it and I'm hoping that in those moments you discovered that it was powerful. What do you think?

Yeah. I definitely felt more… more powerful in the scene. I felt like I could stand tall, be sure in myself and be more playful.

Good. I like how you're folding that into your process. Does that feel actionable moving forward?

Yes.

Shawn, I really think you have a gift for this and I encourage you to focus on it. If you feel like launching yourself, headshots and all of that, I think it would be appropriate for you. You're marketable and naturally charismatic. I think you should take advantage of that. You don't necessarily need a big plan or to know what you're doing. Just be open to the possibilities.

I think a big part of that, it's a lot of fear. I'm even working on this in other areas. It's just something… I gotta get over it. Even my wife tells me "Hey Shawn, you should try. Go do this." I struggle a lot with confidence. I'm just like "I don't know if I'm all that." If I became more confident and less fearful, I think it would be a lot better for me. I'm just trying to figure out how to do it.

I would never have assumed, to talk with you or watch your work, that you are lacking in confidence. But I really appreciate you sharing that with me because it's one of my favorite things to talk about.

One of the titles I was thinking of for my next book - I'm not going to use it - but the title might have been "Confidence. It starts with F." *(laugh)*

That's hilarious.

You can use the F word any way you want to in order to gain confidence. A phrase which is related to being in front of a camera or casting director is - whenever I'm lacking confidence or self judging and I hope you don't mind if I swear but the phrase is - "Fuck these people." And it doesn't matter if it's Spike Lee and Steven Spielberg I'm auditioning for. Take that on.

And you can say "F my thinking" as well. Being pissed off is one of the best places for an artist to be. You can even be pissed off at yourself for not having all the confidence you need and deserve. That's okay. Get mad. Do anything you can to adopt confidence, even if it has to start with F.

You mention that anger but how do I channel it? There have been times in my life when I've been angry but I've been out of control.

Thanks for the chance to talk about this. The way anger is constructive in our work is this: I'm going to show the audience how ugly they are when they behave in a certain way. I'm going to put in your face - Mr. Guy in the Third Row - how ugly you are when you behave like this. I'm going to confront you with your ugliness. That's a very constructive way to use your anger.

I see.

Maybe in a scene I'm small minded. I get to show small minded people how ugly they are. I'm empowered by that. They're out there. Small minded people are watching, bigots perhaps, are watching. I have the power to show the audience how ugly they are when they behave that way. Small minded, prejudiced, manipulative, selfish, whatever it is. I'm going to show you your ugliness. I'm not going to sugar coat it and let you off the hook. I'm going to enjoy confronting you.

Love is on your side. The powers and forces of love are with you. The universe and currents of love are on your side. To help you powerfully tell your loving story. And sometimes the loving story is an ugly story. But ultimately it's still a loving story. Whether I'm playing a small minded person or a bigot. It's still a loving story by demonstrating the lack of love in these characters. I hope that makes us feel empowered in relationship to these emotional values.

Definitely.

And look how powerful it is for the audience to hate a character. That is so fun. Or for the audience to fear you. It's hard to embrace being hated or feared but when we look at the power of that dramatically, it's so fun. I invite you to relish it.

The other side of that coin is the compassionate side of that coin. To share how difficult it is just navigating life. "It's hard to be a person."

When you're doing this kind of work, it's not because you think you're "all that." It's because the world needs your voice. Your voice deserves to be heard. Loudly and articulately. Through you using your voice, you're adding love to the world. So love is on your side. You don't ever have to doubt that. You don't need to think "Who do I think I am?" The winds and currents of love are at your back. Realize that you're not doing this for selfish or self aggrandizing reasons, so don't make that assumption about yourself, that that's why you would do it, because you think you're awesome. It's not because of that, it's because the world needs more love.

Very powerful.

I hope that stays and resonates with you.

More than I can say. Thank you.

I was thinking about when you said "Help a Buddy Out."

That's a fun and productive way to think about our work. Because we can often feel the pressure and the focus is all on ourselves. But we can be thinking: "How can I make the other actor better in this scene? How can I help the other actors? I'm not even going to worry about me. How can I help you?" The other actor in the scene.

And that can take the pressure off of ourselves, when we "help a buddy out." And it's good that we're identifying little ways we can do that in our scenes.

Help them say their line. Help them have the truth to say their line. Do the thing that will help their truth. If they say "Stop laughing." Laugh. So they can say stop laughing.

That's it fundamentally. If they say "Cheer up." Be down so they have a reason to say "Cheer up."

Those occasions are kind of obvious, probably. If the actor says stop laughing, perhaps any actor can see the need to laugh. But it's more nuanced than that.

We can also "help a buddy out" by being affected by their story. Find them interesting That's really worth focusing on: How can I help this other actor look good? How can I help them tell their story in the most powerful way? And I don't have to focus on me. I don't have to worry about that.

You've heard me say, "Don't say the sad line sadly." And I think it might be appropriate here. The lyrics of the language and the tone… they sort of match. On the nose-ish. Perhaps a bit more variety, vocally, musically. Investigate your perspective on the lines. The inquiry of "Can the sad line be said with hope somehow… the lonely line with affection?" I wouldn't want the piece to melt down into something, I don't know, innocuous?

A lot of people may have difficulty with the idea of confidence. Perhaps out of a sense of modesty or humility. To these people it would feel aggressive or over-bearing to assume confidence. It might be against your nature to inflate your ego - It might feel as if you're putting the other person beneath you.

That viewpoint is admirable. Compassion and being supportive of others are excellent traits. In fact, you are one of the people who most deserves confidence. The world needs more people of compassion to speak loudly. Your voice needs to be heard. Your confidence is serving the world.

As your voice becomes louder, you more powerfully proclaim a loving story. We speak louder to create greater change. Maybe for most of us it's acting, music, dance, film. The social cause that you choose to fight for. In one way or another these are all loving stories. All great art is. Get in touch with the loving story and help us fall in love with it, too. The world needs more love.

Another reason people may avoid confidence is because they fear overdoing it. They might think "Well I would be confident but I don't want to become one of those cocky blowhards." Great. I don't want you to become one of those cocky blowhards either. And it's perfectly reasonable to have that fear. Once you assume confidence, it is possible to overdo it.

For now put that fear aside. The confidence we are seeking is simply to make us comfortable in our surroundings, not superior to them. You are secure in your mind that you don't need to put down others in order to feel whole. Confidence is not based on anything outside of yourself.

EMMA / KIM Scene

KIM
Terrible night.

EMMA
Yeah.

KIM
The cops will be looking into everything.

EMMA
Yeah.

KIM
They'll want to talk with everyone, I guess.

EMMA
Yeah. (pause) Who?

KIM
People who knew Jeffy. People who know Roland. Knew Roland... That will include us.

EMMA
Well, I didn't know them very well.

KIM
You went to Roland's wedding.

EMMA
Three years ago. Since then, I've hardly seen him.

(pause)
KIM
Are you sure?

EMMA
What do you mean?

KIM
I thought I saw you at Hoopers.

EMMA
What? When?

KIM
Yesterday.

EMMA
What did you see?

KIM
The two of you were having a discussion. There was a Caesar salad on the table. You were sharing a salad, right?

EMMA
What else did you see?

KIM
That's it.

EMMA
Well… it didn't mean anything. I just bumped into him. So I sat down a minute. I ate some salad because I was hungry. Is there anything wrong with eating a little salad?

KIM
I don't care about the salad, Emma! I care about why you didn't tell me about it.

EMMA
About what?

KIM
About seeing Roland!

EMMA
I don't have to tell you everything!

KIM
You have to tell me about this! Emma, Roland is dead.

EMMA
It has nothing to do with me. I ate a little salad. I talked about my job. That was it.

KIM
Emma, you are one of the last people to see him alive!

EMMA
Purely a coincidence. I just happened to be going to lunch at Hooper's and he was there. That's all.

KIM
Why were you going to Hooper's? You hate that place.

EMMA
I was meeting some work friends there.

KIM
Who?

EMMA
Why are you giving me the third degree?

KIM
Why are you acting so weird? Did you go to Hooper's to meet Roland or some work friends?

EMMA
I don't know.

KIM
What do you mean, you don't know?

EMMA
I don't know, okay? I don't know.

Oooh. I want to know what happens next. Ann, how's it going?

Okay. I say okay because it feels kind of good. I had fun.

Great. Fun is always welcome.

I have a lot of questions like who are these people?

And what's going on?

Yeah.

Is Emma hiding something?

We come to believe she is. Because of the dialogue.

Good. When I Sherlock Holmes this, I think she's hiding something.

Yeah.

And when Kim says he saw you at the restaurant yesterday, you were like, uh-oh I'm caught. Was that part of your thinking?

No. Not really.

Because I'd like to see this played as, throughout the scene, there's something that you're not saying about Roland being dead. You're not volunteering that you saw him for lunch yesterday, you say you've hardly seen him. You've hardly seen him except for yesterday? So there's something that you're not saying. And I don't know if it's that you were romantically involved or there's some kind of financial dealings or bribery or extortion, but something's going on. And I'd like to see that you have that knowledge throughout the scene. And I don't know what the secret is but I know that you have one. I want to see the wheels turning even though you may be saying "I hardly knew the guy." Okay?

I can see that now.

I want to see your wheels turning. That'll be fun. I want to see that there's a secret there that you don't want to get out. Maybe you're protecting him or his legacy, maybe you're involved in money-laundering, something's up that you're not saying.

You think I killed him?

I doubt it. But maybe you know something, he owes a lot of money or a drug deal gone bad or he's got a little something on the side or you're a little something on the side. You certainly didn't tell your best friend about seeing him yesterday.

And Joe, the whole beginning of the scene, you know too. You know what you saw. I think you're fishing right away.

I am.

I'm not seeing you fishing. I saw it about 5 lines into the scene...

I just came up with something...

OK

I just went with it, that because of her, she's bringing attention to me, too. That I have something to hide. And I know she's involved in it, too. I had that element. Maybe that changed what you were looking for.

Great distinction. Let's break that down. I want to look at the central story. What do you think this style is? May I surmise it's a mystery overall, yes?

Yes.

Mystery, drama, could be a soap opera but it's in that genre of mystery, yes?

Ok.

And I like the approach, Joe. The bringing "The thing that's not the thing" with you that you just mentioned.

But it's not appropriate...

In David Mamet's book (*On Directing Film*) he says something that I think is appropriate here. Basically we don't want to have two mysteries. We don't want to give the audience two paths. Which one of them is suspicious? As Mamet says, We don't need two reasons that we're late for work. You can't say "I'm late for work because I was stuck in traffic and my aunt fell down."

Right.

Which is it? Were you stuck in traffic or did your aunt fall down? We don't need two reasons. One reason is cleaner. It's a really lovely distinction he makes there. We don't need two reasons we're late for work, just one. So in this scene, the second story that you also have something to hide, might muddy the waters. I really just want all the

pressure on her. When I Sherlock Holmes the scene, that's what I see. I just want to put all the pressure on Ann's character.
Because she's the one that's obviously hiding something.
Right. When I Sherlock Holmes it, that's what I see. So we don't want to superimpose a second storyline when the one is cleaner and stronger and tells the essential, powerful story.
And that would fix your earlier note about being suspicious at the beginning.
Right! *(applauding)* You saw what you saw before the scene begins.
Something that might be fun for us to think about: Sometimes the story is just about the other person, it's not about me at all. As much as I love the diametric thinking and the juxtaposition of ideas that we talk about… sometimes the story simply isn't about me,
It's about the other person. We talked earlier about "Help a buddy out." So in this scene, I think your job is to tighten the clamps on Ann's character. Put the pressure on her.

Ann, let's look at it from a different angle. What do the writer and director of this scene hope for? What are they fantasizing this scene can become?
They want to pique the audience's curiosity?
I do agree with that 100%. But by doing what? In addition to being curious, I want the audience to feel a sense of panic on behalf of your character. Not merely be curious. If I - out here in the audience - were her? I don't want to be implicated, I don't want to go to jail for 25 years. We're just finding a way to tell an impolite story. My belly would be on fire as this scene happens because I'm getting caught and my life will be ruined. I don't want to go to jail. And the audience can understand that panic. I want to see what we can do to get their bellies going. And I'm asking Joe to put the screws to you in this scene and your job is to feel that vice tighten. To see how much pressure you can put yourself under.
I sometimes mention the concept of "Impolite story." Joe, here your Actor Brain can think "How do I tighten the vice on Ann?" and Ann you can think "How much pressure can I be under?" And then this scene is ready to explode.
To make the audience curious is an intellectual pursuit but to make them panic is a belly pursuit. You see what I mean? The belly is more powerful than the brain.

Joe, your work is continuing to improve. I want to think about another concept. Let's look at something differently.
I want to think about the yin and yang of communication. Sometimes you're yin-ning really hard but you're not leaving room for the yang. And that can mean you're thinking "I'm going to give you the answer to how I'm feeling right now" as opposed to always leaving room for exploration, leaving room for the audience's curiosity. So avoid answers. Answers are anathema to what we're doing. So bring more yang. Leave room for the audience to explore.

How can I be of help?

How can we make solid, active choices in a short amount of time?

That's a very good, succinct question. A great launching point for today's class. *(pause)* Tension and release. Whatever I'm doing - when it becomes its best - there's going to be tension and then there's going to be release. How you find tension in a scene and how I find tension in a scene might be different, but as long as there is heightened tension and then satisfying release, we're good. Whatever we're doing is good. That's ultimately why we do all the stuff like "arrows" and "meal changes," etc. It is so that we can create tension for our audience and then the smart, satisfying release of tension. That's what powerful acting and storytelling is. Creating tension and satisfactory release of tension and doing that throughout the process.

Bottom line. If the audience's belly is going and then the belly stops going and they go "Aaaah." And then the belly starts going again, that's what we're after. Then we've got them. And that tension can be discovered and implemented in so many ways.

When we approach our work like that, that's the first thing I'm trying to do. I'm not even trying to "act good," I'm trying to create and release tension, productively. Because that tension is what causes the audience to be involved.

Without tension, the audience is not involved, they're observing but they're not involved. Tension makes them involved. That's how we get their butterflies, their goosebumps, their laughter. That's why we do everything else, so that in the moment, there is tension and release.

And I'm on the edge of saying, even if I gave you a script right now and said "Go." and you'd never seen it before, you don't need to know any of the facts of the characters or the situation, or anything. All we need to do is create tension and release tension. You don't even have to know what the lines are, necessarily, Because there are so many ways to create and release tension, regardless of the dialogue.

We have to be smart regarding the style. If I'm doing a show for eight year old kids there's a different tension than for adults. But it's still tension. The joke is "What's going to happen?" and the laugh is "Oh, that happened." So it's there throughout. No matter how you apply it, it's going to be relevant to the audience's experience. Even Jack and the Beanstalk is tension. Of course it is. That tension is drawing me in, and that release is giving me a moment to catch my breath, laugh, enjoy.

Each moment of each scene is either building tension or releasing tension.

Getting back to your question, we see that after some rehearsal and discovery, what we have found when the scene gets good is those moments of tension and release. We might not see those opportunities at first glance or first rehearsal but over the rehearsal process that's what we are finding. Those opportunities for tension and release. And that's really what our job is, regardless of story.

I never really heard that before.

Well, your question got us into an interesting discussion. When everything else is stripped away, we're finding our way to making the audience a participant in the experience. That tension is curiosity so they lean forward and when tension is released they lean back and digest.

And we'll find that, in the equation we're discussing, tension - and creating tension - is about eighty percent of what we're doing and release is about twenty. Just to give you a gauge.

I like that.

Does that feel actionable?

Yes. Yes.

Great.

It takes a weight off my shoulders.

Alejandro, I like the way you are putting things together in your brain. I can see how you are taking all the puzzle pieces and putting them together so they become a craft. Nice work. Fundamentally, tension and release.

Tension and release.

Or we can say "Tension, tension, tension, release." That's closer to the ratio we're after. Great conversation.

How can I be helpful?

In audition scenarios, how important is it that I follow all of the stage directions?

You're in the LA market and when you audition for film or tv, it's very likely the writer is in the room. They'll have input in casting. And keep in mind, by the time you, the actor, have seen the script, it's probably the fourth or fifth draft. If it's made it all the way to the actor? They feel it's significant. Nothing in the script is there carelessly. If the writer wrote something, they might feel betrayed if you don't do it. So that is my counsel overall.

On the other hand, if the writer is not there, I pay little to no attention to the stage directions. The other side of that coin is "I don't want to be told what to feel. I want to do it and see what happens and make it powerful." And it could be that what I come up with is more powerful than what you intended. It can often happen - and should often happen - that the actor surprises the writer with how profound a scene is. Directors surprise writers all the time. "I didn't know I had written that good of a script until the director directed it." And sometimes "I didn't know the scene was that good until the actor acted it."

That's sort of the norm - or certainly a norm - is that the scene improves when handed over to the actor.

But with the politics of the audition process, I suggest you fall on the side of the writer's intentions. If you see other opportunities, we can sprinkle those in but do try to fulfill what the writer has in mind.

And the same thing story-wise?

We can't change the story, the events in the script. The same as it's not our job to improve the dialogue. Our job is to do what we're given but do it powerfully. We don't have to change anything to make the material its most powerful.

Now of course the specialness and uniqueness that is you, that is always welcome in the mix. You, doing it the way you think it should be done. But what you're doing is what they're telling you to do.

It's smart to make a distinction here between things that they're asking for physically - like "He opens the door." and things they are asking for emotionally, like "sadly" or "with regret." But either way they have expectations and we have to sate their expectations. We have to quench their thirst for the moment. Because if they're still thirsty for that moment, then we've missed it, right? So we've got to quench that thirst.

At the same time we might sweeten what we… We can sweeten what they're drinking. To take that analogy a bit too far, *(laugh)* we might sweeten the beverage. I don't want to leave them thirsty for a moment while I also might sweeten what I'm offering them to drink.

I think it's quite common that writers discover the possibilities in their work when it gets on its feet and when actors are doing it, more even than the fantasy they had in their head. Directors also have a fantasy version of what it can be, what it should be and we want to give them their fantasy version. On the other hand, sometimes our fantasy version is more colorful and powerful than theirs. And you might come to that conclusion together. But at the onset, and certainly in the audition process where all of the power is in the hands of the writers and directors, we have to give them the bare minimum at least, as far as what they are expecting in the scene.

During the rehearsal process, if there is one, you might start to be more collaborative in the process or they may start asking you for ideas. You can build on that from there. *That definitely sounds actionable.*

Good. I'm glad to get a chance to talk about auditions in this way.

This brings up something I haven't mentioned in class for a long time.

In auditions, always go in with a "B reading."

You go in with a really strong A reading. You've prepared, you've Sherlock Holmesed, you've shot your video, you're all set with your A reading. But don't let that be the only approach you go in with. Have a B reading ready.

Sometimes, they may say "That was awesome but here is another detail you didn't know." So now you have to make an adjustment. But sometimes we can go in with an A reading that is so strong, we can't find our way to a B reading. The A reading is the only one that makes sense to us. So go in prepared with a B reading. Even if it's not the correct reading.

When they give you a note, we want to show a contrast between our A and B readings. That shows we have flexibility. Even if we don't hit their note exactly, we have demonstrated that we're pliable. It's not necessarily important we make the adjustment perfectly, it is important that we make an adjustment.

If the contrast between your readings is greater, they can see that there is a range of possibilities. They can say "Oh. Look what's available here. We can get to the details later in callbacks or in rehearsal." So go in with a strong "A" and have a "B" ready, just in case.

On the other hand - what is that, three hands now?- consider this: Often the adjustment the director is asking for is merely a flavoring. We might get this type of note when we're very close to giving them exactly what they're looking for. In this scenario, don't change too much. They love what you're doing. They may be giving you the note in a sense of playfulness. So don't abandon what got you there. Just add the seasoning they're asking for.

By the way, don't explain your creative thinking to your director. Let the results be what matters. Sometimes, if you explain your thinking, your techniques, the specificities in your video, to the director, they'll say "Oh no. That's not it at all."

Keep your process private. If it works, it works. Explaining why or how it works isn't helpful. Even explaining how or why it doesn't work. The only thing that counts is the result, the performance.

If it isn't working - that is, if the director wants something else - do your work. Reshoot your video so you can truthfully live the character's life in a way that gives the director what they want. Reshoot the video, make the adjustment. Shoot the video that will give the desired results.

Jen, how's it going for you?

I felt like I didn't have much variety. My "meal changes" didn't contrast enough. I felt like I was "ping-ponging" between two very similar places. I don't know, maybe the character... I don't know.

(Another actor) Can you explain "meal changes?"

To rephrase a bit, meals are basically topics, subjects in the conversation. Our job is to present different meals. To contrast this topic or subject with this topic or subject is to change meals. When the audience gets that breakfast is over, they'll digest breakfast and whet their appetite for lunch. We can't let the whole scene be eggs.

In this scene, you've got the "hello" section, the "I'm sorry this happened" section, the "I think he was a bad cop" section, then the "Maybe we can be friends" section. Contrast each of these meals. To change meals, we change flavors, textures, presentation.

The operative word here is contrast. And greater contrast is always a greater story.

Okay.

Well, I don't know about "always." I got carried away. But the phrase I do stand behind is "Contrast tells a powerful story." The contrast between your meals tells a powerful story. Not necessarily more contrast, more power, but contrast is powerful. Okay?
Yeah.

Jen, I think you're suggesting that you couldn't see a very wide path for this character. One thing I think you could fold in here is vulnerability. You've got her guard up. Her alarm bells are ringing. But if you were to mix in… I would like to assume that the two of you were good friends back in the day, you had barbecues together, you would borrow each other's mowers and what have you, On the flip side of the coin, of hating him and resenting him, is a need for normalcy, and a friend and a hug that the situation is preventing you from. And I would like to see the vulnerability side of that. The loss.

We often talk about love in this class. To identify the need for love here, despite the attitude of "You're a jerk." To see the loss of the friendship that you did have, I think is going to tell a powerful story. Does that feel actionable?
Yes.

Does that feel like it will give you a yang to the yin? A yin and yang for you to play?
It does.

You mentioned "ping-ponging." Yes, it's correct that you're going to shut him down, that you're going to tell him off, but to let us see somehow, sometimes, in some places the pain that you're feeling in regard to losing your friend.

We're always looking for the loving story. And it's not always a happy-ending love story, sometimes it's the loss of love, the denial of love, the absence of love. Sometimes that's the powerful story. And here to see the loss of love, not only of your husband but of your friend. And using impolite story, perhaps the whole police department. Maybe your whole world was wrapped up in the police department and you've been shunned by all of them.

And I also get the feeling that you're playing 100% sure there's no chance your husband was a bad cop. What if it were only 95% sure? Or 87% sure. Or 46% sure.
Right.

Could there be a window there as well?
Yes. I was "ping-ponging" but I didn't have a very clear vision of what the other side was.

(Another actor) Sorry, what is "ping-ponging" again?

Here's how it comes up in class. An actor will do a reading, and I'll say "Hey, that was good. Now try it this way instead." And the actor will try it the other way. And then I'll say "Hey that was also good. Now try one that is "ping-ponging" between the two readings." That's how "ping-ponging" usually comes up. We try it two different ways and they both work. Keep both. But now don't let the two readings melt together like some kind of soup, keep this one here and this one here. In fact I'll often say "Make sure it's a large table." So then you're all the way here to all the way there, to all the way here. Don't get stuck in the middle. That's "ping-ponging."

And to share with you when that happens, the actor "ping-pongs" the scene, and my observation for that actor is the actor has been *playing the game* of ping-pong. Literally playing the game of ping-pong with the emotional values. And that sense of play, causes the actor to feel free and welcome mistakes because they're just playing. Most of the time when an actor takes this approach, the result is a playful performance, which may sound comic but it can be dramatic too. So that's the concept behind "ping-ponging."

Okay. Thanks.

Jen, how did the scene go for you?

It felt better. Once I found the vulnerability as you said, the grief, the loss, it gave me something to bounce off of. Before I was just mad and I couldn't find anything else, but this helped.

I found it to be much more compelling. It isn't the armor, it's the chinks in the armor. And to see the chinks in your armor really opened up the role and gave the audience a way in. Out here in the audience, we cared a lot more about her this time.

Vulnerability, to the audience's eye, is very compelling so it's pretty much always welcome. We spoke recently about "it's hard to be a person" and vulnerability really tells that story. So vulnerability is almost always welcome. It really tells that "It's hard to be a person" story. Okay?

Yes.

Jen, I notice that I've assigned you two scenes that are challenging and downer roles this week. Did you see the other scene where you've been diagnosed with something fatal?

Yes. I saw it.

I am usually careful assigning scenes like this but I felt like y'all could handle it.

It's okay. I'll just have three martinis at lunch. (laugh)

Why wait till lunch?

Right (laugh)

So I think I'll give you a few minutes to rehearse this scene.

I have a technical note for you. Especially in a close-up, I'd like you to use economy in your motions. In a close-up, you don't want to be too continuous and animated because this movement is deflecting the audience's eye and therefore their intimacy. They never really get a look at you.

It takes a lot of courage to be still. Because moving is deflecting but being still absorbs the audience's eye. So stillness has power.

I don't want you to get stiff but I want you to embrace an "economy of movement." For instance, instead of three movements, how about one?
Ok. Yeah.
Those can be little movements of the eyes, a tilt of the chin, little eyebrow movements, or a lip or a cheek. I want you to feel the power of stillness. Especially in a close-up. If you're in a full body shot or a two-shot, it's okay if there are more movements. But as the camera moves in, our movement becomes more economical.
Especially in close-up, I don't want your instincts to allow every facial movement, every flicker of the eyes. Stay economical. It has more power.
It takes a lot of chutzpah to be still. To be really looked at. A lot of times actors, especially with a camera in their face, they're trying to overcome being looked at or trying to compensate for being looked at. But stillness is like "Go ahead and look. Go ahead and look." We want the audience to see us. And having the courage to be seen? That's powerful. Does that feel germane to your experience?
Yes. I definitely understand that and relate.

       Nice job. Good adjustments.
I had asked you to use "Economy of movement" in the scene. How did that work for you?
Good. I did notice some habits that I was trying to contain.
I think you assimilated this note very well. And that stillness gave you more power, was that your experience?
Yes.
Good. I thought you implemented that really well and I'm glad you felt more powerful and perhaps more dominant over the environment of being an actor. Is that correct, do you think?
Yeah. Yeah.
You were in charge and not like "I hope, I hope." I think that movement thing can sometimes be "How about this? How about this? Is this good? Is this good?" As opposed to "This is what it is. Deal with it." which I think that economy gives us.
That adjustment was very powerful.

       How did that go for you?
I had some trouble with the props and business. But overall I thought it went well. I tried to bring charm and thought it went okay. It felt smooth.
I'm glad you mentioned charm because I was aware of that. He was charming, and I liked that. There's no reason why he shouldn't be, he's on television. *(laugh)* So charm is always welcome, especially if you've got it. So I thought it was appropriate for the character and the scene. Good job in that regard.

I like very much who you're being in the scene. I like that guy. It felt however, that there weren't a lot of events in the scene, in your discussion with her. In a "help a buddy out" way, I think you can be more hit when she tells you about her husband, and you might be more amused when she says something funny.

Your character was great. Warm, safe, smart, respectful, compassionate. I really like him. I wouldn't want to change him. But I'd like more dynamics and in a "help a buddy out" way, you can help her story get more powerful by how you are affected by it.

Okay. I can definitely make that adjustment. I didn't see that until now. But I did see that the way I was playing it was, I don't know… kind of flat.

Because you were being reassuring and respectful and compassionate - all of which was lovely and appropriate and I wouldn't want to lose those qualities - but you're right. It resulted in something kind of tepid. A bit lukewarm. So we need you to percolate more at moments in certain areas. Does that feel actionable?

Yes.

I want to say something about the last line in the scene. Keep in mind, the last line of the scene is usually designed to bait the hook for the audience. You've got this "Tell somebody" line at the end of the scene and our job is to make the audience desperate to find out if she tells somebody, who she tells, what happens. In the parlance of the olden days, trying to get the audience to stay through the commercial. Stay through the ad to see what happens next. Do you see how you're baiting the hook there for what happens after the commercial?

Yes.

Great. Bait that hook. That's what the writers and producers want. Bait that hook. See what you can do to make the audience desperate to find out what happens next. That's our job - especially in episodic television.

At the end of a scene, the audience' reaction should be either: "I can't wait to see what happens next," or satisfied and reflecting on what just happened. We're trying to put the audience in one of those two positions. Either looking back and being satisfied or looking forward and being curious. That's where we want the audience to be at the end of almost every scene. Most often, curious is better. The final line is always an opportunity.

JESSICA / SUE Scene

JESSICA
Take my wine.

SUE
What?

JESSICA
Just take my wine.

SUE
I don't like wine. It gives me a headache.

JESSICA
Just put it near you. You don't have to drink it.

SUE
What is your problem?

JESSICA
You see that guy over there?

SUE
Where?

JESSICA
Over by the salad bar. No, don't look. (Sarah ignores her and looks anyway) Real smooth.

SUE
Shut up, he didn't see me.

JESSICA
He almost did.

SUE
So what? What about him?

JESSICA
He goes to my meetings.

SUE
You're not supposed to tell me that.

JESSICA
Guy is seriously messed up. Sometimes he comes in high.

SUE
Oh my God. Is he high now?

JESSICA
How should I know?

SUE
Is he stumbling or anything? Behaving erratically?

JESSICA
He seems to really like olives, but I don't think that's a symptom of anything. I don't want to talk to him. If he comes over here, let's be talking about opera or something.

SUE
I don't know anything about opera.

JESSICA
He won't know that. It's just so he won't try to join in our conversation.

SUE
Poor man.

JESSICA
What do you mean poor man? The guy crashed his wife's car. He broke his best friend's nose in a fight over paying for beer. When he was a kid he stole money from the church's collection box.

SUE
Remind me to never tell you anything.

JESSICA
You hear a lot of stuff in those meetings.

I have notes for both of you. I'm only trying to open and unlock avenues for everybody. So here are some thoughts.

To me, the style demands a quicker pace. And I want to remind you of something we talked about recently - that "help a buddy out" approach. In this scene it felt like you were almost having a boring lunch with your friend. We need you to get excited about what's happening - just in a "help a buddy out" way. It's like "What? There's a guy? Where? Oh my god" That's just helping a buddy out.

Okay.

Alejandro, you have a very winning sense of comedy. I like it. You have good timing, good diagramming. I love how you recognize the punch lines and find a way to make them stand out in a way that's fresh. Does that feel germane to your thinking and experience?

Yes.

You diagram those moments really nicely.

Okay.

Right now, I just want to push the "help a buddy out" button again. Think about how, for you to get excited about this guy, helps the story be exciting. If you're not excited, if you're bored by the story, it's a boring story. So we need to help the audience to understand it's an exciting story.

Okay.

So for you to be excited about it is a key fundamental part of that

Right.

And yet I like your laid back, kind of clueless guy. I like him, But if we can add more excitement to what's happening in the scene, we'll be doing ourselves a favor.

For both of you guys, I want to talk about the concept of "As if."

The way I might look at that here, is playing the scene "as if" you guys are secret agents, trying not to get caught with the secret formula. Now, it looks like, "Oh, we're having lunch, I think I recognize that guy, etc." It's rather mundane. It needs more of a "Ohhmygod! Don't look! Don't look!" We can really add excitement if we use "As if."

I don't know that I read her completely right.

Often the answer to these kinds of professional roles - cops, lawyers, doctors - I will often put those roles under what I call "heroic" style. The central detective on a cop show is obsessed with justice. The central doctor on a medical show is obsessed with a cure. They are driven by their work, striving for excellence. That's what I call heroic. Here you're playing a mental health counselor, and we don't know much about her. She may secretly be addicted to gambling but we don't know that. I wouldn't assume that. But it's in our best interests to make the assumption that my character is heroic. And to play it heroically would be with utmost compassion. I would want you to raise the level of compassion until it's spilling from you. Raise the need to figure him out, to cure him.

We can think of heroic style as "Good people trying hard to do the right thing." You're just a good woman, a good doctor, a good person trying hard to do the right thing. Trying in this scene to help a cop who doesn't know how troubled he is.

Another aspect that sheds light in the same area: Sometimes the story can be "I don't like my job." But I don't want that to be our default. If that is the powerful story then I'll go to that but if not, I'll assume I love my job.

For our character to not care or dislike my job - in improv terms that would be "No and."

Right.

"Yes and…" would be "This case is the most fascinating case I've ever had and I'm desperate to help this man." The more invested you can be in wanting to figure out what makes him tick? How can I help him?" The more invested you are, the more invested our audience will be. Does that feel actionable?

Yeah.

Great. The audience doesn't tune in to see "a day" in your character's life, they tune in to see "the day" in your character's life.

How did that go Joe? I thought it ended strong. Thanks for coming up with a monologue in about 90 seconds.

I've done it before.

Thank you for being confident enough to do that. I thought you did a good job overall.

Maybe it was… I don't know. Go ahead.

No you go. I think you've got it.

I was going to say, maybe I did it too "good" in parts?

Yeah.

That's what you were thinking?

Yeah. That's probably the best way to put it. I think you're right. You were trying to do it "good" in the first part of the monologue. Later on, the video took over and the truth became how you told the story, the video was doing the talking. In the beginning, the acting was doing the talking but in the second half the video was doing the talking.

Okay.

Before we had this little sidetrack conversation, I was going to share my observation that when I first said "Hey Joe, do a monologue." You bowed your head for like 5 seconds and I thought you were in a perfect place to begin. But then you asked for like 30 seconds and I think when you came back you were focused on doing it "good."

I haven't said this in class before, I don't even know how to phrase this. Actors for some reason seem to need like 15 seconds and sometimes it would be better to just start.

I'm going to remember this. Because you nailed it. I was using that time to think about how I was going to present it. Presenting rather than I guess, representing.

I like the way you put that. I'm really excited that you're starting to understand how powerfully the video can work. You're really tasting that. You're beginning in moments to give me my fantasy reading on this monologue. When the video speaks, it's so strong. When the video stops talking then you have to do the talking.
I need to keep focusing on the video.
What's exciting to me is that I think you now have a practical understanding of the process of video.

I was trying to set the environment and who I was talking to in my video.
Just to articulate, the video isn't what my eyeballs are seeing necessarily, 90% of the time I'm talking about what the mind sees. The memories, hopes, dreams and fears. Not a lamp, a window, a beach. When I say video, I'm meaning that inner thought.
And that's what's lacking when I'm doing it "good."
We're in agreement. Good, good, good. When one is diminished, the other has to fill in.
Exactly.
A fantasy I have Joe, of you at your best, will be when you don't give a fuck about how "good" you are... about being "good," convincing anybody, gaining anyone's approval. When you don't give a damn about any of that, that's when you're going to be your most powerful. And you're getting there now when you live in Character Brain, because Character Brain isn't worried about doing it good.
When you eschew all of those ideas - that you have to impress anyone or make them think you're a good actor, you flip the bird to all of that - that's when you can truly "Fight harder for the character than you're fighting for yourself." And you're getting close to that now.

Ann, you have a performance tomorrow. How is it going?
Pretty well, I think. Any advice?
Here is something I'm a bit worried about, you're going to get laughs. And that's challenging because we didn't rehearse with laughs.
I think the actor knows where they think the laugh is but a lot of times the audience is going to surprise them, by laughing at the "wrong time."
One hundred percent. You don't know where the laugh will be and you don't know how long it's going to last. The more disruptive the audience's laughter is - the longer you have to wait for them to stop laughing - the better the show is. So we hope the audience feels free to disrupt our rhythm. We need to let the laughter become the star of the show and we don't want to do anything that would steal the spotlight.
Wait for the laughter to start to come down right?
Yes, and sometimes wait longer than that.
Here is my basic approach to holding for a laugh: As soon as the laugh happens, you grab onto the line. Grab onto your next line - or, if the audience didn't hear you because

of the laugh, grab onto the line that was interrupted - and hold on tight. If you don't, while your actor brain is playing the laugh, you might forget the line. So grab onto the next line. That's the first thing you do.

The second thing you do is nothing. Nothing. The first thing you do is grab onto the line, the second thing you do is nothing. You wait to let the audience have their laughter experience. That whole time they're laughing, you're holding onto your next line. And we can be very patient in this process. We don't want to interrupt their laughter. And we certainly don't want them to not hear us because they're laughing. So laughter is always the star of the show and we're going to work in service to it. So we can nurture laughter and encourage it and create an environment where laughter builds on itself.

Often the audience will laugh twice at the same joke. They'll re-laugh, if we're patient. Or after laugh A, a slight motion or movement may get a second big laugh. So we always want to err on the side of patience when it comes to playing the laugh.

We just rehearsed your monologue and it was about two minutes. With an audience's laughter, it might be three minutes, it might be two and a half. So we have to leave breathing room for those laughs.

More than 90% of the time, when I'm talking about video, I'm talking about the character's thoughts. Not what the eyes are seeing, what the mind is seeing. Not a table, a chair, a lamp but the memories and hopes the character sees in the mind's eye. It's a personal, private video, not the exterior things that everyone can see.

PAUL / MRS DILLON Scene

PAUL
Mrs. Dillon?

DILLON
Yes?

PAUL
I have the 2:15 appointment?

DILLON
Oh. You're early.

PAUL
Yes, well something came up and I have to pick up my kid at 2:15 today so...

DILLON
How did you get in here?

PAUL
There was no one out front.

DILLON
Ah. It's lunchtime.

PAUL
Yeah, sorry about that. I am having an unusual day. I'm usually quite responsible. It's just that today my daughter…

DILLON
Have a seat, Mr…?

PAUL
Paul. Jeremy Paul.

DILLON
Have a seat, Mr. Paul. I'm a Mom so I know what it's like. And a Grandma too, so…

PAUL
Congratulations.

DILLON
Thank you.

PAUL
There's always something, isn't there?

DILLON
Oh yeah.

PAUL
Sure is.

DILLON
You're here for the job?

PAUL
Which job is that?

DILLON
The warehouse job. (pause) Don't you know what the job is?

PAUL
I just heard you were looking so I made an appointment.

DILLON
Oh.

PAUL
2:15. But I'm a bit early.

DILLON
Well Mr. Paul, I think we're going to continue our search. So if you'll excuse me, I'm going to eat my sandwich.

PAUL
Don't you want my resume?

DILLON
I don't think we have anything for you.

PAUL
Please, just look at my resume.

DILLON
Mr. Paul, we have a lot of applicants.

PAUL
Mrs. Dillon, just have a look. (He hands her his resume) You'll see there I worked with Tucker Pharmaceuticals.

DILLON
Okay.

PAUL
As a matter of fact, that's where I first heard of you. You used to work there, didn't you? In the nineties?

DILLON
Yes, I did but I don't see what that has to do with…

PAUL
Your work in accounting was quite extraordinary. Legendary, even.

DILLON
Mr. Paul…

PAUL
Yes Ma'am, you certainly have a way with numbers.
(pause)

DILLON
What is it you want, Mr. Paul?

Shawn, how's it going?

Good. When I first read this I couldn't figure out where this was going. I thought it was just a guy going for an interview but working with Jen, painting a clearer picture, I could see what was really going on. It kind of fell into place.

Perhaps the takeaway from that experience is that we often don't see it at first. But it's there. There'a a way to make every scene fascinating. It's there. We don't often see it. We think "It's only this. It's only that." But no. There's a way to make the scene fascinating. And to keep looking until we find it.

And once that clicked in for you, you see all the possibilities, how the whole scene blossoms and opens up for you.

Yeah.

Great. There's always a way. That little hook or twist is always there, we just have to find it.

Jen, how's it going?

Good. It's a terrific script. It's short but it has a lot of twists and turns in it. She's irritated, then she's sympathetic, then she's irritated again, then flummoxed that he's such an idiot and then of course she's scared at the end. So it's a good script.

I'll confess, I wrote it. Jen, you really carved out… a phrase we use a lot is "meal changes." You went through a lot of meals and they were all different. They all had different texture and flavor and presentation. I thought you did a great job, powerfully contrasting those meals. Super good. You guys did a great job with that scene.

That line "I'm having an unusual day" I was thinking that line is suggesting I have something on her.

That's a good impulse. Think about your video. Does your line mean I'm having an unusual day because I'm blackmailing a corporate executive or are you having an unusual day because your daughter sprained her ankle? Or both?

I feel like it's both. Here's an example, let's say it's Joker and Batman and Batman is tied to an electric chair or something and the Joker says "You know the funny thing about chairs…"

(Laugh) I like that reference. That's an iconic way to turn the scene, to have something nefarious in mind but put a pleasant spin on it. That's a terrific example.

Shawn, I think I saw you making use of those ideas but I think you were just dipping your toe into the water. I want you to dive in. Paint a bolder picture of what you're discovering. Does that feel actionable?

Yeah.

Good Sherlock Holmes-ing. It ties back to what we were saying earlier. That there is always something fascinating to uncover. And it's not in the language. That's another point worth making. It's not in the language. It's not in the words, it's somewhere outside of the words. So when we're doing our investigation that's where we want to look, outside the words, not within them.

The word blackmail doesn't appear anywhere in the scene but that's what it's about, isn't it? We don't look within the words. It's outside of the words.

Something worth remembering here is what we call the "intimate glimpse." That means that the audience knows something about you that the other character in the scene doesn't. When you come into the scene, she thinks "Oh poor man, a single dad, I want to help him out." But the audience is thinking there's something up with this guy. She doesn't see it but the audience does. That's what we call the "intimate glimpse." The audience can think there's something up with this guy and later on they think "Oh I was right!" So they receive a reward for their investment.

I think I get it. So something's off. It feels uncomfortable. Something's off.

Uncomfortable is one of my favorite words. We want the audience uncomfortable because that means they're invested and that they care about what happens. That's when they get butterflies or tears or goosebumps. Because it's uncomfortable. I'm leaning forward, I care.

If it's comfortable I'm sitting back sipping iced tea but if I'm uncomfortable I'm leaning forward and invested.

Jen, you're having a really great day today, acting-wise. What techniques are you employing that are paying off so well? Let's look at what you're doing so well. What do you think it is?

Well, I feel like I'm really present today, which is great.

Good.

And something that really resonated with me was that whole idea of being a person is hard. And it's something that applies to every single line of the script. It's hard to even answer the door, she's exhausted, she's been grieving, opening the door is hard. That's something that really resonated with me.

I'm glad that concept is working so well for you. You're having a solid day.

How is memorization coming?

Slowly. (Laugh)

There are certain things outside of the video that can help us memorize, things like rhythm... patterns can help us memorize, alliteration can help us memorize.

What's annoying is when you think you've got it and then discover you don't.

Our system here is to link it. I like to tell myself - it's not always literally true, but - the second time I forget that line, put a link there. And I won't forget that line anymore. The second time, put a link there.

And remember the fundamentals of the link: the silly image, intersecting with the silly image.

For instance from the holding hands line to whatever follows.

I'm feeling comforted by holding his hand.

In your Character Brain, yes, but what about your Actor Brain? That's where memorization happens, certainly that's where linking happens. So for the purposes of linking, for instance from the hand holding moment, I'll create a big silly cartoonish image of clasped hands and then have them intersect with whatever comes next, even if it's broccoli. I'll create a big silly image of clasped hands and then a huge stalk of broccoli intersecting right through the two hands together. It's a silly image. If it's logical, I'll forget it but if it's silly, I won't. So use that process as far as your linking goes.

It has to do with physically feeling...

Logically yes. But for linking we're not going to use any logic at all. Yes?

Okaaaay.

Do you understand the concept of linking, as far as the silly, cartoonish images?

I do. I'm not sure I know how to apply it.

You have to step outside of Character Brain, back into Actor Brain. That's where linking and memorization will take place. Your Character Brain doesn't want to treat these subjects in a silly way, nor should it. But in Actor Brain, when you're performing and have the question "what's my next line?" which is an Actor Brain question, your next line is waiting for you because you linked it in Actor Brain. And then you can immediately dive back into Character Brain. Instead of searching around for the line, you have it.

I just did it right now, it takes a few seconds and when I see clasped hands, I know what's next, it's broccoli.

The Character Brain is about 70% of memorization. Here we're talking about the other thirty percent as in linking and other Actor Brain tricks like rhythm, alliteration, etc. But I can't get to 100% without that concentrated work on linking, that getting from here to here, without linking.

I remember in a play I think you saw me do, I was playing a lawyer, and I remember linking Abraham Lincoln to envelope. I know what's next after I talk about Lincoln, I talk about an envelope. I still have the image now, two years later, of a big silly image of Abraham Lincoln and an envelope intersecting with him. And I've got it, years later.

So that's what I'm trying to espouse here. Those silly cartoonish images, not logical ones like Abraham Lincoln holding an envelope, that makes too much sense. It won't work for linking. The logical ones are for the character half of your brain. But when we're linking in Actor Brain, be outrageous and therefore memorable. I've got it: clasped hands, broccoli. Got it. And if I need it, I'll still have it tomorrow and next week. And again, it's because of that silly image I created, that I'm able to make that transition smoothly from one to the next.

Because what is memorization but always knowing what's next? That's what memorization is, it's a series of knowing, over and over again, what's next. So when we use this method, we always know what's next, clasped hands, broccoli, got it. Abraham Lincoln, envelope, got it. And if I go from broccoli to let's say, "September," from broccoli I intersect a big silly calendar with a big capital SEPT and I've got it. It's silly, it doesn't make any sense, but now I know: Clasped hands, broccoli, September. And we can go on and on like that.

This is how we can get the whole piece memorized - and actually get it - as opposed to trying to get it. I hope that sounds actionable.

And again, it sounds difficult but it isn't. It only took thirty seconds and I've got it, clasped hands, broccoli, September. It doesn't take long to create these images and when I do, I know what's next. Because it's silly, it's also memorable. Okay?

Yes.

Good, I'm really excited. I look forward to seeing how this approach works for you. I'm here to help.

Shawn, good job overall. I'm glad to see you diving into the material. I wonder if you're feeling a little tentative. I'd like you to use more muscle regarding the emotional values. It's a little polite. I'd like you to get impolite in your thinking.

I'd like you to raise the closeness between the two of you. So now the loss is even greater. Create a past relationship where the two of you were like family. That way, the

loss of that relationship leaves a greater void. We need for you to feel as great a loss as she's feeling. Does that feel actionable?
Yeah.
That's the impolite thinking I'm using here. How do I create relationships where the loss is greater? That makes this into a greater tragedy. This is what I mean by "impolite." A lot of times actors may get that note and start yelling or being rude in the scene. That's not my meaning.
Other acting schools might say to "raise the stakes." Impoliteness is what raises the stakes.
Does that feel actionable and hold together as a concept?
Yes.

Jen, nice job with that last line. I could see your heart was in your throat. The last line is always useful for one of two things. Or even both. A summary of the scene, and also baiting the hook for the audience as to what happens later.

Shawn, I enjoyed seeing you play the game of letting us see behind the mask. That intimate glimpse of letting the audience see, but fooling her. Were you conscious of that?
Yeah.
And how did it go in relation to confidence? How did you feel this time?
I feel like I gained a lot of confidence because I know what the scene's about.
Cool.
And also what you said about starting with F. That helped.
Awesome.

Regarding getting started in your acting career, if you wait for the perfect moment, you'll wait forever. If you're waiting until you have all your ducks in a row and have a babysitter lined up, you'll spend a lot of time waiting.
Let's say you get your headshots and submit yourself for projects, it still may take a month or more for anyone to even respond to you. It's not like all of a sudden you have to quit your job and move to Hollywood. I encourage you to take those small steps. It's not going to change your life in a major way just because you submitted for some stuff, or even get a callback or even get the gig. In television and film, they may just need you for four hours on a Saturday.
It used to be that for auditions you had to drive somewhere on a Thursday at one in the afternoon, but now almost everything is done virtually.

You're having trouble feeling confident in your lines. You went up, etc.
Right.

You mentioned in your email that there's no cognitive loss, etc.

Right.

It's a mind game, a head game. Pardon me for launching right into it. When people have trouble remembering lines I always ask them "What is your technique?"

Just go over it and over it and pound the lines. I've recorded them and listened to them over and over. I could always learn lines. My problem is, when I get up there I'm a deer in the headlights when I get on stage. Now. I'm like what the heck? I've been doing this for decades. I walk out there and I experience this blankness. I don't experience this in any other walk of life.

Well, memorizing lines is a unique task.

Yes.

You mentioned in your email that you were living in about 90% Actor Brain.

Right.

I'm glad you can identify that. I think you're successfully diagnosing yourself. So our task is to get you to dive deeper into your character's waters when that is happening. I don't think we've worked together on memorization have we?

No.

First let's address the idea of diving into your character's waters. Here I'd like to use something we call a "mantra." And your mantra for your character might be "I hate this job." Or "I'm leaving my wife." Or "I'm going to steal this money." "I'm secretly in love with you." Whatever that thing is that is unspoken but is a dominant thought of the character. That's what we call a mantra.

What is that huge pool of water that I can dive into? If I force myself to think "I've gotta quit this job," I'll find myself swimming in the character's waters.

So what would be the mantra for the character you just played?

Umm. (pause)

How about "I couldn't believe it."

Right.

At any point during the performance, when your Actor Brain is thinking "What's my line?" You can self-impose the thought "I couldn't believe it." and you're back in Character Brain. Back in your character's waters.

Keep in mind your mantra can change throughout the scene.

Another thing we have to go into is video. It's the main component of memorization.

(Long conversation about the specifics of the lines)

I didn't do any of that work, Duane. What was I thinking to prepare for this role? I was just trying to get from line 1 to line 2 to line 3 to the end of the damn thing. In front of the audience. I was white-knuckle the whole time.

Well, I think it's fixable.

Do you?

Yes.

I hope so.

Unless there's cognitive problems which can sometimes happen but we don't think that's the case.

No.

Well, let's look at your technique. From what you described, your technique was kind of terrible.

Actor Brain can be a spiral. We need the answer to the question "what is my next line?" to be in your Character Brain. So let's take on a new technique. By shooting the video, I'm creating a new truth.

Memorization starts in our Actor Brain. It is simply always knowing what's next. Over and over again, what's next? At the end of the show, you don't need to know the beginning. At the beginning, you don't need to know the end. You only need to know what's next, right now, over and over again. At any given moment, you only need to know one line. This one. And you do that for the entirety of the performance.

Here is the idea behind linking. I'm going to take one ridiculous image and a second ridiculous image and have them intersect and link together. For instance if I said school bus and then I said broccoli.

I'm going to create a silly cartoonish image in my head of a school bus, a big yellow school bus and then a huge, cartoonish stalk of broccoli, as big as the bus itself, shooting out of the windshield of the bus. Ok?

We have two silly - not logical, logical is forgettable - but silly cartoonish images and they are linked together. So now when I see a school bus, what do I see attached? Broccoli. It's already there. So if I have a line of dialogue about a school bus and then I say a line about broccoli, if I do this process, when I see a school bus, there's already broccoli there. I don't have to remember what's next because it's already there. I've linked it.

The broccoli line follows the school bus line?

Yes. Or the broccoli speech follows the school bus speech. Or "school bus" is my cue line and my line is "broccoli."

How does that stay consistent with your video?

It doesn't. This is technical. This is Actor Brain.

This is non-video stuff…

Correct. This is not Character Brain. We're acting and in Character Brain and then suddenly we say "Uh-oh. What's my next line?"

Right.

We're turning on our Actor Brain. And our Actor Brain says "Oh. School bus? Broccoli's next." And then we dive back into Character Brain and our video of broccoli. So it's just a way to solidify what's next in your Actor Brain - not Character Brain, Character Brain is all video based - but when Character Brain isn't enough, we have to dip back into Actor

Brain. We'll use linking to find the answer to my question. I'm talking about a school bus, what comes next? Oh, Broccoli.

I was using lots of alphabetical tools like "after leaving" "A.L." and stuff like that which wasn't working for me. I can see now there was no imagery.

Exactly. There is a place for lots of techniques but the one you mentioned isn't the best. So let's make sure we've covered linking. I really want to make sure you grasp this concept. So if I'm talking about a school bus and your line is next, what are you going to talk about?

Umm. Broccoli.

Right. And you'll still have it tomorrow. When I say my line about a school bus, you'll go "Oh, broccoli is next." Because you did that link.

Yes.

So keep in mind, the link is an Actor Brain device. Not logical. Don't make it logical because if it's logical, it's forgettable. If it becomes "I drove a school bus and then I went to the store and bought broccoli." It's completely forgettable. So what we want is non-logical. Anti-logic. Silly and ridiculous. So when we wonder "what's next?" we dip into Actor Brain and the answer is right there and we can get back into Character Brain.

And you use this technique when you're not getting the memorization through the video, right?

Right.

There are always phrases, like awkward phraseology where the tongue does not want to say it that way. It's not logically thinking that way. We're like why does he say that in that way? And my brain thinks "that doesn't come now, that comes later," so I resist it.

In the Actor Brain sphere, when it comes to memorizing, There are several different tools we might use that are technical. Alliteration, alphabetizing, reverse alphabetizing, rhythm… but these are last resorts, they are the least effective.

I want you to do a linking exercise. I'm going to give you five things to memorize.

Should I write these down?

No. Just use the linking that we have been using. Keep the example we used of the schoolbus and then broccoli. Because if after broccoli the next line is about a stop sign, what do I do? I link the broccoli to a stop sign. So now I create a visual of a stop sign sticking up through the broccoli. So now what do I have? I know it's school bus, broccoli, stop sign. And if we continue like that, we could go on virtually forever. Because we don't need to remember fifty things, we just need one at a time.

And we can use this wherever and whichever. It can be topics or subjects or maybe a cue line; they say "school bus," I talk about broccoli. And we'll employ this any time we're having line trouble. The second time I have to call "Line!", I'll put a link there.

So I'm going to give you five things to memorize. Use the linking technique.

Squirrel

Tic-tac-toe

Denver
Mashed Potatoes
Hurricane *(repeated the list twice)*
(Pause)
The first thing I want to do is link them using the first letter.
Don't. Use the images. Take 60 seconds.
(Pause)
Do you have them?
Roughly.
What are they?
Squirrel, tic-tac-toe, Denver, mashed potatoes, hurricane.
Great. I'm going to give you five more.
From hurricane, go to:
Australia
Golf club
Steering wheel
Pot of gold
Exercise. *(List repeated twice)* Take 60 seconds.
What's the second one again?
Golf club.
(Pause)
And the fourth one?
Pot of gold.
(Pause)
Got it?
Australia, umm, golf club, steering wheel, pot of gold… Can't remember the last one.
Exercise. I didn't give you a lot of time. Also, exercise isn't an object, so to picture it is a bit different. I'm picturing a little man icon with bulging muscles pumping a little weight. This approach is a bit different when the image you need isn't an object. I don't want to get too specific because we're just worried about simple links for now.
I feel like the fact that you even have to go "Umm" means that you are not specific enough with your images.
Maybe with a bit more time…
You're right. This is awfully quick. But when I see a school bus there's broccoli right there. So it's not "What should I say next?" But "What is there?" I create the link and it's there. So I don't have to conjecture about what it should be, it is.
So that's the specificity we're talking about. Like here I see a steering wheel but what's it intersecting with? A pot of gold.
Here's what I did: Australia was first…
What's your image?

The great outback.

But what's your image? Describe the image.

The image of this enormous… the largest island in the world, the vast expanse of the largest island in the world, the interior of the… I've never been there but…

In the example of the school bus, to do it the way you're describing would be, "well it's used for transportation and it takes kids back and forth…" No, what's the image? A big yellow bus. And in this case what's the image of Australia? It's the shape of the continent, a big map and there's Australia dominating, the shape of it. A snapshot of that.

Against the Indian Ocean.

Right and then is the golf club.

I'm picturing the vast expanse of Australia and the vast expanse of a golf course.

Golf club.

Oh golf club? Not a golf course?

No. Golf club. So here's the image I recommend, sir. I've got Australia and then a huge golf club, as big as the continent itself sticking right up through eastern Australia. It's a driving wedge or whatever - I don't know golf - but it's sticking straight up through the continent. And it's silly and it's sticking right up through eastern Australia.

I see. Okay, what I was doing was looking for similarities between the two things. I was thinking, what's similar between Australia and a golf course? The vast expanse. But you're suggesting it's more… more imagistic than that.

To do the process you're doing you're having to put logic together and we need logic in our Character Brain but not here. Here we use a big-ass golf club stuck right through the eastern part of the continent. And then we have a steering wheel so we intersect those as well. So now we have Australia, golf club, steering wheel.

If we bring any logic whatsoever into it, it's going to become forgettable.

That's my modus operandi.

Logic is the enemy of drama in a number of ways. But especially when it comes to linking. Because you might say "I went to Australia and I bought a golf club. And then I drove a car and it had a steering wheel." Nothing, boring. Instead, go "Australia, golf club, steering wheel."

So now, when I'm doing my piece, and I hear Australia, or I have my Australia monologue or a comment about Australia and then I wonder what's next, I know golf club is next. So I'm using linking in that way. And then the specificity of the video in Character Brain covers the rest.

Okay.

When we were doing squirrel, tic-tac-toe etc. What was your process then? Was it what I'm talking about or were you adding little bits of logic?

More the latter.

A squirrel is a big cartoony squirrel and the tic-tac-toe is huge and intersecting right across the body of the squirrel.

Yeah, I was envisioning a squirrel with a pen in his hand and he's playing tic-tac-toe.

That's too logical. Logic is forgettable. But a continent intersecting with a golf club, intersecting with a steering wheel... Once I take that snapshot, it's going to be memorable.

Or what about a squirrel foraging for nuts and he finds a...

No.

Don't even do that?

No. I don't want you to outsmart this. By being more clever than the exercise. The exercise is simply, one silly, cartoonish image linked to another silly, cartoonish image. It's called linking. Not "tell a good story" or "fill in the blanks." That's not what we're doing, we're linking.

Your image of the broccoli shooting out of the windshield of the schoolbus is very vivid.

And what's after broccoli?

Umm. Ha ha...

You might not have done the link there but I did and it's a stop sign.

I didn't create that image, no.

That's okay. You have a better concept now than then. I don't want us to be smarter than the exercise, okay?

Okay.

Don't outsmart it, don't make it logical, don't worry about Character Brain because this is outside of Character Brain. This is for when Character Brain doesn't know what to say next, we shift over to Actor Brain, we go "broccoli's next."

Okay.

So if you don't mind I'd like to give you all ten images again with this process in mind. Well, just the first five. Squirrel, tic-tac-toe, Denver, mashed potatoes, hurricane.

(repeated)

(Pause)

Have you got them?

Squirrel, tic-tac-toe, Denver, mashed potatoes, hurricane.

Good. Here's the next five. Australia, golf club, steering wheel, pot of gold, exercise.

(repeated) Take 30 seconds. (pause) You have those five?

At least four, I think.

But not the fifth?

No.

Exercise. It's not really a thing, it's an activity. An image that works for me is a little icon man lifting weights with bulging muscles. And I'll remember that the word is exercise. I won't say like "working out" or "little man with weights'," I'll remember that it's exercise.

Okay.

So what are the second five starting with Australia?

Australia, golf club, ummm, australia, golf club... I'm confusing it with the first set.

What's intersecting with your golf club?

Steering wheel.

There you go.

That's what did it. I saw the steering wheel spinning on the golf club.

Okay. They should be intersecting or come in contact with each other. That is the visual link. Like the broccoli jutting out of the windshield of the school bus. An image that is ridiculous enough that I won't forget it. Every time I see a school bus, broccoli will be there. Any time we have to use "ands" or "therefores" or "this makes sense because," we're trying to make it logical. Don't. Keep it ridiculous.

I think I understand. It's just my logical brain wants to impose logic on everything I'm doing.

And that is not welcome. Logic is anathema to this exercise. In Character Brain, to some degree, things have to make sense. But not in our linking in Actor Brain. In Actor Brain, we want them to absolutely not make sense. So they don't get confused. You're trying to make Actor Brain similar to Character Brain. Don't. Make it more different.

Gotcha. Okay. I'll practice this over the next week or so.

The only practice I want you to do is the linking and you should do it right now. So that the next time I see you, you'll know these words and you won't have them written down. But if at the end of your golf club, there's a steering wheel there, what's to remember? It's right there. It's like the Character Brain video. If I have the truth, I don't have lines. There's a steering wheel there. What line?

So now I'm going to give you the list once more. Don't write them down. And when I see you next week, I'll ask you to name them. *(Repeats list of ten)* Whenever you're ready, start at the beginning.

Australia, golf club, steering wheel, pot of gold, exercise. I think that's the last five.

Okay. What are the first five?

Ummm. I connected the others, but not the first one.

That's okay. We don't have a connection to the first one so it's a bit trickier. I'll give you the first one and then you'll have the transitions to the next, okay? So the word we started with...

(Suddenly) Squirrel!

(laugh) Great, so go ahead.

Squirrel, tic-tac-toe, ummm, Denver, mashed potatoes, hurricane.

Okay so what are all ten?

Squirrel, umm, tic-tac-toe, Denver, mashed potatoes, hurricane, Australia, golf club, steering wheel, pot of gold, and umm, exercise.

So I'm going to ask you right now to take about 60 more seconds with that and then we're going to put this away. But I want you to solidify those images. You just

memorized 10 random things in perfect order in about 4 minutes or less. Now that you know the process you can go even quicker than that. So once more please.
Squirrel, tic-tac-toe, steering wheel..
No.
Squirrel, tic-tac-toe, Denver, mashed potatoes, hurricane, Australia, golf club, steering wheel, pot of gold and ummm, exercise.
The last two times in a row you've had trouble with "exercise." So you need a better image of a little man lifting weights. It can't be vague, it has to be specific. Also last time you went from tic-tac-toe to steering wheel and that's not correct. So you need a better link from tic-tac-toe to Denver. That link right there is a bit weak.
I see that.
Don't take anything for granted. Not to belabor it but I think you're letting yourself get away with vague images. Make them specific.
Next time I see you I'll ask for these ten things and you won't have written them down. You can run through them when you're driving or in the shower or whatever. You can go "What were those 10 things? Oh yeah…" and then run through them.
And I'll make those images concrete.
Great. So anytime I need to remember what's next I can create a link. Maybe it's from "gallery" to "Susan." So I create the linking images from gallery to Susan. Got it. Moving on.
Now that we know what linking is, moving forward, what's at the end of your golf club?
A steering wheel.
Right. If there's nothing there, you won't know. But if there's a steering wheel, you'll know. What's at the end of your golf club? A steering wheel. What's at the end of your steering wheel? A pot of gold. What's at the end of your pot of gold? A little guy lifting weights. It's that simple. That easy.
Hopefully I won't need to use this technique a lot.
I don't think I've articulated this before but I don't see any reason we couldn't do a link at every line. I don't think it's cheap. Because Al, tomorrow you'll still know this list and you'll know it next week. If you remember to remember them. Go over it. And for very little work you've gotten a great deal of return. It's easy. After broccoli for me is a stop sign. After Denver for you is mashed potatoes.

Getting back into Character Brain, I want you to depend more on video than you have depended on in the past. You've been using a lot of other tricks that aren't video based. The only truth is in your video. If it's true, you know what it looks like. If you don't know what it looks like, it isn't true.
I didn't do any of this work. I don't know why I…
Listen. I know you feel terrible about forgetting lines in that show. I'm sure it's a bigger deal to you than to anyone else. But moving forward, using video and using linking

wherever needed will give you a much more solid technique moving forward and you'll be stronger than you ever were.

I'm glad I thought of reaching out to you on this. This is a problem that, if I don't address it, it's going to short circuit everything else I'm trying to do. If I don't have the confidence when I go out there in front of an audience, something I've done a million times.

You'll have the confidence when you cover the right bases. When you use video and linking you're covering the right bases. It won't fail you. What's at the end of your golf club?

It's that steering wheel, every time.

Who needs a line? We have truth. The video gives you truth. You don't have to remember any lines. Give me those ten items again.

Squirrel, tic-tac-toe, umm, Denver, mashed potatoes, hurricane, Australia, golf club, umm, pot of gold, exercise.

Okay, very good. Those umms worry me a little bit. I'll remind you to get more specific with your images. If we do that, there's nothing to remember, it's just a picture. I'm just describing what I see. Not "what's the thing I'm supposed to say?" Screw say. See. What you see will tell you what to say.

Okay. Thanks. See you next week.

It's been a pleasure.

I don't mind telling you, I was in a bad place.

It's 100% fixable. It isn't ability, it's technique. Another thing you'll discover is that images are much more complex and interesting and profound than words. So images are a win-win. We're using linking here in Actor Brain but when we use video in Character Brain we're going to discover things that are even more important.

Okay, we'll see you next week.

Here is the -ism that I think applies here: "Don't say the funny lines funnily."

I was doing that?

It's not something that I would usually say but there are too many arrows. It became disorienting. If I lose my bearings on the crux of the line, there won't be a payoff.

I always have to watch out for tipping off the punchline. When I do it falls flat.

The funnier the line, the less funny we say it. The audience feels smart when they figure out it's funny. If they figure out it's funny, not only is it funny but they're smart. If you show them it's funny, you take the smart part away and maybe it's funny and maybe it isn't. So tickling their smart bone, it's just as good as tickling their funny bone. And I'm sure I've never said that before. *(Laugh)*

A YEAR IN ACTING CLASS

March/April

Natasha, one thing I'd like to ask of you overall, is to energize your verbal energy. That's articulation. A bit more energy in your articulation. A phrase I like to use is "Consonants are opportunities." Even here, we wouldn't want the opening line to be, and I'm exaggerating here, but it sounded a little bit like "Tae my wine." We're like "What?"

The K in take, it's gotta be there. That K is an opportunity.

That is something that in high school, I remember being told. I think that's just a matter of trying to get to the end of the line. I should instead take time and enjoy my line!

Yes! Why not? You love acting! *(laugh)* Remember "consonants are opportunities."

(After being given a scene from Heath Ledger's Joker)

Alejandro, anything rattling for you today?

Yeah. One of the pieces you sent me was something I've seen before and I was thinking how can I not copy it? How can I do it my way? When I was putting together my video and thinking about the role, it was bringing me back to the film I had already seen. It's a very famous scene. I thought maybe you would have seen it.

How specific is your memory of how he did it?

Pretty specific.

First of all, this situation is unique to acting class. This is sort of a simulated experience. I don't think they are going to remake this movie anytime soon. So this isn't something you'll come up against in casting. In theatre it might happen more often, that you're reading for something you've seen before or that you've seen the movie. Television and film will only rarely be a remake of something. For the most part you aren't going to be challenged with this.

If I was in your shoes - I'm going to sound like a braggart but I'm going to say it anyway - there have been times when someone saw my performance and said "You were better than the original guy. Better than the guy in the movie." or "I saw it on Broadway and you were better than that guy." There's still room. Regardless of what the precedent is. There is still room for you. Fight for your space. Maybe you can do it as well as the original guy. Maybe better than the original guy.

Obviously, it's considered by many to be one of the all-time great performances so good luck with that. *(Laugh)* But there is still room for you. Fight for your space.

Don't imitate. I think that your impulse is to avoid that. Don't give your power to Heath Ledger. Don't give your power away to somebody's Academy Award. I don't need to give my power away. I'm going to do it my way and it is what it is. You deal with it. You tell me if it's better or worse or the same or different. I don't care. That's not my job. You, out there in the audience. That's your job. I don't have space for that.

You have such a lovely reverence for the art of acting. It shows in your discipline, how often you come to class, how prepared you are, how hard you work. And I think that's really great.

Sometimes actors who are that passionate can create what I call a "Glass museum in the sky." That's where we can sometimes place the greatest performers and performances, whoever you think is the best. But if we put it above ourselves it becomes out of reach. I'm placing it above me because of my reverence for it. What we want to do is take that glass museum down to earth and smash it.

Allejandro, how's it going?

This piece is relatable. I can connect with it. It's a short piece and I wanted it to be understandable.

Nice work. You have so many good habits. Really good work. I want you to try it again. I think you were telling the story rather subtly. It was understated. See if you can help me out a little bit. I'd like you to carve a bolder path for the audience with that language. I'm not sure I'm saying this well. A word I sometimes use is to "impose" your language on the audience. Don't give us the opportunity to miss it. The point, how you're feeling, what's going on. Does that feel actionable?

I think I could amp it up a bit.

Make sure that we get it… really hit us with what you're saying. Don't give us the option of tuning in or tuning out. Don't give us that option. Paint a bolder picture so that we are confronted more by what you're illustrating. Does that feel actionable?

Yes.

Take fifteen seconds and then try it again.

Natasha, how's it going?

I've been working on diction like we spoke about last time. Paying attention to the consonants. But also trying to have some fun with it.

Great. I saw that.

What I'd like us to work on moving forward is shooting the video. In this monologue, you're describing a scene in an office and a coworker who is popular. What does that look like? What does it feel like in your belly when that is happening? How do you feel left out? Shoot that video and then when you live in that world, it becomes an experience. It becomes an experience and not lines that you have to say.

I think that's a challenge for me. Not focussing so much on the lines but on the experience.

The great part is when you focus on the experience in detail, then the lines will be there as a result of that. You end up with the best of both worlds. You know the lines, not

because you memorized them or practiced how to say them, but because you really "know what you're talking about."
Right.
I'd like you to take about thirty seconds and shoot some video. Then we'll try it again. Make sure your video precedes what you say. See if you can use the video to drive your language. Does that feel actionable?
Yes.
Whenever you're ready.

"Last stop on the emotional train."
Totally exasperated and broken down?
For me, it's self-loathing. That's the last stop on the emotional train. When you think about Philip Seymour Hoffman, great, tragic roles, Pacino in anything, Sean Penn, they all have an element of self-loathing. It's very powerful.
I was watching the other night, Glengarry Glen Ross…
Perfect example. The whole film is self loathing. Jack Lemmon gives one of the all time great performances in that. And self loathing is at the core of it.
I've been trying to work on impolite choices.
Look at the impoliteness and stakes and un-presentability. Great opposing ideas between self and hate. Beautifully opposed. Anything can happen, it's so juicy. And self loathing comes from some sort of wound and the audience can sense that. This makes them either want to give you a hug or run away. Either way is compelling.
And this can give the audience something to know about me that I might not know myself.
Right. 100% right. The "intimate glimpse." That intimacy of the audience to know you loathe yourself but you don't even know.

Al, Have you had any ruminations about what we talked about?
Yeah. I liked a lot of what you said, Duane. If I can just really connect with the video. Really run it and breathe it and experience it, the lines will not betray me, evade me.
I like the way you put that. If I've filled in all those blanks in Character Brain, the lines will not betray me.
I'm counting on that. If I do my homework, this shouldn't be happening, forgetting my lines.
I agree with you. And I think you're focused in the right area. The video is going to cover all those bases for you. Real quick bit of housekeeping. Do you have your ten objects?
Yes.
What are they?
Squirrel, tic tac toe, Denver, mashed potatoes, hurricane, Australia, golf club, steering wheel, pot of gold, exercise.

Cool. Tell me about your process during the week.

A couple times a day I would think "what are my ten things? What is the correct order? What's the image that is going to help me remember what a squirrel and tic tac toe have to do with each other?"

I'll remind you of the word we use: "linking." That the images are physically linked, one after another.

Natasha, anything rattling for you today?

Yeah, shooting the video. I don't know why it's such a challenge for me.

Here's a quick exercise. I'm going to give you a line of dialogue. You should shoot the video and whenever you have the video, raise your hand. Take as long as you like. So I'm going to give you a line of dialogue.

"Amanda is such a rude person." (*Joe takes 5 seconds, Natasha, 30 seconds*)

Great, now say the line. "Amanda is such a rude person."

(Both say the line)

I think I'm still having some trouble. It's going to take time.

Pardon me, I don't want to minimize your process but I don't want you to overthink it. We can get a fundamental video to give us some basic truth to say our lines in a very short period of time. Even if it takes thirty seconds or so to shoot the video for a line, once you've shot that video then we've got it and we can recall it, we can use it. Maybe we discover later that Amanda isn't really rude at all, I'm just trying to put her down for some reason. So then we can reshoot that video if we need to. But for now the video that we've already lain is going to serve the purpose.

In your reading a moment ago, I saw a relationship to video. And a relationship to video is actually more important than the details of your video. Just that there is one is more important than it being the right one. Because we can't read your mind. We don't know what you're thinking, we just know *that* you're thinking.

Fundamentally, I could give you a scene that you've never seen before, ice cold. You look down at the page and your first line is "That morning, I was nervous." Can you shoot that video right now?

I'm not sure how.

If I really want to simplify my process, I can think to myself "What does morning look like?" And I see the sun streaming through my bedroom window. And I ask myself "What does nervous look like?" and I look down and see my hand is shaking. Right now I have enough. I know what morning looks like and I know what nervous looks like. Fundamentally, I have all I need to say the line truthfully.

As we continue down the path of the video, we can blossom into things that might be more powerful. Why you're nervous will matter at some point, but right now you have what you need fundamentally. We can't read your mind - to some degree I think we can - but overall, that you have a relationship to morning is more important than what that relationship is. And by using your video, by seeing it, you automatically have a relationship to what you see.

Knowing what morning looks like is what's important. Later on we can figure out if it's sunny or cloudy, or if it's raining. Later on, we can make all of those decisions but right now we just need to say morning truthfully. Later, we can decide if it's November or July.

Also, we can spend a lot of time shooting that video and decide it was raining. But ultimately, will that matter? Perhaps the opportunity of morning is more powerful than the finite choice.

The word "that" is also a video. What is the video of "that?" For me it's choosing one out of many. Here it's one day out of many mornings. My video includes a calendar. With a focus on one of the days. It could be a Tuesday or a Friday. It doesn't matter. Ultimately, it may matter, but not yet.

Now I have a video of "That morning…" We always have a video of "I" (laugh) And "was" is just past tense and I have a video of nervous with my hand shaking or heart racing.

So the process is to be sure we see "morning" before we say it. Before the "Mmm" of morning. First we see the sun streaming through the window, now I say "morning." We see our hand shaking and know what that feels like and now we say "nervous."

As we fill in the details, that's great. We fill in the blanks. Later on we discover that we're going to rob a bank today or have a job interview or I'm going to break up with my significant other. We don't know why you're nervous. We're welcome to shade in those colors later but right now we just need "Morning - Nervous."

I'm tempted to say this a few ways but one way is: If I don't make the decision about why I'm nervous yet, then that leaves the possibilities open. A phrase I use a lot is "avoid answers." We don't need the answers, we need the inquiry. I'm hoping this holds together as a concept?

Hmmm.

That by not defining it, I'm allowing it to be what it is, as opposed to what I'm trying to make it become. And perhaps being open to possibility, I'll find something more powerful than that thing I had figured out. I just want that to be part of our instinct and intuition at some points. This is certainly nothing you're doing wrong.

I don't know if we've talked about this, Natasha, overall in acting, we're not looking for answers, we're looking for good questions. Answers are really dead ends. So it's all about the explorations, and we save the answers to the last page. Questions are fertile. Does that sit with you conceptually?

I think so.

One thing I have found is people who, before they were actors, were in certain professions like medicine, law, finance… They are answer driven. If you're an accountant, you've got to have an answer. You add those numbers and there is an answer there.

But in our work as soon as we zoom in on an answer, there are more questions there. That's what we want to do: keep asking newer and better questions in our work. Does that feel actionable?

I think so.

Let's send the two of you into rehearsal.

Here's a concept we sometimes use: "head, heart and gut." The head is intellectually understanding the scene and the character, the heart is caring about what the character cares about, but the gut is the hardest one to get to. That's the belly. That's where involuntary emotional reactions happen. The gut is where butterflies and goosebumps come from. It's where we get excited and it makes us sweat or cry. That's gut.

So head is intellectual, heart is empathy but gut is involuntary emotional reaction and that's the hardest one to get to.

I'm tempted to not tell you this, to keep it a secret but currently you have movements and facial expressions that are not really needed. They are not the essence. I think when I ask you to get in your gut, some of that movement that we don't need might go away. You see how that might work?

Yeah.

You'll become more centered and rooted. Does that sound fun and actionable?

Yeah.

If you'll forgive me, in that monologue you were talking about something but you didn't "know what you were talking about." You said it but you didn't know it. See the difference?

Yeah.

So you've got to know it. Sometimes I'll say with a "Capital K." You've got to *know* your Mom, know your history with her. Otherwise - as I'll sometimes rather pithily say - "you don't know what you're talking about."

I'd like you to care more about what's happening. I'd like you to care more about the guy at the salad bar. Be more curious about these meetings your friend goes to. By you caring more, it signals to the audience that they should care too. Does that feel actionable?

Yeah.

Get more excited about whatever is happening. Let's try this scene again from the top.

A YEAR IN ACTING CLASS

There were several places there, where I thought you had a stronger opinion and I hope you were having more fun.

Oh yeah.

It happens pretty often when people read your role in this scene that actors play it as if they're a bit bored or put off. But we're going to try to find ways to energize the situation and by getting more excited about what's happening in the scene, you're sending the audience a signal that they should get excited too.

And perhaps we're finding through this inquiry into getting excited, that we're getting to your gut as well. What do you think? Do you think the belly is doing more of the work now and not your brain?

I think it's not there yet but it's getting there.

Me too.

Joe, how do you think it's going?

I think it's moving in the right direction.

Good. Once again Joe, I think that take is viable. On set, the director would say "print that. We're going to keep that one."

Okay. Good.

So that was a good one. Where I'm having a bit of a problem is that at the end of the scene, it seems like you forgot the predicament you were in, that you don't want to talk to that guy. You don't want him to see you. He might smell booze on your breath. And so the stakes of what is fundamentally happening kind of frittered away by the end. Like you had everything figured out. But I still want the consequences of the scene itself to hang in the air. Okay?

That's pretty good.

Good. Let's not lose the...

I think I got sidetracked when she felt empathetic toward that guy. I'm like "What do you mean, poor guy? Let me tell you about him." And I think I got all wrapped up in that part.

I agree, Joe. And I can see why. We had a conversation recently and it was a rather unusual conversation that I don't have very often but because your acting is getting so good now, we're starting to have new conversations.

We were talking about comedy at the time. You were doing a monologue and we both agreed that there might have been too many arrows. And it was disorienting because I didn't know which one I needed to remember for the joke to pay off. If we lose the foundation then the payoff is in relationship to what? And so the payoff isn't as strong. Okay?

I get the concept but how did I do that here?

Well here, we forgot at the end of the scene that there was still a guy here that goes to AA with you and that you don't want to talk to him. It became about how much you disapprove of this guy but without the consequences of the scene.

I think my mantra got lost.
That's a good way to put it.

There are places where you aren't really finishing the line. You're interrupting yourself before you finish the line. In a scene earlier you did it a couple of lines in a row and in that case I thought it worked. Perhaps the character was so overcome with emotion that he didn't finish the sentence. That works for me.

But now you're doing that again in this scene. I understand why you're doing it. It's in the interest of syncopation. That's what is driving you to make that choice. Your instincts are telling you to syncopate in order to create more momentum in the language. I like that instinct but I want you to be careful where and when you use it. I wouldn't want it to become a habit. And in this case the line itself lost value because of it. This time, the line itself was more powerful than your syncopated choice.

It's interesting how these habits come up.

Natasha, how is your relationship to video on this scene?

I feel like it's going well. It still needs some work. Shooting that video of me drinking wine and how it gives me a headache. It definitely needs some work but I think it's going good.

It's interesting you mention that line. I was noticing that. In a sense, I have the same note I gave Joe a minute ago. And that is yes, wine gives you a headache and yes, you need a video of wine giving you a headache. But it also needs to be in relation to the scene. Which would be not simply that wine gives you a headache but also, "why are you making me take your wine? You're acting weird." I don't want to forget that. I don't want the thought to be isolated from the scene. Does that make sense?

Yeah.

I agree with you. I saw you had video and I believed wine gave you a headache but I don't want us to forget in relation to what?

There's a fine tuning to our idea about video. Not only do we need the truth about what we're saying, but we also need a reason to say it. That's another video. My reason to say it is also my video. And usually my reason to say it is so that you will understand. So my video is of you going "I understand." That's what is driving my language. I have a video of you going "Got it, Duane."

Maybe I'm talking to you because I want you to give me $500.00 to bet on the horses. And my video is of you going "Okay, Duane. Here's the money," while I'm talking about why the horse will win, whatever those details are. But along with that video needs to be the video of why I'm saying this. And that video is of you giving me money. *(Laugh)*

Joe, how'd it go for you?

Not good.

Why?

I was completely in Actor Brain.

Why do you think that is?

I guess I let my video go.

That's true. Fundamentally, you're right. I think a bit of it might also have been "I got good notes."

That's true too.

You might think you're done in your exploration but keep exploring. Even if the notes are "That's perfect, Joe." Keep exploring.

Don't rest on the laurels.

Yeah. And what I was complimenting was the blood coursing through your veins. Not the finished product but the way you were playing the game. So keep playing, keep exploring. Avoid answers. The blood is always moving.

Anything rattling for you Allejandro, my friend?

How do you repeat a performance exactly the way you did it?

Great. Alejandro, I just started coming to you to begin almost every class because you always have something quite compelling to discuss and it always gets us off on the right foot, so thank you. Here is the way I would be thinking about that, please.

A way I like to summarize it is to "relive not recreate." So that's my little -ism, my little Duane-ism, is "relive not recreate." So we want to go back to Character Brain. Your Actor Brain has a performance to recreate but the Character Brain has a performance to relive. When I'm doing my performance - not really a hundred percent true but overall and theoretically - I'm not worried at all about what happened in yesterday's performance. I'm not worried at all about what happened on the earlier take. I'm just the same person in the same circumstances with the same memories and the same hopes and I just start fresh.

I'm going to live as much as I can in Character Brain and not worry about repeating things. We'll set aside the thought of continuity right now, which is important on a set. If we set that aside, what I want to do is completely and simply live the moment again without the knowledge that I have ever done it before. Because the character hasn't. Only the actor has done it before. And if you're really, thoroughly shooting your video and knowing what you love and who you love and why - and do that powerfully - you don't have to worry about how you said the line. You don't have to worry about a head turn or a vocal inflection or a gesture. Let those things all happen organically for the first time.

Only continuity will get in the way of that. I'm not going to change my blocking, right? On the second take, I'm not going to move to the window if that's not the blocking. That's not going to work. So for continuity and the understanding of the process of shooting a film, there are certain things that are the same, but they're very minimal. It's really just where are you physically in the space and you know, do I have a drink in my hand? Am I holding the drink in my right or left hand? That's really all we need to preset or predetermine. Now I'm going to live my life again. I'm going to relive not recreate. Live. Start fresh. You've never done this before even on the 30th take. If we're thorough in our video and our hopes and our dreams and our wants and our fears and what we love, then it will look similar to the outside eye. But for us it really isn't.

I want to keep in mind please, that our blood is always flowing. That's one thing that actors try to do sometimes. They try to stop their blood from flowing, like "Hold it a minute. I'm going to act!" *(Laugh)* Right? As opposed to understanding that your blood is always flowing. Our cells are always replicating. And this take is different than the take I did 5 minutes ago because I'm 5 minutes older. My synapses have been firing. I've lived more life. I'm a different human being. I'm going to let life live and I'm going to participate in it and I'm not going to try to control it. Relive, not recreate.

Maybe I got a great laugh on a line in a comedy. Now I'm thinking "What do I do when that line comes up again?" That's kind of the question, right?

Yes.

Once again I'm going to ask us to relive, not recreate. Maybe in last night's show, I got a big laugh when I said "Your mother-in-law is in the bedroom!" So tomorrow "Your mother-in-law is in the bedroom!" *(exact same inflection)* Okay, that's how I'll say it: "Your mother-in-law is in the bedroom!" *(exact same inflection)*

But if I do that, what is saying the line? My ear. I'm trying to sound the same and that's my ear talking. Instead, really be thinking what you think about the mother-in-law being in the bedroom. Maybe your character is excited and nervous and maybe there's about 10% of you that thinks it's funny. If that is the "juxtaposition of ideas" that makes the line powerful, then use that "juxtaposition of ideas" to say the line, not how I predetermine the line should sound.

A phrase that has been popping in my head and hasn't quite made it to language yet in this conversation is that we don't want answers. So "Your mother-in-law is in the bedroom!" *(same inflection)* would be an answer to how that line is said. You don't want an answer. If you have an answer, ask a better question. Ask a more informed question. So we are in the state of finding out while we perform instead of a state of knowing. That's a phrase I haven't used in a long time. "State of not knowing." Which is what we're trying to create. If I know how I'm going to say that line and I'm saying it that way over and over again, if I know how I'm going to say that line, that's an answer. Let's get rid of answers. The question is, your mother-in-law is in the bedroom, how do I feel about it? Perhaps in our Actor Brain tinged with a little bit of comic timing, speaking in-between the beats. As we know, a bit of Actor Brain is always okay to manage what we're doing.

But remember that percentage we're going for is 90% Character Brain, 10% Actor Brain. Character Brain is not worried about getting a laugh. Actor Brain may be and that's okay. Actor Brain is welcome. But Character Brain is worried about the Mother-in-law in the bedroom. And if we're living 90% there, we'll be okay.

Keep in mind, If we have the answer, that's going to be 90% Actor Brain. That's like "the audience will believe me if I say it like this. I'll be a good actor if I say it like this." All of which are Actor Brain thoughts. We want to think Character Brain thoughts as much as possible.

Whatever actors and actresses you admire - whatever faces you might be seeing when you think of a great performance - one thing I think they're doing is they are so committed to the characters that they are kind of saying "F.U." to the camera. You are so dedicated to the character, that you are daring the camera to watch.

There's a disdain for the camera and the trappings of the camera. There's a big F.U. to the status quo on set so the actor can overcome all of this disempowerment around us; the equipment, the microphone, lights and cables, it's 100° and it's supposed to be winter, right? So much disempowerment.

Another phrase I haven't used in a long time is "the aggressive act." When it's time for me to start, I have to start with an understanding that I need to overpower everything around me. I need to overcome everything. The director, standing there watching. The camera person. Overcome the camera which is right in front of you and sometimes as big as a human person. All right there in front of you. I've got to overcome it because if I don't I'll never get to the prairie or whatever the scene is. Because there's a big-ass camera right in front of me. And a crew of technicians and designers all looking at you. I have to have enough of an FU to get rid of all of that so I can get where I need to be. Without the FU, it's like "I hope you guys like the way I take you to the prairie" as opposed to with the FU, it's like "We're going to the prairie whether you like it or not."

Polly, anything rattling for you?

I think tonight I'm committed to demonstrating more confidence and living in Character Brain.

Wonderful. I'm with you. And you know, living in Character Brain will give you confidence. Because Character Brain isn't worried about acting "good," doing a good job acting or trying to impress everyone or getting a good review. Character Brain doesn't care about any of that. Actor Brain is where the lack of confidence lies and the more we're in Character Brain, the less we need confidence. Because Character Brain either has confidence or doesn't, but Actor Brain is where the struggle lies. So we can quiet Actor Brain by diving deeper into Character Brain. Character Brain doesn't care about the scene or the line of dialogue or impressing an audience. The harder you fight

for your character the more confident you'll feel because you'll quiet those un-confident voices in your Actor Brain.
Right. Okay.

As I was considering working with you tonight - and as you know I've been applauding your growth recently - I just wanted to remind you of something we talked about last week. It might look like we need an answer, but instead we're just going to raise good questions. Explore but don't come to an answer. An answer such as "my character is…" fill in the blank. My character is stern and we get a stern reading of a stern character doing stern things. If we get rid of that, we might be stern here but here we're compassionate, here we're loving, here we're reflecting, here we're anticipating. Now, because we avoid that answer, we leave so much room for exploration.
Right. In playing with these, that's one thing I noticed. Wait, I can't do it like this because that's my preconceived notion.
Being confident will mean you're willing to do it without a net.
That's the tough part. I like a net.
That's like surfing on the sidewalk. Who cares? Nothing is happening. You've got to get out on the ocean. A so-called answer might give us a false sense of security, as in "I know what I'm doing" but to be truly confident means "I'm okay with not knowing." I think you are making strides in that direction.

Alejandro, my friend, I know something is rattling for you this evening, what is it?
I've been thinking about something you said a couple of classes ago when you said "I don't believe you." That alone, that sentence… makes me want to zone in more on the scene. That one sentence gave me more focus, more motivation.
I don't remember saying that to you, it sounds kind of mean, but if it inspired you, I'll take it. *(laugh)*
I actually liked it. This is kind of a shark world so… I remember you saying "This may sound mean but…"
I think I might have shared with you that sometimes when I'm watching acting and they say "Yesterday I went to the supermarket," I'm thinking "No, you didn't." And they're like "and I saw Susan there." And I'm like, "No you didn't." You did not go to the supermarket yesterday, you did not see Susan. You have no truth. You're saying lines of dialogue but there is no truth there. Because you don't know what it looks like.
"I ran for governor in 1974." No, you did not. No, you did not run for governor in 1974. You're lying. If you ran for governor in 1974, you would know what it looked like. If you don't know what it looked like then it never happened. You're lying to me.
If you ran for governor in 1974, you would know what it looked like. Shoot the video which gives us our truth.

So if you really have a video of running for governor in 1974; you're seeing rallies, and meetings and wearing a suit and its lapel is wide because it's 1974 - whatever the fashion would be - and knowing what it was like to make speeches and do interviews and to hope you win. If you don't know what all of that looks like, then you absolutely did not run for governor in 1974.

And we use these videos to generate our dialogue. We need our language to be generated by truth and what is truth but video?

And we can create a video for anything. We can create a video of running for governor in 1974 or seeing Susan at the supermarket yesterday. We can create a video for anything and then we absolutely know what it looks like. And when we know what it looks like we don't have to pretend it's true anymore because we know it is. We've seen it.

Real quickly, shoot a video of running into Susan at the supermarket yesterday. Take a moment.

(pause)

Lisa, your first line of dialogue in our class: "I saw Susan at the supermarket yesterday."

(3 students say the line)

(laugh) Those were three very different Susans. *(laugh)*

That's our challenge for whatever we ever say. To have a video that generates and makes truth of the line of dialogue. And that the video precedes the things we're saying, the video drives the language. If we're doing that then we have truth.

And look at how interesting your video is. As far as who Susan is, what she means to you, what it means that you saw her. Has she been missing for six months or maybe you haven't seen her since 4th grade. Is she your best friend? Is she your rival? As we move forward, if we discover she's a rival, we simply reshoot the video to reflect it.

If I have truth, I don't have to convince anybody. A waiter doesn't try to convince people they're a waiter, they simply take your order. Without trying to convince anyone. I'm just going to take your order. I'm just going to show you to your seat, I'm just going to offer you water. I don't have to pretend I'm a waiter, I have to take your order.

And if I really saw Susan at the supermarket yesterday, I don't have to act like anything. I really saw her. "Creating a new truth." That's what the video will do for us.

Alejandro, how did it go for you?

I really tried to put arrows in there and change up the tone in my voice in some lines… That's what I was focusing on.

That was a really good take. You've developed some great skills and you're comfortable in the process of figuring out a role. You're like "I think he's this kind of guy and I can inhabit this kind of guy in this way…" Your technical stuff like eyeline is getting quite good, your rhythms are quite good. As you mentioned you're using arrows. I think that might be where we should explore.

I think certain moments could be mined a bit more. Your instincts are to use arrows to change it up but I'm not sure that you're changing it up smartly. I'd like to refine a bit of your use of arrows. You're changing it up to change it up but where and when and which directions you go is also part of the equation. If you make the change here, it might be more powerful than if you make the change there. If you go from an excited tone to a hushed tone, it may be more powerful to make the change in this moment than in this moment. Does that make sense?

Yes, it does.

Great. I think right now you're using all your instincts but you're using them independent of the script itself. You're really doing well. I think you can compete. To take it to the next level would be getting smart as to where and when we make these choices. Does that feel actionable?

It definitely does.

Good. Your work is viable. Viable is a great word. That means "give this guy a callback."

Polly, how's it going?

I tried to not look at my script and I know I messed up a few words but I kept on going.

How did you feel about your video?

Most of the time it was there. Sometimes it would wander.

I think it was very good in some places. And when the video is strong, who needs acting? We don't have to worry about acting, we have truth. And you're finding your way to that. Now the only time I'm pulled out of it is when you don't have the video. Like when you said the word "grim" and also when you said "sooner or later" I felt your video was lacking.

I liked her. I thought she was strong.

I felt more into her this time than before. I felt more confident.

Good. If that monologue is two minutes long, it's a matter of maintaining the highest level the whole time. To me as a coach or director, partly because you're having to look at your script, it sometimes will look kind of like this: "I'm saying my line and I'm acting!" break, "I'm saying my line and I'm acting!" break. Not that that's what is happening for you, but at our best we're going to fight through those moments. We might have to look at our script but can we fight for our character the whole time?

I was also taking some pauses and I was afraid I was dragging.

I don't think you were. Keep in mind, it's about tension. If we go too fast no tension can happen. You're forcing us - when you go slowly and take your time - you're forcing us to confront what you're talking about. In this monologue, you're forcing us to confront your dead husband hanging in the closet.

Tell me about the video on your taxidermist. Would you say you have a good image there?

Umm. No. I don't think I have one.

Going back to our earlier conversation, "Wonderful taxidermist I know." No, you don't. Don't let me catch you in a lie. In fact, why lie at all? Shoot the video and then tell the truth.

I felt in that scene the rhythm was predictable. Here is a thought. "Establish a rhythm, upset it. Establish a rhythm, upset it."

(laughing) It's so much easier to just establish a rhythm and stay at it.

That might lull the audience into falling off to sleep. Instead, by upsetting the rhythm, we are helping to keep the audience's ear awake.

Don't let the audience get comfortable. Keep them in a state of surprise. And rhythm is a way to keep them awake and alert. "Establish a rhythm, upset it. Establish a rhythm, upset it." Rhythmically, if you've been in the same pattern for a period of time, find a way to change it. That sudden abrupt change in rhythm keeps the audience alert.

Got it.

In this material, in this style, in this scene, I don't know the answer. I'm not familiar with this scene beyond what you're doing.

Sometimes Alejandro, I feel you're really comfortable in that emotional mid-range. If it were a scale of 1 to 10, you seem to fall in that 3 to 7 range. I wonder what would happen if we started exploring more nines and ones. More the nines than the ones. I want you to feel free sometimes to 9 out. Feel free stylistically, comically perhaps, to be more freaked out that you cannot dance, that you don't have the courage to dance. I feel that you're very comfortable in that 6 area, but what if we needed a 9? What would that look like? Does that feel actionable?

Yeah. I think I know exactly what you're talking about.

Does it feel fun?

Yeah.

I just want you to have options. I don't want you to get locked into that six-y area. At times we might want to raise the stakes for you. In this scene how heartbroken you are that you can't dance, that you never learned how to dance. How much you wish you could be a dancer. Can that be more unreasonable? There certainly wasn't anything wrong with what you did but I want to make sure that we recognize the other possibilities, how to get there as well. Does that feel germane to you when I suggest you're getting comfortable in that 6 area?

Yeah. Like I'm holding back.

I like your technique very much. It's coming together nicely. It's more of the exceptions to the rules that I want to cover here. I want to make sure your technique would include going to what right now feels like too far with these emotional values. It might feel like too far right now, but if we needed them to be that high, what that would feel like and how to get there. That we are aware of that and that that's part of our diagramming as well. For us to get unreasonably upset that we can't dance. Not reasonably, unreasonably.

That's a word we use often. Unreasonable. Too far gone.

This brings back a memory with an acting coach, I had done something over the top and I remember the acting teacher going whoa, whoa, whoa. I didn't understand why he was telling me to hold back.

Your coach was probably right in a certain way.

If you were to ask me to define overacting, I would say it's when you don't have truth. When the video isn't driving the moment. If the stakes are genuinely high enough, it's not overacting. Overacting would be from the outside in, not the inside out. We can overact by pretending it's true but if it is true? That's not overacting. That's raising the stakes. Overacting would be when we don't have the truth to back it up. We're just going to raise the stakes and do it truthfully.

I understand that.

I think I'd like you to take a few more chances. I want you to be able to take more chances and not be so secure with what you're doing. Fair enough?

Yeah. Okay.

Again, it's not that you're not truthful or adventurous. At the core of it, your athletic skills are good. If you're up on the wire let's say, you're really walking the wire well. But now I need you to get out your unicycle and still be up on the wire.

Okay.

You're walking the wire great but now we need you to get up on a unicycle and start juggling. Take more chances.

Lisa, I see that your focus is on accents and that's fine. You're really good at them. What I will sometimes say as a caution is don't let the accent do the role. I might also say don't let the mustache do the role or don't let the wig do the role. In terms of the accent, if this was a radio play, we'd be fine. If I was just listening. But acting is more than how we sound. Is that a fair thing to say?

Absolutely.

Thanks.

Alejandro, what were you working on?

I was really just thinking "eff it." Just go for it. I was just focused on her and my mission.

Great. That all worked well. I especially liked your line "Sure is." You may remember how you did that line. You were thinking, "Yeah. I'm going to extort some money" while she was thinking about a little kid with the sniffles.

If I was on set filming this, I would make a note and say print that take. That's the one we'll probably use. That was strong. Again, you're developing a lot of good techniques and avoiding bad habits.

That's exactly what I'm hoping to do.

Part of me rails a bit, when I think you might be intimidated by a role because of its size. A bit of the hair on the back of my neck stands up if you think that because of the size of a role, it may be beyond you. Okay, maybe Hamlet. *(laugh)*

Part of putting one foot in front of the other is that you don't have a problem unless someone asks you to play the role. That's when you have a problem. When someone says "Will you please play this role for us?" That's when you have to decide if you can do it or not. Don't be afraid to try to do it because you don't have a conflict until someone says "You're the one we choose."

Right.

At that point, you have to make a commitment. And then you look at what the commitment is. Wait until they ask you. Then you have to know whether you can or can't.

So go ahead and audition for anything?

(Laugh) Well, I don't know about anything, but yeah. Go ahead and go for stuff, whatever it is. That could be a play or whatever and then you see what's offered to you. And if it is Hamlet, you might raise your hand and say "Hey, did you know I've never acted professionally before?" But if they're asking you to do it, that's what putting one foot in front of the other is.

Okay.

So what's the next step? If someone says "Will you please play this role? Rehearsals start Monday and we open in three weeks." You look at the script, talk to whoever you have to talk to in your personal life and then you either say no or you get to work and you have fun.

One thing about doing a short film for instance, is that sometimes that's just a Saturday from noon to five. And it lasts forever! In ten years you'll still have the footage from that movie you did for those five hours that one day.

Wow.

And in theatre, too. It looks like a huge deal but it's "Okay. If I can commit, January 15th, kind of clear my schedule from mid January to the end of February. Four nights a week and Sundays... someone will have to walk the dog..." If we can do that, then for the rest of your life, you'll have done that.

You've made those connections and you've gained that experience. Sometimes for a short term sacrifice we get a long term reward. For the investment of doing it, forever you'll have done that.

It's okay that you haven't really done it before, everybody has to start out at some point. I don't want us to be intimidated by it, until we're confronted with having to do it.

Polly, in addition to all of the acting skills that you've been building, it seems to me that you're just a smart person. I don't know what your real-life career is but I would bet that you are above average and that's going to be the same here. Don't be intimidated because acting is new for you or because it's acting you're out of your element. You'll be fine. I have a great deal of confidence in you. Whatever your career or expertise, that's going to serve you here as well. So don't hesitate because you're lacking. You're not lacking, you're ready.

Okay. I have a trip coming up but after that…

Sometimes it seems like it has to be all of a sudden and everything. Like "Starting Thursday I'm only going to eat salad." So I want us to avoid "I'll have to wait until after the first of the new year" or "I have to wait until after the wedding." We can just spend an hour on the computer looking for what's out there. It's not necessarily a big lifestyle change that we go to an audition.

That's great and you're right. I know exactly what you're saying.

You're getting to the point where you're viable and can compete.

Yep. I'm ready.

I'm excited about that. Good, good, good. Great. Good conversation.

Largely your video was good but there were places where it wasn't.

Did you think I went too introspective?

No. No, I didn't.

Okay.

It's not about the experience that you're conveying to us, it's about the woman this happened to.

Okay.

That was strong. I think that can get stronger. That aspect of how you're affected by this. It's more about that than the things you're saying.

How the whole thing affected me.

Yes. For us to see the person this happened to. The effects of this experience on this person. And I think you're already on the brink of fighting for that, Polly. That was very good work. To make it great is this next little precipice. It's great that you give me the opportunity to talk about this. When you can make it about who you are as a human, rather than the story - like this happened and then this happened - but about you as a human being.

More on what I'm feeling…

Yes, but I worry a bit that you might be seeking answers.

Yeah. Okay.

A phrase that comes to mind is what we've been saying a lot recently: "It's hard to be a person."

Yeah.

It's hard to be her.

Mm-hmm.

It's hard to have this resentment over a guy who died.

Right.

It's hard to hate somebody who's sick.

Right.

It's hard to be sick. It's hard to have compassion. It's all hard to navigate.

I think in this one I felt more of that than I have in the past.

Good, Polly. And it's great because it leads me to say ultimately, you're more interesting than your story. And that's a great place to be. To be fierce enough to be interesting enough that you don't have to embellish or sell. Just because you're a human being and we can read you and feel you, where you're at. Where you're feeling scared and where you're feeling triumphant. We read and know you inside. Not outside - what we're hearing or even seeing - but what's happening inside. You're on the brink of doing something very nice in that very way.

And that's what I think the best actors do. It doesn't matter what the story is, they're fascinating.

It's what you're feeling inside to convey.

Convey scares me but okay.

The feelings…

To strip away anything that isn't at her core and to make her core more vulnerable and aware.

Okay.

But I'm afraid that you'll say "I'll make this choice and I'll make this choice" and I don't think it's about her choices, it's about her.

Right. I know when I first started this piece it was "this is the part where I start getting angry, I soften up here…"

And now you're being brave enough - we just saw an example a few minutes ago - of not having to have those answers, to not make those decisions but to live your life. We talked about without a net and that's what without a net is. It's to not make those decisions but fight hard for her anyway.

Right. Yes. I felt like I didn't have a net most of the time.

Great. That's something we're looking for. At its core, Actors shouldn't have nets. And when you're doing your best work, that's when you're way up on the wire. Good, good, good. Polly, that's really nice work.

I have a bit of a technical note for you. I don't know exactly how to express it but I'll try it like this. Regarding your verbal and vocal energy, It feels like you're mostly in the five to seven range, and I'd like more fours and threes.
Oh, okay. I felt I was going too soft.
I felt there were places where you were giving vocal energy and I didn't feel that your video would support that energy in that particular moment or that particular line or that particular word.
Okay. I see what you're saying. Yeah.
Think about not only projecting your character out but also think about drawing us toward you. It feels a little too yang-y and not enough yin. Draw us in a little more, don't just give and give and give, take too. So that we're on a string with you.
Okay.
Does that feel actionable?
I feel like I would have to give it a whirl.
Okay, great.
Great.

How's it going Joe?
Alright.
Joe, you'll have to tell me if I'm right, but I feel that your video and your words may be happening kind of simultaneously. That your video wasn't preceding your language.
Yeah. You're right.
I'd like you to get your video further in front of your language.
Yeah. I haven't gotten that note in a while, but you're right.
Again, the video needs to precede the language.

In a way, I'm looking at the similarities between you. For both of you, there's such vulnerability, human frailty. I'm really just finding other ways to say "it's hard to be a person."
Your characters are just trying to figure it out and doing their best, even though the deck is stacked against them. Who's prepared for Polly's monologue? Who's prepared for that moment in life? When the person who ruined your life is now dying in a shopping center parking lot and you confront him. There's no playbook for that. There's no playbook for this stuff, we're all just flailing about, trying our best. And when we see that in our characters, when the audience sees that in our characters, They go "Yeah, I know

that. That looks like my Mom." "My sister." "Myself." "I felt like that in college." "I felt like that last year." "I feel like that all the time."

It's when we understand, we're more than the things we're saying. We're more than the circumstances our characters are in. We're people. We're human beings. And that is already powerful and frail. Especially dramatically.

It's a pleasure working with you both tonight. If this were an audition you'd probably both get a callback. Nice work, both of you.

We talked about Sherlock Holmes-ing. When we look at the clues in the script, what are we finding? Natasha, what assumptions are you making about your character? What kind of a young woman is she?

I feel like I'm a hypocrite. There's a bit of deception there.

Great! Character's flaws are much more interesting than their positive attributes. To see that she's petty enough to say "Let's be talking about opera," duplicitous enough to be drinking wine even though she's attending AA meetings, selfish enough to tell stories that shouldn't be told. There's a lot going on with her and I'm really fascinated by who the woman is that makes those choices. I think she's kind of fascinating. And I don't know what the answers are, but I think those are great questions.

I'm trying to think of how to do that.

A phrase I like to use: "Who we're being." I think it's who she is, not what you're doing. It's the person who makes those decisions, not the decisions themselves. Perhaps she's entitled. Perhaps she's always had wealth and so people kow-tow to her. There's something about her and I just want to investigate who she is.

I think she's such a gossip, that she enjoys telling this story. Right now I feel it's kind of lukewarm. As opposed to "Hey, you won't believe what I've got to tell you about this guy." And if she enjoys telling this story, what does that say about her? I think that's worth investigating. Let's try the scene again.

That line "He seems to really like olives but I don't think that's a symptom of anything." We can see that that's a punchline, right? That's a joke. That somehow, some way, the author is expecting a laugh on this line?

Right.

I think there's a couple of ways to go for it. One is, it would be ridiculous that olives would be a symptom of addiction. You can say it like you know it's ridiculous. As if to say, "wouldn't it be funny if olives were a symptom of addiction?" Or the other would be "He seems to really like olives and I'm pretty sure that means he's on heroin." I think right now you haven't really decided, you're somewhere in the middle. It's just a line of dialogue but your perspective on the line is important. Either approach might work, I don't know which it is, but it's in there somewhere, you see what I'm suggesting? Seriously considering it might be a symptom or wouldn't it be funny if it were a symptom? But somehow or other I don't want the line to just melt into something innocuous.

It's a good opportunity.

Good. And that's a great way to look at it. The writer is giving us opportunities and if we take advantage of them, we're serving the work well.

Natasha, how is it going?

Good. I really like this scene. I'm being a bit more playful and just sort of moving through the scene. It was fun.

Good. I saw you having fun and fun is very easy to watch. It's easy to watch people having fun. We delight in watching people have fun. Even though the character is a bit freaked out about the guy at the salad bar that she doesn't want to talk to. But you, the actor, having fun playing these moments is really appealing. I invite you to keep relishing in that idea.

Natasha, a word that comes to mind for me is playful.

There were moments there when I felt you were really in the waters of the moment, right?

Yeah. And even now I keep seeing different ways to just be playful with the scene. It just sparks new ideas. It just makes it fun.

And to put a cap on it, when it's fun for you, it's fun for us.

You said that you're judging your work while you're doing it, and that is something we want to avoid. A phrase I like to use is "one-way street."

That self judgment is watching yourself, something outside of yourself watching and saying good or bad. But that's a two-way street, to be watching yourself. This is a one-way street, my performance is emanating from me. And powerfully going in one direction. My performance goes out and away and toward the audience. There's nothing observing me. Nothing coming back at me. It's a one-way street.

I forget how you put it but earlier you said you were being hard on yourself or judging your work and what was or wasn't working during the scene. When you're playful it helps you keep out of that mindset.

Mm-hmm.

And that one-way street idea, was that something that made its way into your thinking?

Yeah. That definitely resonated with me. It's hard to not have a second part that's watching or judging or critiquing. It's such a feeling to feel fully immersed in the scene, in the moment and when that second part goes away, it's easier to feel really in the moment.

Ann, regarding memorization, I was observing that you're a little reliant on your script. You have that line "Where?" You shouldn't have to look at your script for that. If your line is "Where?" we need to quickly find a way to not need our page for that line. There's a couple of "gimmes" in the script. There's always a couple of gimmes. So let's identify where the gimmes are and take advantage of the gimmes. Which is a golf term guys, for a like two-inch putt.

Not to be confused with gummies.

No. *(laugh)* Gimmes.

Natasha, One thing I'm going to ask you to do is to slow down a bit. In Actor Brain there's this "Keep going" motor. "Keep going. Keep going. Keep going." But in real life that motor is usually slowed down a bit. There's no motor going "Oh my God. I have to keep going. My scene isn't over yet. I still have more dialogue. Keep going." I'd like you to slow that "actor motor" down. If the scene is 30 seconds longer that's okay. I want to see what happens if you luxuriate in the pace a bit more. I had a couple of notes but I think I'll just give this one for now. We'll see what happens when you take that note. I have a feeling that by slowing down and confronting your language a bit more, the other notes will take care of themselves. Okay?

Okay.

Let's see what happens this time through.

Thank you, Natasha. In terms of what we've been discussing this morning regarding playfulness - or as you put it, being in the moment - this time felt even better as in you finding yourself more immersed in the scene. It was happening more often, more reliably. Was that true to your experience?

It was kind of hard to manage. I was focusing on slowing down and where and how to do that, where to take a pause. And finding new moments like when I leaned in. I felt like the playfulness suffered a bit because I was focused on the other part of it. So now I have to kind of combine the two.

I think you totally nailed it. The moment that you leaned in, etcetera. That was a strong choice. To illustrate, we talked about events earlier. When you leaned in like that, you carved a bolder path for that moment. It became an event.

We sometimes talk about arrows. You can get a little bit confidential with her or you can get all the way confidential with her by using longer arrows. A longer arrow creates a larger event. Does that make sense?

Yeah.

Cool. Super fun.

We talked about gimmes. I haven't identified that idea before but I'm excited about it. Gimmes are lines we can memorize almost immediately. Someone asks you a question, "Where did you go on your honeymoon?" And your line is "Kansas City." *(laugh)* Probably not a common destination, but that's your line, "Kansas City." Then we can very quickly shoot a video that will give us the answer to the question. We want our video to be where the line lives, not on the page. Some lines are just "gimmes." I shoot five seconds of video and I'll have the line forever. Someone asks me where I went on my honeymoon, I'll say Kansas City. I've got it. I never ever need to look at my script again in that moment.

And you don't even have to think, right?

Well you don't have to think "What's my line?" You might be thinking what a bad choice Kansas City was for a honeymoon. *(laugh)* Or "We had to because my wife's father lived there" or whatever. But that line we can consider memorized in about 5 seconds. That's another gimme.

Now if we expand on that idea, maybe my line is "Kansas City and it was July." That's a longer line so it's harder to memorize? Not really. "Kansas City and it was July." Now I shoot the video of July and it's probably hot and humid or there are mosquitos everywhere. I don't know what the real weather there is like - maybe it's beautiful - but I can still shoot my video and have my lines.

The video will memorize the line for you. We don't need to memorize anything, all we have to do is have the video to give us our truth. And therefore we can get rid of the script sooner. Look for those gimmes. Understand that by shooting a simple video, it will give you your line. Where did you go on your honeymoon? Kansas City and it was July. Got it. I have truth now, not lines to memorize.

All I have to do is remember my honeymoon. I have truth now and it took me like 5 seconds. The video will give you your lines. If we use a video, we can cover so much of our memorization and we can cover it so much quicker. In a way we don't memorize lines at all, we memorize images. Screw lines. Lines are hard. Lines are typing. Images are what we have to memorize. And it's so much easier. Kansas City and it was July. Got it.

I know because I was there. The video gave me the experience. And it's truthful. I feel right now I could take a lie detector test and pass it. *(laugh)* Because I shot the video, I have the memory. I've created the memory and I no longer have lines to memorize, I have an experience to recount.

Shoot the video. Have the truth. That's what the video does for us.

We're trying to take memorization from an Actor Brain task and turn it into a Character Brain behavior. The video does that.

I feel I may need to parse this out. We're looking for the first person experience, not the third person observation. Not the experience of saying your lines but the experience that then tells you what to say.

In my real life, I was in the play South Pacific when I was in tenth grade. If I were to tell you that story, I've got to see myself doing it. Here I am at sixteen and I'm on stage! My clothes don't fit but I'm playing the lead! Right? The memory is the truth. Now if I was acting in the role of someone who was in South Pacific at sixteen - which I really did but if I hadn't - I would need to create the memory of having done it and use that memory to drive my language. I, as the actor playing the part, would need to create the memories that I, the real person, really have.

I, Duane, really have that memory. But what if you were cast as Duane? What are you missing? You're missing my memory. You need to create that memory of having really done it. Not of saying the line "I was in South Pacific" but of having been in South Pacific. That's the video that I'm talking about.

Often, our characters' video was created twenty-five years ago. Or five years ago. Or yesterday. But it's not me now, saying my line.

Let's check in. Joe, anything rattling for you?

Yeah. Stuff we have been talking about. More detailed video work. Better details, word by word. As much as possible. Glad to be here.

Good. Does it feel actionable? You say you're working on video. Do you think you know how to work on it? Do you feel you have an approach to that?

Yes, I think so. You'll give me feedback but I've gone through the scenes you sent me, at least one of them, with that in mind. At least on one of them. The shorter one. It feels like it's coming along.

Good. I'm glad. Thanks for getting us started today.

Alejandro, anything rattling for you?

I was hoping you could go over what you were saying about "Word emphasis."

Good. Well, let's look at it from 2 different sides: First, look at Actor Brain. The Actor Brain might say "Which word should I stress?" But over in Character Brain, we hope that the word gets stressed because it is most important to the character, not because we figured it out in Actor Brain.

On the technical side of it - the Actor Brain side - the word we stress will automatically imply its opposite. Again, the word we stress will automatically imply its opposite. The example I use here, and forgive me if it's redundant for a couple of you, is "I went to the bank."

If I stress "I." Here's the reading: "**I** went to the bank." What is that implying? "**You** didn't." Right? What's the story behind that? "I told **you** to go to the bank but you didn't so **I** went to the bank." So if that's the story that we're trying to tell, then that word would be the one to stress.

If I stress "went," it goes like this: "I **went** to the bank." Now what am I implying? "I didn't **come from** the bank. I **went** to the bank." You see how the implication there is of the stressed words opposite?

I think so.

Moving on, "I went **to** the bank." Again, "I didn't **come from** the bank, I went **to** the bank."

I went to **the** bank." Which implies "I didn't go to **a** bank or **any** bank. I went to **the** bank."

And "I went to the **bank**." implies "I didn't go to the **store**. I went to the **bank**."

So you see the implication? We're bringing the opposite idea into the storytelling by whichever words we stress. Does that hold together for you so far, Alejandro?

Yes.

So in another sentence like "I came to see you." "I came to **see** you. I didn't come to **listen** to you" is implied. Or "I came to see **you**. I didn't come to see **her**." Or "**I** came to see you." implies "I could have sent **someone else** but **I** came to see you." Does that feel actionable?

Yes.

Now those exercises we just did, that's all Actor Brain stuff. Here is the more important thing to be thinking about: What does my character care about? Am I mad at you for not going to the bank? If I am, if I'm mad at you for not going to the bank, I'll say "I **went** to the bank." Not because my Actor Brain figured out blah, blah, blah, but because of what I care about. I'm mad because you didn't go.

So the character is making those decisions but when we go to Actor Brain it's good to understand the technical side. So I'm not going to go "Stress this word and then stress this word." I'm going to use Character Brain and think about what matters to me and let the stresses fall where they may.

Is it always something that's important to me? Can it be used comedically?

Yes. There's lots of ways to apply what we've been talking about. But ultimately, we want the lines to be said by the character, not the actor. Is that holding together, Alejandro?

Yes. It's good to get the repetition.

Here's another side of that coin: If we stress words that don't need to be stressed, we're implying something that doesn't need to be implied. Artificially stressing words can lead the audience down a path that doesn't bear fruit. So that's the caution aspect, if you're going to stress a word, be sure that you intend to imply its opposite. Because the audience is going to see the implication of its opposite. But if that doesn't result in clean, powerful storytelling then don't stress that word.

Sometimes actors will artificially stress words in order to look like they mean it, or to add energy or rhythm, but we want to be careful that we don't stress words where the audience goes "the opposite of the stressed word is this, I wonder where that goes," and it doesn't go anywhere. So we want to be careful about where the stresses are happening and not make them happen artificially, which we sometimes do - our Actor Brain goes "Oh, make it exciting." so we stress things that don't need to be stressed - but if our Character Brain cares about 'I'm mad at you for not going to the bank." then let that be what says the line, not "which word should I stress?" Is this all coming together in a useful way?

Yes. Very much.

I'm so glad.

The video is a memory and the memory is a video. That's why we shoot video. Backstory? It's in the video. Motivation? It's in the video. History? It's in the video. The memory of when your daughter was two, the fight you got into with your husband, those are videos that we have to shoot so we can remember these events. The video will inform everything you're saying.

May I interrupt the scene? We'll go back to the beginning of Gianna's speech. Joe, sometimes a good opportunity to break your eyeline is when the other person is talking.

Okay. I consciously broke it a little earlier. I don't know if it was the right time or not.

Okay. I'll take that.

It was a bit mechanical for me.

Okay. I could see that. It's going to be like that for now. You'll make that transition. But it was the right idea and even at the right moment. Though you're right it was a bit mechanical.

Regarding that, if you're staring at her, your eyeballs are seeing but not necessarily your brain's eye. But if when she says she wants her child to know her grandpa, you look away from her, you're letting the audience see the effect her words have on you. You're being introspective. We can see how her words resonate with you. And you'll find it resonating more, too.

May I interrupt you?

Joe, I can see in this take that you're thinking about your eyes.

You're right. A hundred percent.

Don't think about your eyes. Think about being a grandfather and a dad. And how you messed up. Impose that thought upon yourself.

Okay.

Go back to where I stopped you.

Don't show me anything. Let me watch you. Anonymously. Let the audience be a fly on the wall. Obviously, sometimes the audience is a camera and sometimes it's 500 people in a theatre but don't even know they're there. The more you can convince us you don't know we're here, the more intimacy we will feel with you.

There were moments there when you thought about being a Grandpa, and maybe that helps you to think this character's thoughts. Impose those thoughts. Not Joe's thoughts. This character's thoughts. Impose those thoughts.

"From now on, I'm going to be better. Next Christmas I'm going to bring presents, etc." Think his thoughts, not Joe thoughts like "Duane told me to look over here..." And by the way, when you took your eyeline away and thought the character's thoughts and came back to us with your eyeline, you were swimming deeper in the waters of the character. Weren't you? Did you feel that?

At one spot, yes.

Good, not Joe's thoughts "I hope everyone believes me when I say this" but the character's thoughts. "I've been a jerk. Why have I been such a bad father?" Look how deeply you can swim when you think what he thinks, not what you think.

Gianna, How's it going?

Good. I was thinking more about the video.

I thought so too.

Did that work?

Yes!

Okay, cool.

As we move forward, I would suggest we follow that path and get really specific. There were moments when it was good but as we work with video, I find we cannot get too specific. I want to shoot a movie and then that movie generates our language. So we want to get really specific. Words like "in" and "of" and "though" and "maybe" and "sometimes" and "until" and "you" and "me." I want you to have a video for e-ver-y-thing. But I thought there were moments there when you had much better video. For sure. And again, I think I'm kind of a mind reader in that what I'm looking for is, "Is the language generated by the images in your brain or by the external input of a script?" Or "Because I memorized it, I'll say it." I'm looking for "Are you someone who's speaking your truth and not the script's truth? Not the actor's truth but the character's truth?" And the video is what gives us that.

Okay. Thank you.

Perhaps even if this is a dim light, I hope a light bulb is lighting. It will get brighter as we go along.

The phrase I might use here is "first person." If I'm going to tell you a story about yesterday - let's see, what did I do yesterday? Oh, I saw a show! - if I'm going to tell you about yesterday, my first person video is of driving to the theatre and parking and putting on my mask and getting a program and seeing the show. My video is not of me telling you that or where I am when I tell you I saw a show. It's the first person memory of being there. It happens to be true but if it weren't I'd use shooting the video to make it true. Does that sound actionable?

It's something I'll have to spend more time concentrating on...

Gotcha, and I think just now you had a video of yourself sitting down and getting to work and concentrating, right?

(laugh) Yeah.

You had a video of yourself doing that. That was your thought: "Tomorrow or later this afternoon I'm going to get a notepad and I'm going to get to work and I'm going to take a script and I'm going to try to do this exercise that I'm thinking of from Duane's class." That's your video. That's your truthful video. Later on you're going to do that and you shot a video of yourself doing it. You probably saw yourself sitting in your favorite chair. Then your language reflected what you were seeing and you said "I'm going to spend time concentrating." Your video told you what to say.

Okay.

Good. So that's video.

So video is something that can be present or future?

And past.

I meant as well as past.

Let's take the focus off of present. Present might be the environment. The video we're talking about here is either what happened when I was twelve or twenty-five or whatever and that's an experience and that's in the past. And the other part of video is what I hope for. "I'm in love with so and so, one day we'll be together." And "One day I'll live in Hawaii." And "I hope I get the job." And "Please give me that $20 you owe me." That's all future. So really, present isn't useful. Let's be thinking past and future.

Okay. Yeah.

Even part of my video here - I've been conscious in this conversation - my video in explaining this concept to you is of you nodding and going "Oh. I get it now." That's my video. I'm trying to get to that point. You guys going "Got it, Duane. That makes perfect sense to me."

That's why I'm telling you this stuff. Part of my video is what I'm saying, part of my video is why I'm telling you, which is you understanding what I'm saying. I hope that holds together. There's a lot to discuss as we delve in.

Natasha, I still want you to luxuriate more in the tempo. Don't let yourself gallup on your horse. Feel free to amble more in your tempo. This will create more space that you then have to do something with. I want to see how you take advantage of that space you're creating for yourself. Does that feel actionable?

Yes.

And fun?

(laughs) Yes.

For instance on that line "I don't like wine. It gives me a headache." Here's something I noticed, Ann. You looked at your script for that line. Shoot the video. Why don't you like wine? You've got to shoot the video of the pounding headache every time you drink wine. Now if someone offers me wine, I don't have a line, I have a reaction. "I don't like wine, it gives me a headache."

You mentioned being uncomfortable. The phrase I use here is to "Get comfortable being uncomfortable." Instead of "I'm not comfortable. I need to get somewhere where I feel safer." It's "I'm uncomfortable and I like it." It's like the difference between being on a highwire or the sidewalk. The sidewalk is safer but we like the highwire. And when there's a breeze and it's windy, I really like being on the highwire. Getting comfortable being uncomfortable. There's tension and humanity and vulnerability in being uncomfortable.
Yeah, I like that.

You said something earlier that set off the alarm in my ear, when you said you wanted to "be real." And I was thinking, "Well, you only have to try to be real if you're not real. What's missing?" And I think what needs to be real here is your need to present your argument. And then, you don't have to try to be real because you really have something to do.
So you don't have to worry about being real, you get to fight for your cause, and as an artist that's better than a role. That's way better than a role. And you get to say some important stuff. There may only be fifty people watching you but you can help each of them. You can really help these people as they watch this play.
Very exciting.
Change some people. Make them think. Confront their norms. Actors have always been at the forefront of change. We have the opportunity as artists, to create a new future.
Okay.

Your role in a way is to be a trial attorney. You get the chance in this role to present your case to the jury and the jury here is the audience. There's a debate in the story as to what's best. Whose concerns outweigh the others concerns. The point is to make your case to the jury.
We can take license to make our argument strongly. You're making an argument. Think of yourself as an attorney and you're making your case. I hope that's helpful.
It is helpful.
Great conversation.

This note falls under "Who we're being." I want to see a man who has been shaped by this experience and right now I see a nice guy. If you have been shaped by this experience it's a more profound experience than "Oh by the way, this happened."

I see that that would make it about more than just this experience.

Right. Maybe he has chosen a heartless career. He's a landlord or whatever the stereotype might be; an inside trader, a lobbyist or something dishonest. When I Sherlock Holmes this role, it makes me think "How can I use this monologue to show a lifelong predilection?"

I see. I was just limiting it to what happened when I was in school.

Right, and that makes it about one day, many years ago. But if the event had a greater impact on you, the event becomes more impactful. A lasting impact will tell a more powerful story. If this event affected you when you were fourteen, that's one thing. If it still affects you today, then it's a bigger deal.

But that "Who we're being" aspect... You're really good, Joe, at being that favorite, nice uncle and I don't want you to lose that, but look for opportunities to carry more weight, more pathos. A little more "It's hard to be a person."

We want to use the material to reveal something about our characters. It's not "This happened then this happened then this happened." It's about how the events changed me. If an event has a profound effect on you, then it's a profound event. That's dramatically powerful.

Okay.

Good. That's a fun conversation.

Debra, I was tempted during your scene to give you a note, and it's a weird note. You may feel a little put off by it and I apologize. I want you to start the piece again and here is my note and again it may sound mean and unfiltered...

Do that. Please.

I can tell you're acting.

I know.

So now your job is to do the monologue but don't act. Don't let me see you acting. Why would you let me see you? Don't let me see you acting. No acting allowed. Do the monologue but don't act. No acting. But do the monologue.

That's such a bad habit of mine.

It's a difficult dichotomy because you care so much about it. It's hard to not want to do it good. You care so much about it, of course you want to do it good. But we have to care so much that we're willing to not do it good. I know you get the equation, I've seen you avoid good acting.

When I do it's such a wonderful thing, Duane. And I know you go over this. (laughing)

You must be thinking "Don't you get this? We go over it and over it. How long have you

been taking my class? I've been telling you and telling you, don't do that." But it's like you're naked in front of everyone if you don't act good.
In a way you are. That's the sort of vulnerability that we might need in order to avoid the safety of good acting.

Our characters cannot know that they are being poetic or profound. Let's tear all of that down. The audience decides that. Our job isn't to please the audience. Our job is to give them something unexpected and jarring. Out of the ordinary. And they are expecting poetry, because they're going to the thea-tah. Which is where people talk endlessly for two hours "When will this be over?" But to jar them and surprise them, we're not catering to them. So watch out for that safe, "I'm trying to please you" approach. Don't make her into a hero or whatever, she's just a woman with jelly on her lapel.
(laugh) Okay.

Okay. Good. I don't mind saying excellent, Joe. Great adjustment. Could you tell?
Well, I was uncomfortable and I was okay being that way.
Good!
But during, it was a little bit… weird.
Great. Being uncomfortable when you're out there… you should be uncomfortable. You're on a tightrope. You'd better be uncomfortable. I thought that was much better. That was an important story. To see a man who was affected by the story he's telling. Which makes the event when you were fourteen relevant today. Now that's important, rather than "Oh, incidentally, this happened." Now I see a man who's been changed by that experience. Could you tell?
Yeah. And my video was better this time.
Everything is ultimately about something important. It's never just a story. We use the story to reveal something about ourselves. And that is usually something universal, like in this story, you learn to stand up for yourself. That's universal and important. We all have to learn that. Or if it was the other character it might be "Don't be a bully." At some point everybody has to learn these things. We can all identify with that because it's part of everyone's story. So it's really not the details of the story but how you were changed by the event.

"Bracketing" is when you mention something earlier and then bring it up again later. I illustrate it by suggesting that in act one you say "No thanks. I don't drink." and then in act two you say "I'll have a martini." If the audience doesn't remember the moment from act one, the moment in act two won't have significance.

Another thought: It's better for the audience to see your story than to hear your story. So we're really using our language to illustrate for them. So they're not hearing you but actually seeing the story. How do we use these words to paint pictures? To make them see what you're saying is powerful communication. Draw me a picture. It's not about the audience hearing what you're telling them, it's about them seeing what you're telling them.

This is all very helpful.

Good Debra, thank you.

Good scene. Anything rattling for you, Alejandro?

I felt like when I first brought up the eraser, I'm not sure it came across.

What do you mean by that?

I feel like when I said it, if I was listening, I would not have understood.

Good, Alejandro. That's an "Aunt Enid." Remember "Aunt Enid?"

I remember you mentioning it but…

"Aunt Enid" means sometimes you have to over-articulate certain words. Like I can't say "Tomorrow we're going over aneenids house. You wanna go?" Because the audience will say "What? You're going where?" I have to say "Tomorrow we're going over AUNT ENID'S house. You wanna go?" I've got to add articulation to certain words.

"Aunt Enid" is used for surprise words. If I were to say "Can I eat that grapefruit?" it wouldn't be as surprising as "Can I eat that eraser?" So we want to carve a bolder path with our consonants. Sometimes we'll put a slight pause before and after our Aunt Enid moments. Okay? But the first time you say eraser, if you add articulation, you'll help the audience to know that they heard you correctly. And in this scene that helps because after you say eraser, sometimes you just refer to the eraser as "it." So you're helping the audience in a fundamental way by using "Aunt Enid" there.

I'm very excited because we both had the same note in that moment. Good fine tuning and instincts. Excellent. Anything else?

Not really. That was a hurdle and I kept thinking back to it in my brain, thinking "I don't even know if they're understanding the rest of this."

(Laugh) Got it. That's a good note for yourself. "Aunt Enid" can help there.

That brings up a good point and I'm glad because it doesn't come up too often in class, but you mentioned you were "thinking back."

I'd like to give us the counsel, please, that during a scene, in our Actor Brains, we don't think backwards. Only think present and forward, don't think back. You might have to sometimes - like in a play if someone says the wrong line and you have to think back in order to help fix it - but otherwise don't reflect on a scene while you're doing it. Wait until after the scene is over to reflect on it. Don't reflect while you're in it.

I mentioned this in a class recently but this scene is a real example of it. Comedy is really a re-thinking of logic. What's logical to me is if some guy says he wants to eat an eraser, I'd be like, "Wow. This is a serious situation, maybe a mental health issue." But for Joe's character it's like "Well, that's very impressive that you want to eat the eraser." Comedy is really a "Tilted logic." That's not the only thing it is, but it's one thing that it is.

And Alejandro's character, thinking that this picture of an athlete is a proper resume, again a unique take on logic. Nobody else would have that logic but this character does. So comedy is often a spin on logic. And that is super fun.

Joe, there were places there in the scene where I thought you were balanced as far as who you were. But there were places where I think you were falling back on "I'm a happy guy and here I am," and it didn't have the complexities that you had at other points in the scene. It was a bit too easy.

Sometimes for you, it's an easy go-to for you to play that happy guy. I want you to challenge yourself and not let you go to that "answer." Watch out for those types of answers that feel too easy. Challenge yourself. Play gray areas. Don't let it be black and white. Don't let it be easy. If it's easy for you, it's too easy for the audience as well. Okay?

Yes. Very good, thank you.

Here's a thought: Awkward moments are valuable. Awkward is gold. In real life we try to dissipate the awkwardness. But on film or on stage, awkward is money. Take advantage of the awkwardness. Awkward equals tension equals drama. So whenever we get the opportunity for an awkward moment or conversation, in real life we would try to avoid it, but here revel in it. It's dramatic currency.

I think there were places there, Joe, where you let yourself talk without the video to support it. That can cause you to artificially stress words.

Joe, how's it going?
I don't know. (both laugh) I think maybe, not great.
I don't often share this Joe, but when I ask an actor how it's going and they say "I don't know." In many cases, from my perspective it's going very well. When I ask you how it's going, I'm asking you to reflect in Actor Brain. "I don't know." is a response we give when we've been living predominantly in Character Brain.
Now that I think about it, I think I said I don't know because the whole time I was feeling awkward…
Yes! Avoiding answers is awkward, playing the game is awkward, putting a spin on the ball when you're playing is awkward. It's about awkward.

I guess that part of me that wants to do it good was disappointed. So when you said "how's it going" that was where my answer was coming from.

Exactly! And you put that very well, you look back and go, was my Actor Brain pleased? Did I do good? You know what? You didn't. And that's one of the reasons I'm so excited! Because it wasn't good, it was truthful.

Truthful isn't good. Good is easy and plastic. In a lot of that scene - and it's a long scene - you were avoiding the good way. So instead it became complex and textured and nuanced.

So that pleasure center in your brain, let's shift that. Toward that awkward, not sure, a bit confused, a bit afraid, unknowing, that's life! As opposed to the good way which is what I practiced in front of the mirror - which I know you don't do but you see what I'm saying - instead you're living the character's life and that is unsure. I'm unsure, you're unsure, everyone in this room is unsure. We're all unsure all the time, this is real life. We're unrehearsed.

Again Joe, I thought that was pretty good. And it seems that actor pleasure center in your brain didn't get tickled. Great. Leave it un-tickled.

I'm okay with that.

Now we're really playing the game. We're playing a complex game, not an easy game. This isn't some game I can figure out and dominate, I've got to play a complex game. If I can dominate it and figure it out, and understand and make sense of everything, it's not a very interesting game. Make it a complex game and then you really have to play it - not win, play!

No winning required. We don't need to win, just play.

I was quite pleased with that take. I thought about 70% of that was money.

Alright.

And it's not an easy piece. I hope you're recognizing how being driven by the video is better than being driven by your actor pleasure center or your ear: "How do I sooouuuuuunnd?" No. Let the video do the talking. And I felt there you were letting the video do the talking for quite a bit of it. Is that your experience? You were letting the video talk, right?

Pretty much.

Bang! So rethink where your pleasure centers are located in your brain. I don't think I've ever talked about pleasure centers before.

Not in class. (laugh)

Here's a technique that might be helpful, to make sure we have video. There's a technique called lifting the line off the page. You have the script in your hand, you look down, read the line silently. Then look away from the page and then say the line. That's helping us get from typing to images. We're starting to force ourselves away from the typing of the words and into my video of the images that can cause that line to happen.

It's easy to basically read out loud and act. This lifting technique helps to take the reading part out. We're saying the line out loud but we're not reading. The typing, the shape of a W has no meaning to us. We're getting away from the page and into our brains.

Line by line?

Line by line. And again, the shape of an H has no meaning to us. Really fun. Thank you for a great class.

Alejandro, here's a note I forgot to give you but I wanted to come back to it. You have the line "but then something happened." In that moment I don't want you to go "but then something happened. I gained weight and ate terribly." I want to go "but then something happened. *(pause)* I gained weight and ate terribly." Make the audience want to know what happened. Dangle the bait and wait for the audience to get hungry. Build tension toward what happened. Make us hungry for what's coming next. You see how I might diagram that one line of dialogue?

Yes.

Awesome. Thanks for a great class.

Alejandro, anything rattling for you?

I was thinking about words and lines of dialogue that you have to repeat, in the same scene. Trying to make it not sound the same.

I'm happy to try to address that, Alejandro and thank you for always bringing up worthy things to consider.

I think the conventional wisdom for actors is "make sure it sounds different the second time." I don't really agree with that thought. Instead I suggest you use your video and let the video tell you how to say it. Don't let your Actor Brain decide how to say it. I think that's an artificial decision to make. In real life if I say something twice, I'm not thinking "make it sound different." In real life, I'm probably saying it twice because I really mean it and I want you to know how much I mean it. Not because I'm trying to provide variety for you. Let the video make that decision for us. Let your video decide how to say lines and if it's the same there must be a good reason for it.

We hope to let the Character Brain speak. We're not letting Actor Brain or the so-called rules of acting be in charge. When you're in Character Brain and fighting hard, these decisions will happen on their own. As I often say, let the video do the talking. And if it's different it's different and if it's the same it's the same. Regardless of what the conventional wisdom may be, we shouldn't make things different simply for the sake of making them different

That sounds actionable.

Great. Always a pleasure.

Jen and Alejandro, overall I thought it was pretty terrific. Alejandro, I'm not going to check in with you, as much as ask you to reflect on what you were doing. What were you prioritizing that gave you such a good take?

I was trying to make sure that everything I said was understood. A slow patient delivery of what I had to say.

Good sir. The first time you mentioned "Big Aubrey," it needed a bit more articulation. Of course that's an "Aunt Enid" moment. Right?

Oh yeah.

"Big Aubrey" is an "Aunt Enid" moment. We recognize why that is right? It's because we're surprising the audience's ear.

Here's a thing that I will observe: That the investment you made in articulation gave you more investment in your belly. More investment in articulation will give you more investment in the belly as well. So it's a win-win in focusing the way you are. It helps fuel the belly so that's a win-win… Win-win-win. We keep winning.

The "Aunt Enid" stuff I found was really helping.

What is the "Aunt Enid" thing again? I think I've heard it but I'm unclear.

"Aunt Enid" refers to over-articulating words that surprise the audience's ear. I can't say "After work, we're going over a neenid's house. You wanna go?" the audience will be saying "What's a neenid?" We have to articulate "Aunt Enid's house." so that the audience is secure in knowing they heard you correctly.

Alejandro, I'll also commend you on being playful and making him funny and charming. Charm is something we've discussed on a number of occasions and you found it here. It doesn't say on the page that he's funny and charming but why shouldn't he be? After all, he's on television. *(laugh)*

Yeah. (laugh)

Jen, I am not sure how to address this but I feel somehow that you're dependent on the printed word longer than you need to be dependent on the printed word. I think if you found a way to avoid the printed word, you'll fill in some blanks. What do you think?

Do you mean get off book or…?

Less dependent. I don't mean you have to get memorized, but In that moment where you're thinking, "What's my next line?" just wait a second. Maybe the script is where we find the answer, sure, you can go to the page but maybe there's another answer. See if you can avoid the process of "What do I say next? I'd better look. What's he saying next? Now what's my next line? I'd better look at my next line." Right?

Yeah.

Instead challenge yourself to be Emily and say what Emily says and if you need to look, go ahead, that's fine. But I think your cognition of the scenes and the story and the character and the lines, is perhaps way better than average. But I don't think you are challenging yourself in that way. Is that appropriate?

Yeah. I could stop double checking. There are tons of lines that I do know but I double check first.

It would be fun to see what happens. There are times when you're stuck and that's okay. But if you're not stuck, just be in the scene. See if you can find the lines in your Character Brain. Is that fair? Thoughts or comments on that? Is that a good thing?

Yeah, I think that is a good thing. Yeah.

Super good scene from both of you. I was talking in class the other day about awkward moments and there were some really awkward moments here. So powerful. You see the power of awkward? That's dramatic money. Comedic as well.

Right.

Everything is going very well in this scene. For both of you.

Alejandro, a bit of an adjustment. I'd like you to demonstrate a bit more compassion. There were a few moments where you sprinkled it in, but I'd like you to live more in that place. More vulnerability and warmth. Is that actionable?

Yeah.

Compassion, warmth and vulnerability are almost always good things. I think you made the decision that this doctor was professional and he is professional. But that's not the first thing he is. First I think he's compassionate and vulnerable and after that he's professional.

There was also a moment or two Alejandro, where we could have used more "Help a buddy out." Part of that is, in your Actor Brain, recognize what great lines she has. She's got some great lines. So don't let yourself flow too easily into the next moment. You can "Help a buddy out" by being affected or perhaps taking a slight pause before moving on. Give everyone a chance to recognize the great line, including the writer. *(laugh)*

One way to "Help a buddy out" is to be affected by what the other person says. To have what they say affect you and resonate and reverberate with you. Really take in what's being said to you. Don't deflect it or disregard it, really take it in. And here that will "Help a buddy out."

Alejandro, how did those adjustments feel?

I definitely felt more connected to her.

It often happens that the roles of a therapist, social worker, doctor, nurse, sometimes police… Oftentimes our job is simply to fill the role with compassion, as much compassion as we can bring. If I go to a therapist and they're a great therapist, they have compassion. If I go to a doctor and they're a great doctor, they have compassion. Nurse, same thing. Compassion. And I really don't think we can go too far in some of these roles. Think about a Mom or maybe a teacher. Those types of roles. For many of these types to be at their best, compassion is ruling the day.

I sometimes refer to "good people doing their best" and that's what I mean here. If a doctor or nurse are great at what they do, they have compassion. Same with a social worker or teacher. Think of a running river of compassion and we want the audience to get splashed through the screen.

There are plenty of exceptions; sometimes our characters are not good at their job or have other issues but at its core, in these roles, unless we see a good reason not to, we're going to bring all the compassion we can find.

Heroes are filled with compassion and if we are compassionate we can be heroic. So if I'm playing a therapist, unless I see a reason otherwise, I'm going to fill that role with compassion. If we can exemplify that and make it tangible to the audience, that's what we're after.

I have sometimes defined warmth as a combination of humor, humility and compassion. In these types of roles, it's important to bring warmth.

It seems easier to stay in Character Brain in the early stages of rehearsal but then what happens when you add blocking, like cross to the sink and get a glass of water or you have to open the blinds?

Great question. I think in the doctor scene you're probably seated but in the office scene there might be blocking. You do some filing or something.

Right.

Blocking can get really complex but essentially, but if the director tells you "Get up and cross to the filing cabinet on this line," it is technical in Actor Brain at first. Now we find a way to shoot the video to need the file you keep in the cabinet, so you're staying in Character Brain when you cross to the filing cabinet. The video you shoot will fill in the blanks. If you shoot the right video, then the blocking will follow.

We're taking notes from the director and turning them from an Actor Brain task, into a Character Brain behavior. At first, it's Actor Brain: "When? Open the file on this line? Cross on this line?" But when you get to Character Brain, you're like "Oh. I need that file." Or "I want to avoid your eye contact so I'll distract myself looking out the window." You'll figure that out on your feet when you get your blocking or notes from the director.

Just because I'm having so much fun reflecting on the scene - it was quite good - Jen, so much of the scene was mostly about what you were not saying. You were thinking things that were completely not what you were saying. And that is fascinating. To watch you swim in these waters and they're choppy and difficult and even disorienting. Well diagrammed and very well played.

For each of you the word viable comes to mind. If you were up for these roles, you would definitely get callbacks. Well done

May/June

Polly, we're working on your audition monologue tonight. Anything rattling for you before we get started on that process?

I'm just really excited to have you do the first tweaks because I do much better after you've critiqued me.

I appreciate that. That's interesting. You know, I've been looking at Joe's material for the show he's working on and I already have notes. I haven't given him a chance to do it yet but I already have notes. *(Joe laughs)*

Joe, you're working on a Neil Simon play and Polly, you've been asked to audition with a monologue by Oscar Wilde. For both of these pieces, I think our initial inquiry and Sherlock Holmes-ing is in the question of style.

Everything is style and everything has a style, Gilmore Girls was a style. Friends is a style. All of this stuff is before your time, Alejandro. *(laugh)* Going way back, Gilligan's Island or Twin Peaks was style. Breaking Bad, Cheers, Sopranos… More recently Ted Lasso… ultimately everything has style, whether it's easy to define or subtle.

To give ourselves a really good awareness and understanding of how to embrace the style of the material, will get us 50% cast. If an actor hasn't embraced the style, it's hard to fit them to this particular opportunity. They might be really good but they're not necessarily good for this. Style helps us be good for this. Not just good - because we're all good - but can we be good for this project? This thing I'm auditioning for, do I understand and embrace the style? The thing I'm cast in, do I understand and embrace the style?

A lot of actors seem to want to say "I don't want to play that cliche.' No, often the cliche is what's needed. A cliche is a cliche for a reason. If you're successful enough, long enough, you too can become a cliche. *(laugh)*

Style gives us permission. Gives us permission.

We can also just call it inspiration. What am I inspired by? I don't know what to call it but Katherine Hepburn had style. I don't know what to call it but it inspires me. It's okay for me to use that inspiration, especially in the pursuit of style.

You can take a type and fill it out. A type helps give expectations. Look at the adults in Ferris Bueller's Day Off…

Ben Stein.

Right, he was great in that and the other guy, I think Jeffery Wright is his name. They're playing types and types help the audience have expectations. Later we can fulfill or deny those expectations. Types create dramatic energy.

As Polly was saying very astutely - I felt it led us into a good conversation - that she always improves after my first round of notes. Typically, my first round of notes is probably going to be centered around style. I say "Do you see the style opportunities here?" and you say "Oh! Okay." and you go away and embrace the style and when you come back everything starts working. That's probably a good observation to make. The adjustment would be to make style part of the early Sherlock Holmes-ing of our material. Does that feel actionable?

I have a question. I thought I had a grasp on style a few weeks back but I'm not sure I have it...

First, let me suggest, Alejandro, that overall in your work, you get style. Nothing lacking there. I'm glad you want to pursue this intellectually, but you already recognize instinctively that this is this kind of script and this is this kind of script.

Like playing the guy who's clueless...

Yeah. You have your more confident guy next door, your more professional person, then you've got your more brooding and pissed off characters, right?

Okay.

If you're doing Teenage Mutant Ninja Turtles, if you're cast in that, that's going to be different than like Breaking Bad on network TV.

Okay.

It's partly in how we invest in the world of the character. That's a way to fill out style.

Okay. Like High School Musical or something.

Right. For that style, I might be a little brighter or perkier, smile more. That's the way I might stylistically embrace that. Embrace the world of the character and that will help us fill out style. Or if I'm poor and it's Russia and it's wintertime, embracing that world will help us find style. With really good video, you're covering the base of style.

I sometimes define it in the ratio of, "In this world, what is it like to really hate someone?" Mixed with, "Who is this material for? Who's the audience?"

Let's say I hate someone named Steve. If I'm in a drama, it might mean I would kill them. But in PG rated stuff or a romantic comedy, I would maybe spray-paint their car. Or if it's more for kids, I might hate somebody by tricking them into eating broccoli.

Yeah.

So if I'm doing something for a young audience, killing wouldn't really be an option.

(laugh)

We're looking for the limitations and new rules of the world we live in. The limitations and the new rules. How is the world of our characters different from our everyday life?

Okay, that's really helpful.

Good.

All those examples were really helpful. Especially the Ninja Turtles one. (laugh)

Good! I finally got one you can identify with. I'm glad. I've never actually seen it by the way, I was just guessing. I didn't know. *(laugh)*

In a way I'm hoping that through your insightful comment, Polly, we may be pre-empting our first round of notes. That's good because I've talked so long we're almost out of time. *(laugh)* I think I'll send you all into rehearsal. Thanks. What fun.

Good, Alejandro. Even your work that isn't my favorite is still pretty good, so congratulations on that.

In this one, I was a little bit worried about that cadence again. *(Using a leading tone/up inflection)* "I went to the *(up)* restaurant. I saw her across the *(up)* room. I said I would be *(up)* back. I don't think I'm going *(up)* to." Right? And I really want you to have that resolve. *(Using a resolve/down inflection)* "I went to the *(down)* restaurant. I saw her across the *(down)* room. I said I would be *(down)* back."

I think that's what I was thinking about. It didn't feel right.

Here is what is happening when you do that, Alejandro; First it's an old habit. And that leading tone that you're using is an excuse for the point you're making. One reason you're doing that is I don't think you're using the video. You might have the video as you say the line, but make sure the video happens before you say the line. First is the video. So in my video, if I remember what it looked like to see her in the restaurant, I'll say "I saw her in the *(down)* restaurant." instead of "I saw her in the *(up)* restaurant."

That leading tone is like "Just give me a second. I'm almost done." It's a bit of a deflection. But I don't want to deflect, I want to confront with my language. Right now it's a bit polite and excuse me. *(Up inflections)* "Excuse *(up)* me. I'm *(up)* sorry. I'm saying this *(up)* line." Instead of "I'm saying this *(down)* line."

Right now you're letting yourself do that because it's a habit for when you don't have strong video. You do it most often when you have a lot of lines in a row. You're intimidated by paragraphs a bit. You're using that cadence as a kind of crutch.

One thing I was thinking the other day when we were talking about monologues and that they can be intimidating. One of the reasons it's intimidating is because in our brains - our "actor motor" I call it - our "actor motor" is going "Keep going. Keep going. Keep going. Keep going. Keep going." And instead when that is happening I want you to go "Stop!" Just "Stop!" *(pause)* Right in the middle of the monologue, just stop. *(pause)* Start again. Stop. *(pause)* Start again.

We can get rid of that "keep going" mentality. That's a default setting that actors get to when they think they have a big speech. Stop. Just stop. Right in the middle. If you have a five minute monologue, say two lines and stop. You don't have a five minute monologue, you have ten-second monologues thirty times in a row.

Okay. Yeah, I felt like I was pushing it.

I think the main reason was that you didn't have your video. Using the video will take care of that.

Okay.

Sometimes I think you're trying to come up with the line reading and not using video. That line "I saw her in the restaurant." For that to be truthful, what did it look like? She was sitting by herself, she was wearing this type of clothes, there's a glass of water on the table, her purse in her lap, her face looked like this, she looks in my direction but

doesn't see me. Those are all part of our video. We have to see all of that and then we can say "I saw her at the restaurant." and have truth to support it. You see the video we need in order to say the line truthfully?
Yeah.
Let the truth tell you how to say it.
Okay.

Debra, what is rattling at the end of class?
You've been very helpful. I appreciate the help you gave me so much. The video is so important. It's… what did you say? 87%?
Roughly.
It's so helpful. I've never heard that in other classes.
Right. It's not a part of other acting techniques. I can't figure out why.

Alejandro, anything rattling at the end of class?
Looking at both scenes tonight. I'm noticing the more video I have, the easier it is to say these lines.
Right. The video will say the line for you. So we don't have to worry about what our voice sounds like or what our lips and tongue are doing, our video will do all of that. And then we have truth on our side so it's a win-win. If we have video, we're good.
Besides being 87% percent of what we're doing, it's also the rule I ask you to never break. You can break all the other rules but don't break this one: Video.
It's a standard I can't really hold you to. I have to go "Hey, did you have video in that moment?" And you go "No, I guess I didn't have video for that moment, sorry." *(laugh)*
Just know that if you say it, you're responsible for the video. For everything. If you say it, you're responsible for the video. So now that we know that, we can hold ourselves to that standard so it doesn't become incumbent upon me to tell you that it's missing. Like we said earlier, if you're wondering what my note is going to be for you tonight and if your video is missing, it's going to be "shoot your video."
Great work, everyone. Thank you.

Alejandro, what's rattling for you today?
I'm thinking about my eyeline. In this scene there are two other (virtual) characters. I don't know how it looked but it's something I'm working on. But I think I had pretty good video.
Great. Going very well.
As far as eyeline goes, Alejandro, I think you're doing it exactly right. In a scene with two other characters, put one character on each side of the camera.
I don't know if I've articulated this as much as I might, but bring that eyeline as close to the camera as possible without looking into it. The difference between here

(demonstrating eyeline further away from camera) and here *(eyeline closer to camera)* is important. As I bring my eyeline closer and closer to the camera I give more and more access to my eyes.

The director and the DP *(Director of Photography)* will set up shots like that and stage the actor you're working with closer to camera. Often on set, they'll even move furniture in order to keep the actor's eyes available. So when we are staging our own work, like for a video submission, we do that also. We're always trying to fudge our eyeline toward camera. By the way, to the left or right of camera, and slightly higher than the camera. In most cases avoid directly above camera. And of course, focus directly into the camera for your slate.

Of course when you're working in person, use the other actor for eyeline. Don't fake it if the real person is there. A generous actor will cheat toward camera in order to help you stay open.

If you really want to fine tune, when you are looking at the other actor for eyeline, they presumably have two eyes. Focus into the one that's closer to camera as opposed to the eye further from camera. This puts your eyeline a couple inches closer to the camera, providing more access for the audience.

Welcome to class, Talia. How do you think your scene went?

Okay. I feel like it was okay. I think I could do better.

You probably heard Joe and I talking about video. Do you understand that concept? I like to describe it as the movie that plays in my brain. Not what we're seeing with our eyes but with our brain.

And I can't read your mind but it looked like you had some video. Right? You saw your dad, or at least a dad. You saw the restaurant. You knew what it looked like when he said these mean things to you, yes?

Mm-hmm.

Good. I like to identify that as the video. And that the video precedes our language. First is the movie, then is the narration of the movie.

Okay. Yeah.

And it seems to me you're kind of doing that already. So I just wanted to put into words what some of your good instincts already are. That gives us a language for that so later on in class I can ask "Hey, do you have video for this?" and we know what we're talking about.

We call that video. It can be memories, hopes, fears. If I'm worried my significant other is going to leave me, then I have video of them gone, right? And that I'm miserable. Then I can say "Please don't leave."

It's a way of working in Character Brain instead of Actor Brain. Actor Brain is trying to "say the words good" and Character Brain is worried about what the character cares about. And you're already falling on the right side of that equation, which is that you're thinking character thoughts.

Well done.

Thank you.

Good start. Let's go into rehearsal.

That scene between the two of you was hilarious. Talia, what do you think? How is it going for you?

I don't know. I feel good about it. I'm just happy to do it. It was really fun.

Talia, as I work with actors, once I get to know you a little more, I might begin to see if you have tendencies or limitations that we can work on. But right now, your path is pretty good. I don't want to get in your way, frankly. But from your perspective, if there is anything I can do to be helpful, I would love to do that. But I don't see a lot of shoulds or shouldn'ts. As always, from your perspective, if you're like "Hey, what about this?" then that is something I'd be happy to address. Is there anything like that rattling for you?

Not at this moment. I'm pretty picky with myself so I'm sure I'll have stuff in the future and I'll be sure to ask you about that.

Okay, great. Things will come up as we refine but I don't want to mess with things right now. Again, I'm always happy to help.

Alejandro, how's it going for you?

The video was way more detailed than in the last scene.

Just some fine tuning here. I really like a line you have in the scene where you give a picture of Lance Armstrong and say you "don't have a formal resume." I might suggest you stress the word "formal." As we discussed, the word we stress will imply its opposite. So if we say "I don't have a **formal** resume." What I am basically saying is "this is an **informal** resume."

Okay.

I just thought that one line was an opportunity like "I didn't have a tuxedo so I wore a thong." Or "I didn't have a tuxedo so I wore socks." So the word we stress is going to imply its comparison. Do you see how we might use "formal" to enhance the joke?

I think so.

If I may, I'll remind you in this same thought here that comedy is often a "tilted logic." So if you stress the line in that way it becomes "I don't have a formal resume so it's perfectly logical that I give you an informal one." So I want you to take away from this a couple things: One, that the word we stress will imply its opposite and two, that often comedy is embracing a tilted logic.

Okay.

Do you see how those two ideas fit together on that particular moment?

Yes.

So comedy is often a tilted logic. If we have a tilted logic, let's highlight my logic as opposed to your logic. My logic is "I didn't have a **formal** resume so here's a piece of paper I found in the gutter." "My **formal** one, I don't have. Instead, I have this empty Pepsi cup. Makes perfect sense to me."

So let's be sure to look for those kinds of opportunities in our material. Does that hold together as a theory?

Yes. I definitely think I understand that.

It's really fun when we can demonstrate how our logic is different from the rest of the world's logic. Quite often that's the foundation of comedy or comedic characters. How is our logic different and how can we powerfully demonstrate that? Good conversation.

I remember you talking about comparisons. Could you explain that again?

It's said to be the greatest line of dialogue ever written in English. "To be or not to be." You could say "to be or not to be" anywhere around the world and people will go "Oh. You mean drama."

"To be or not to be" is the most powerful line of dialogue ever written in English. Wonder why that is? It's a comparison. Of the two most polar opposite things; being and not being. Polar opposites. Not the opposite of up and down or red and blue, but being and not being. And it's done in the most succinct framework possible. Six words.

So it's a comparison of the most opposing ideas possible. In the most succinct framework. That line of dialogue has lived as the definition of drama, as the cliche' of what it means to be dramatic.

That makes sense.

Comparisons are super powerful. In a way I can be saying, not only what I'm saying but I can be saying what I'm not saying. I'm giving you both sides of my equation when I bring comparisons into my work.

It's hard to put into words but I believe you're getting the concept, Alejandro. I trust that that is happening for you.

So it's like when you're saying something but you're really saying something else.

We could put that in comparisons, Alejandro, but I'd rather think of that in terms of juxtaposition of ideas. Very similar ideas.

The line of dialogue "I love you." said loving-ly, is redundant. But the line "I love you." said as a reminder? Oh. So it's not only love but it's also fear of losing love. Now love is relevant because of that other idea.

We call that the juxtaposition of ideas. I'm saying I love you but what I'm really saying is "I love you. Don't forge-et!" And the audience is left to think "Something's happening. He said I love you but…" If I'm afraid you're going to forget I love you, then maybe you're going to meet your other lover or we had an argument this morning. Something is happening. If I say I love you lovingly, nothing is happening but love. If I say "I love you."

as a warning? Or as a reminder? Or as a confession? Something is happening. So that's the basic concept behind juxtaposition of ideas.

It's interesting because it came up in my brain to talk about it in class the other day. I think it was yesterday. I was about to address this very thing. It was specific to something I was working on with Joe.

What if I'm saying these lines, but say the words as if they were these words? I have a line of dialogue like " I'm not going to the mall." But say it as if you were saying "My life is over." Now there are some consequences to not going to the mall. Not simply that I'm not going to the mall but it's relevant to something important.

Yes. Okay.

So that is an interesting exercise, Alejandro. When you are looking at a line of dialogue, think "what if I was really saying this line Instead of that line?" How would that line be affected if I brought on that juxtaposition of ideas? Then those words that we're saying resonate somewhere. They resonate, they reverberate, they repercuss. Because there's some idea for those words to bounce off of. As opposed to my words just being my words and what I say and what I mean is the same. If what I'm saying and what I'm thinking is the same then it doesn't reverberate. It doesn't bounce. It doesn't repercuss, it doesn't affect. There's no resonance. We need those two points for a spark to happen. Sometimes I may discover that, that may even be my reading of it. That line "I'm not going to the mall" with the reading of "My life is over." There's something behind what we're saying. Otherwise, it's not relevant to anything. Okay?

Yeah.

Sometimes I'll even suggest that the juxtaposed idea is 51% and what I'm saying is 49%. I'll do more of this than this.

That makes a lot of sense.

I'm so glad. I'm glad you can make sense of all these ideas. They're a little bit hard to grasp. But you seem to be doing well and Talia has been nodding her head as if she's getting it as well. Yes Talia?

Yeah.

That's terrific.

Good scene. It's worth mentioning that comedy is dead serious. I was laughing out loud for most of the scene, but you guys were like, "this is really serious stuff." Alejandro, you even had a tear in your eye when you got the job of cleaning toilets. I thought it was really well played and keep in mind the more serious you play it, the funnier we find it. Comedy is dead serious.

Alejandro, anything rattling?

I've been putting in more time, especially on days when we don't have class. I've been thinking about bringing value.

Alejandro, I am so in your corner. Things are going very well.

I'm going to jump to a different topic. Something I didn't talk about in class the other day. It's something I wanted to mention to you, if it's alright.

There was a scene you were doing and your character laughed quite a bit. Remember that scene?

Yes.

I kind of loved it. But. If I were an actor in the scene and you were laughing over my line, I might get mad at you. You understand that balancing act?

Yeah.

And secondly, the sound people who are editing the scene after the shoot, they need the other actor's dialogue to be clean. If you're laughing while that actor is saying their line, they don't have clean sound on that line. They might have to come in later and re-record. That's something we need to be sensitive to in a professional environment, that the sound department needs clean copies of everyone's dialogue. Do you see how you can contribute to that?

Yeah. Definitely.

Terrific, sir. I love the impulse, the unreasonableness. I thought it was kind of awesome. But the technical aspects and then the other actors point of view. They may have something very specific they want to do with that line of dialogue, and you may not be giving them the opportunity to do that if you're laughing while they're speaking.

That makes sense.

That would apply in theatre as well, right?

In theatre, it is usually called upstaging. To upstage is to draw attention to yourself, at a moment when somebody else should be getting the attention. That's what upstaging is.

One of the great stories of upstaging, if you want to hear a fun, legendary story… I think it was Bette Davis or some old-time actress, appearing on stage with another actress that was a rival, and she said "I'm going to upstage that actress, even when I'm not onstage."

What she did was she had a glass of whatever beverage it was, and she set it downstage on a table but she left it half on the table and half off the table. She put it there and she left and the other actress is doing her thing, but the entire audience is watching the glass to see if it's going to fall. *(laugh)*

Actors can do it, sometimes in a spiteful way, such as that example, but also unknowingly.

The word upstage comes from the theatre. Picture two actors side by side on stage. Now one actor moves slightly upstage. *(away from the audience)* The other actor must turn their back to the audience to address that actor who has moved upstage. So the upstage actor is more open to the audience than the downstage actor. Quite often, the downstage actor will make an adjustment by moving upstage as well.

Often when I'm staging something, I notice a scene moves imperceptibly upstage until, if it's unchecked, they'll end up at the cyclorama. *(laugh)*

So you get the points here, Alejandro?

I definitely understand that. After class, I was thinking it wasn't right.

I like that you have the chutzpah to make big things happen for your characters but we have to be sensitive to everyone else's interests.

Okay. I didn't even realize.

I have no doubt. Well done. We have a lot of material today so let's get started.

This is an important dynamic. The emotional values can be extremely high but we don't want our presentation of those emotional values to also be high. That tension can't be sustained. There's nowhere to go.

So the higher the emotional values, the hotter your kettle is boiling, the tighter the lid. So it might blow but it doesn't blow. Once in a while it does, of course.

Right now your approach might be "The emotional values are high so the presentation of those values should also be high! I'm feeling hugely about this, so I'll present hugely about this!" No. Instead "I feel hugely about this but I'm not… willing… to show… you." Keep the lid on like one of those pressure cookers. When you release the pressure, everything starts to cool. So keep the lid on. That way the pressure is higher and it burns hotter.

That's beautiful, man!

Aww. Terrific.

Debra, here's a thing. It has to do with video and the concept of video, and your employment of the concept of video.

Ultimately, once I have video, I no longer have to pretend I have video. But when we don't have video we have to *(overdone)* "pretend we have video!!" If I really have video, I don't have to pretend I have video. I don't have to convince you I have video. I don't have to present to you. I don't care whether you believe me or not, you don't have to believe me. I believe me. Screw you. *(pause)* Pardon my language. *(laugh)*

It's so hard to employ that… I default back to my usual tricks. Especially when I'm learning lines. I start getting all jumbled.

The way we sometimes address this is, for a lot of this there's a big capital F. Without the F it's "I hope you like what I'm doing, you guys. I really hope you think I'm a good actor. I hope you like me, pleeeease." With the big capital F it's "I don't care if you like it or not. Sit down and shut up."

(laugh) I know!

Can you employ that big capital F?

I can. I have to.

If you don't employ the big capital F, you're giving us out here in the audience your power. But as soon as you put a big capital F in front of it, you're taking your power back.

All of us - out here in the audience - we need for you to have the power. We didn't come here to be powerful, we came here to watch you be powerful. That's why that big capital F works.

Don't think that by using the F, you're being mean to your audience, you're not. You're serving them. It's ultimately loving and compassionate to put a big capital F in front of your work because you're serving your audience. So make that F even bigger.

Yeah.

You have the opportunity to fight for her. Don't fight for you. Don't fight for Debra "I hope you like me. I hope you think I'm good." No, fight for her instead. She cares about love and beauty and art and compassion. Fight for her.

How is that sitting with you? Does that feel actionable?

That was great.

I'm so glad that is resonating with you.

Especially the big capital F. I don't do that enough. I'm like "Is this okay? Is this okay? What do you think?"

A proposed title for our book is "Confidence. It starts With F." Starts with F. Fonfidence. *(laugh)* Because we can give our confidence away to everybody; casting directors, audiences, critics, your Mom and Dad who are in the audience today, your sister-in-law who has never seen you act, the camera… Oh my god. We can give our power away to everybody. But if you put a big capital F in front of all of it, you can keep your power.

Keep in mind, our job isn't really to please the audience. Not even really to entertain the audience. I mean sure you can do a school play for 4th graders and entertain. What we're doing here as artists is more subversive. The way we are teaching our audience and making them aware. Helping them see love and beauty and possibility. Not by saying "Hey everybody! Love and beauty and possibility!" But instead, subversively, telling them a story that hits them in the belly. That they didn't see coming. You see the subversiveness of that?

Yes.

I'm not here to entertain you or have you enjoy yourself. I'm here to hit you in your belly. In a way that you don't expect and in a way that's going to move you. And probably toward being a better human being.

I'm here to do that subversively. You don't even see it coming. Does that feel actionable?

Yeah.

Don't politely give us the story, subversively give us the story. See what I mean?

Yeah.

How fun is that?

Very fun.

Joe, how's it going?

Okay. I think I need to add a touch of regret.

You said "a touch of regret" but I think a lot of regret is needed. We have the opportunity to bring angst and regret and loss. It's hard to be a person. That's a way to make the stakes higher. If you barely care, the audience barely cares, too. You've got to care a lot. You're desperate.

If we have the option, care deeply about what your character cares about. Don't care a little. Caring a little lets yourself off the hook and it lets the audience off the hook, too. At the end of the scene, we need the audience to desperately want to know what happens next. Let's make these events larger. Much more need from you.

Got it.

Alejandro, how's it going?

I feel like take two would be rock solid.

Good, Alejandro. A lot of nice things going on.

I think in this scene that you are the star of the show. Did you ever notice that often, the star of the show is a regular, everyday-type person and everyone around them is wacky? Like Jim and Pam are normal in The Office and everyone around them is wacky. I think that's what is happening here. You are the central character in the story and your job is to be identifiable for the audience. Kind of a quote-unquote everyman. It's really all about diagramming. You're the central character. Let the wacky stuff happen around you. Your job is to bail them out, reign them in. Let them be wacky. You're good at being the wacky friend but I don't think that's what this is. You stay centered.

Makes sense.

Ann, anything I can do to be helpful?

I was just appreciating what you said about the central character being normal. I hadn't thought of that before.

It happens that way a lot. We have our central character and then there's the wacky neighbor, the wacky doctor…

The wacky Mom. (laugh)

Exactly.

More video. The video is where all the answers are. People say "What's my motivation?" The video will tell you. Go to your video, you'll find your motivation there. Use your video. Okay?

You're right. I just didn't do it.

You talk about the flyers that are hung in the streets, "Have you seen my dad?" If you pull back a little, there's dust in the streets. That's dust from the buildings. That blanketed the city of New York. Once you have a video, the video is fascinating. The words aren't fascinating. The words are never fascinating. The video is. Okay? So use your video.

You're getting there. Does that feel actionable?

Yes.

We'll come back to that scene a bit later. Good, good, good.

Okay.

Talia, when you start talking about your husband, I'm going to ask for what we call a "meal change." First you're talking about your daughter, then he says what he says and you say "My husband…" When you introduce the topic of your husband, can you change the flow of the scene? Make it separate and different and distinct from the earlier conversation. We call that a "meal change."

I see.

If we change flavors and textures and presentation, we're changing meals. This signals to the audience that they can digest breakfast, we're moving on to lunch. Sometimes a pause will help as well.

Got it.

Let's try it again from the top.

Talia, can I check in with you? How's it going?

Umm Good. I think it was better that time. I'm curious what you thought about it.

I think it's going very well. I like, Talia, that you are not doing the bare minimum in your role. You're more well rounded of a woman than the script gives us. You're finding ways to make her interesting beyond the language, beyond the circumstances of the scene. She's just an interesting woman and you're not being limited by what you say. Do you see what I mean?

Yeah.

And I really want to encourage that from you. That's welcome. You let that blossom in any way you see fit. Okay? The unique way that you do it. Not just doing it but doing it the unique way you do it. I want to applaud that and ask you to continue in that vein. Okay?

Thank you.

Absolutely. You're doing very well, perhaps even surprisingly well.

Talia, I'd like to talk to you about your musicality. At one point you say three things in a row. You say "Learning issues, behavioral stuff. All of it."

Right now you're saying "Learning issues. *(up inflection)* Behavioral stuff. *(up inflection)* All of it. *(up inflection)*" Notice the difference when I say "Learning issues *(down inflection)* Behavioral stuff. *(down inflection)* All of it. *(down inflection)*" Isn't it more weighty?

Yeah.

That's what we call "five-one." That's a musical phrase that sounds like this *(singing)* Five, One.

Basically, I'll suggest that through that musicality, our language can land, as opposed to floating. It will land when it resolves musically like that. If it doesn't resolve, it doesn't really land and if it doesn't land, it doesn't have impact.

Got it.

That musicality that you chose there, that's okay from time to time. But for the most part, we want our language to have impact and it won't really have impact when it floats. It will have impact when it lands.

Got it.

What a pleasure. Thank you.

Getting there, Debra. What do you think?

Oh. I don't have the video.

The second half of it you didn't have much video. The first half I thought you did. You were talking about JFK and I thought your video was pretty good there. What do you think?

Yeah. In the beginning.

Great. In those moments, I would say maybe the first third of the scene, you had video. That might have been all the video you had time to shoot. We just talked about shooting video here a few minutes ago, that's all you had time for. Right?

Yeah.

You had video and you were using your video and it was entirely viable. And then you didn't have the video and you had to go to other actor tricks.

Right.

But at first you had video. If you can hold yourself to that standard, you'll be fine.

I know.

So don't let yourself off the hook. Don't let yourself talk without knowing what you're talking about. Knowing what you're talking about is to have knowledge. Knowledge is in images and the investigation into those images.

Force us to confront what you're talking about. When you confront it yourself, that will help.

I agree.

That first third of the scene you had video but when you don't, it forces you to use other actor tricks.

I know. I can hear my voice raise.

It's like a lie detector test. The first third, you're passing the lie detector test, the second two thirds, you're not. Hold yourself to the standard of truth. When you had the truth, you didn't have to do it good, you didn't have to be believable or convince anyone. Don't let the stress of being a quote-unquote "Ac-tor," keep you from being real. Hold yourself to that standard. That relationship to your video was exactly what we're after. Now that we have isolated our problem, you have to go back and exercise that exact muscle for the whole script. Once you have video and know what you're talking about, everything else will fall into place.

When you do that you don't have to try so hard. If you don't have the truth you have to try and pretend. To heck with that. Just have truth. It's more fun and more powerful. Don't even worry about memorizing lines, specifically. Just make sure you have visual images to help drive everything you say.

Just now, in a short time, you did that for the first third of the scene. It took very little time. Follow that path and hold yourself to it. Okay?

Okay.

Don't worry about sounding real or looking real or being natural or any of that. Just hold yourself to that standard. You have to do that. Feel actionable?

Yes.

Ready to get to work on that?

Yes.

Can't wait.

And I can't get lazy about it. I feel I have to get these lines down, I don't have time to shoot video, I have to memorize my lines.

The video will make it five times easier to memorize your lines. Literally. The lines will come so much faster. It's the biggest win-win possible. Using video. Not only does it give you truth, it also will help you memorize your lines because you know. You don't have to try to remember anything. Memorizing is hard. Knowing is easy.

Joe, let's start with you. What's rattling?

Just trying to clear out and get into class.

How's memorization coming?

It's coming along pretty well.

Why? What's going well?

The first eight or nine pages. What tricks do you have for memorization?

Video.

That's it, huh?

Video covers all the bases. What's my motivation? Check your video. What's my backstory? Check your video. What's my next line? Check your video.

Of course, nothing is perfect. Even what I'm saying about video. Nothing is 100% perfect. It's going to be a combination of Actor Brain and Character Brain. To memorize a script in Actor Brain is a lot of work. To memorize it in Character Brain is easy. But you need both.

I was working with an actor who had the word "choir." I think it was you, Joe. There are two videos for choir. One is a bunch of people in robes, singing religious music and the other is "C-H-O-I-R."

Okay.

Why would I go "C-H-O-I-R," when I can see a bunch of people singing in robes? That's the difference. You're right, we can go "C-H-O-I-R." Okay, what's the next word? Okay, what's the word after that? Okay, what's the word after that? *(laugh)* The line was "choir and it was beautiful." I'd rather see a beautiful choir singing and be moved. And then I'm done memorizing that line. Actor Brain is "C-H-O-I-R," but Character Brain is the experience of being moved by the music in church. One is difficult, one is easy. It looks like we're supposed to memorize "C-H-O-I-R" but that's not it. The experience is more powerful than the word.

I'm going to stay on you because I really want you to kick ass in this role. Thank you for letting me drill down on that.

Alejandro, anything rattling for you?

I was thinking about sacrificing. This work takes more than a nine-to-five mindset. It was making me think about sacrifices.

Thanks Alejandro. I want to come back to that - there's a lot to talk about there - but here's what I will say for now. If you can do what you love in life, you've won.

Okay.

Yes, there is sacrifice but if you get to follow your dream and make that how you live, then it's paid off. It doesn't always pay off. But when it does, it's a blessing as opposed to doing some job you don't like. To be able to do the work that you love is amazing.

Okay. Fun. Let me check in with you Joe. How's it going?

Coming along. (pause) (laugh)

What are you using?

I'm using video. Maybe a couple holes but not a lot.

I'm with you. Yep. Pretty good video. Great video in places. And as you suggested, a few places where you let your words get ahead of your video.

A few. Mm-hmm.

Yep. So those are the only holes in there. Great, Joe. Good, good, good. Obviously, when it's going well, it's going very well. So it's for you to hold yourself to the standard of not letting yourself talk, without the video to precede it. When you've got that video preceding your language, it's quite good.

Sometimes we're acting in a scene and we hear ourself. I might start to talk and I have to go "wait, don't talk. I hear myself but I don't see anything." Just hold a moment. "Wait. What am I talking about? Oh yes." Then proceed. Sometimes all you need is like a one second pause. It's worth it.

There were places where I actually saw you doing that. You would yap for a moment and think "Hold it, Joe. Get back to the video." And then you dove back into the video and the next line was beautiful and textured and layered.

The video gets rid of that thing you sometimes do which is like "Please believe me, you guys! I really mean this!" *(laugh)* But when you use video all of that goes away and we are drawn into this warm, vulnerable human being.

Good, Joe. When it's good, it's very good. Sometimes we have to talk about bad habits but the video gets rid of all of that. And it did in moments here. Really nice. Good work.

Alejandro, how's it going?

I put in more specifics in the video this time.

This is the first time I saw you had video for the line "a series of mistakes." As that line was coming up, I was thinking "Don't forget to give Alejandro the note about video on 'a series of mistakes.'" But then you had video there. And I was delighted. Was that your experience from your perspective?

Yes. I definitely had more video for that and the whole beginning.

Yep, yep, yep. Good, good, good. Great.

As I said earlier in class, the video will cover all our bases for us. Even a question like when to pause. Does your video hold your attention for a beat longer? Then take a pause. Are you figuring out your place in the world for a moment? Then pause there.

Alejandro, another thing I thought went well was your rhythms and how you would establish a rhythm and then change the rhythm. Gallop along here and then canter there. And then take a pause and then speed up for a minute and then take a long pause. You were contrasting your rhythms throughout the piece. I was very glad to see that as well. Nice work.

Joe, there's a certain power that I'm seeing from you today - in both of your scenes - where you are not feeling you have to please us. You're powerfully being you and to heck with the consequences or judgements. You're not trying to please us and I really want to fan those flames.

Joe, I think the first time I said to myself "Joe doesn't have any video." was when you talked about the phone call at midnight.

You're right. I didn't there.

Make sure you have an alarm bell in your ear when you find yourself talking without video. Don't let yourself perform. - that's perform with a capital P.

A YEAR IN ACTING CLASS

Okay (laugh)
There are places where you aren't performing and it's working very well.
Thank you.
You're welcome.

Joe, you're shaking your head no. It's okay. There was a little more Actor Brain happening.
A lot more.
That's going to happen when we try to incorporate notes.
Arrgh.
At least your Actor Brain was telling you the right things. *(laugh)* Which was like "Don't sell. Don't overdo it." So your Actor Brain was giving you good advice at least. And I'm with you. It wasn't as fluid and powerful as it had been earlier.
No.
Even when it's not your best, Joe, it's pretty good.

How was that take for you, Jen?
I didn't notice that time and that's always a good feeling for me. I'm so in it that I don't notice.
Once again, Jen, I really like the way you are seeing your job in this scene. Not taking any undue attention for yourself, yet adding to the scene. And I think it's powerful to see someone who simply cares, a loving, compassionate human being and that is enough for this scene. And refreshing to see once in a while. *(laugh)* Terrific. Thank you very much.

I think my question for you Alejandro, might be in who this guy is. He's obviously off-center. I want to investigate who this guy is and how he's different from an everyday guy. His logic is not your logic or my logic.
Sometimes that is the basis of comedy. How do you skew logic? As we investigate how he skews logic, we can figure out a bit more of who he is. Does all of that hold together?
Yes.
You're getting to the point now, it doesn't matter what you're doing, you're getting pretty good. So don't worry about stuff, okay?
Yeah.
Every time I come to class and there you are again, I think, "there is somebody who is working as hard as me."
The person I am competing with might be better looking or have more muscles than me, but I'm not going to let him outwork me. That's why on Christmas Day, I'm ready to have class or rehearse. Let's work. I'm like "Everybody else is taking the day off. I want to work. I can't let anyone outwork me." That's been part of my focus. And it's forged a career that has been satisfying and certainly a lot of fun.

I think you're going to be able to forge a career in this. Especially because you are spending your time getting good at this. So when you go in and compete, you'll have worked just as hard as the person you're sitting next to. And maybe harder.

That's something that I've been thinking about a lot. I want to compete. This is my career. It's what I've chosen.

A wise person once said, "If you make a living doing what you love, you'll never have to work a day in your life."

Background work is a way to make money. Not much, maybe a hundred a day and you have to be reliable and someone people want to work with. You can even get into the union and do pretty well. For most of us though, that's really just treading water. The question is, how are you going to tread water? Keep on bringing in some money so you can pay what you've got to pay and eat while waiting for something that might pay off in some way. And that can be a long wait. I know several actors who went to Hollywood at twenty and they're in their forties now and just starting to roll.

But not everyone in Hollywood is good. Some of them are. But if you're really good, you'll stand out. And if you stand out, you'll eventually find your path. It might take a year or five years or ten, but at some point you'll get on a roll. You'll play a supporting role on this show and that leads to a supporting role on this show and pretty soon you get some checks in the mail and you're putting things together.

I must share with you, Alejandro, that it's not a good bet. Not a good gamble. You want to bet on something? Bet on something else. This is not good odds. To be a working, professional actor and make a living in film, theater and television. Let alone being a star, the odds of that are extremely small. But the odds of being a full-time actor are also small.

As far as gambling goes; You want to be a lawyer? Go to law school. That's a good bet. You want to be a doctor? Go to medical school. That's also a good bet. You want to be an actor? Go to acting school. That's not a good bet. But hey, sometimes you have to go for it anyway. And that's awesome. As long as you understand the odds.

But you've got a lot going for you before you even start. You're charming and you've really been working hard on your skills and people in the industry who meet you will see that you're already viable. I have a lot of faith in you, Alejandro, that you're in the right place.

I wouldn't say that to everyone. Most people I'd be like "Do you like architecture? Do you like computers? How about medicine or finance?" Not because they aren't awesome and talented but because it's not a good bet. But, some people are like compulsive gamblers and they have to go for it anyway. If that's you then I think you're in the right place. And I personally think your odds are better than most.

I jumped into a career right out of high school and did that for five years and it didn't make me happy. I had money to live life, maybe start a family, but it just sucked.

If you'd had kids at that point, Alejandro, you might not have the choice. When you have a family it's a whole different ball game. Some people can raise kids and then take up acting later in life. After you've made some money, you've got a little in the bank. That can work too.

There's a lot of sacrifice. But keep in mind, you've still got plenty of time for those other things. Right now you're doing this. You're still young. And if it does pay off, it can pay off huge.

A casting director once shared with me this point of view: If you're cast in a major network television show in a starring role, you'll probably make about a half million dollars in the first year. That's if it gets picked up for a season two. Now consider, how hard would a doctor have to work before they make their first half million? There's medical school, four years, eight years, interning, residency... A lot of sixteen hour days, tests and late nights. How hard does a doctor work before their first half million? How much sacrifice? Many intense years.

We're actors. If we get to that level, it's great. That's the game that we'll be playing. That's the poker table you'll be sitting down at.

I'm very motivated. Even hearing you talk gets me motivated.

Go ahead and visualize yourself starring in a tv show. Maybe you have already. Go ahead and visualize that as something you're working towards, so you know what your goal is. That way you'll be able to see if the steps you're taking are leading you toward your goal. I think that's a tangible goal and it's realistic. You're in California and you're an actor and you're good. So let's set that goal for you. I don't care what the timeline is; I wouldn't want you to set one. But at least you'll know if the wind's at your back or if it's in your face. Okay?

Okay. Thank you very much.

What fun.

What's been rattling is repetition. How to find ways to get the words down faster. I know we talked about video and that helps a lot.

Great. You've presented an excellent topic for us. I'll quote an acting coach I respect. He says don't call it memorization, call it learning. Memorize? That sounds scary and challenging, but learning? Okay. Learning is easy.

Okay. Yeah.

As you pointed out Alejandro, start with the video because the video is where you'll create the experience that will then give you your lines.

Keep in mind, we have Character Brain and Actor Brain. The video we create in Actor Brain and then utilize in Character Brain. The character's memory of yesterday when I quit my job. I have to shoot the video of my boss standing up and pointing to the door and saying "get out." And then I have the line "He threw me out of the office." And perhaps in my video, his pointing to the door will have a throwing motion to it in order to help me remember "He threw…" instead of "He pointed." We've created the memory. An experience that will give us our lines.

Let's say I create a video and I say the line a certain way, I like the way it sounds and I think "That's the way I'm going to do it."

May I interrupt?

Yes.

When we repeat our lines, we're not going to repeat the line reading. We're only doing repetition in order to learn them. We don't do it to act it over and over again. I think you know this, We're not going to memorize what it sounds like when I say it.

Here's the process: We work on a line. We come up with a concept of how we think it's interesting and dynamic and powerful. And that's the arrows, right? How long are they and where are they going? Now, keep the arrows but don't keep the music. Keep the consequences but not the sound. Keep the truth of the moment, the arrows, the diagramming. But how it sounds is the end result. Don't skip to the end result. Do all the things that lead to the end result and then let the end result take care of itself.

So there's never a line said the same way?

That would be taking it too far, sir. Keep in mind, My character's point of view, how I feel about things, what I'm seeing, what's going on, performance to performance, I'll keep feeling that way, It might sound the same. That's fine. But I'm not going to make it sound the same to make it sound the same and I'm not going to make it sound different to make it sound different. How we sound should be an afterthought, not a forethought.

To the stage manager, the director, even your co-star, it will look the same and probably sound the same, but your blood is pumping and it's unique to you, this time. So don't make it different to make it different. Don't make it the same to make it the same. Make it the truth. Does that feel actionable?

Yes.

Here's what is happening in your ten minute scene or your two minute monologue or whatever: Hopefully you're in your Character Brain. You're thinking about when you were a child and your Grandpa used to smoke a pipe on the porch and whatever the monologue is and all of a sudden, you don't know what to say. And now, your Actor Brain takes over and goes "What's my next line?" At that point we need Actor Brain to help lead us back into Character Brain.

Here's the process. We're in Character Brain, we're seeing our Grampa, I'm petting my kitten, I'm six years old, and then my monologue moves to high school and I'm seeing my teachers and my friends and it's all good and the lines are rolling and then suddenly I go boom "Uh-oh. What's my next line?" That's a leap back into Actor Brain and in Actor Brain, we have created a link that tells us, "Lawyer is next," which leads me back into Character Brain where I see myself arguing in front of a jury and representing in a big case.

We hope that most of our work is in Character Brain. Remembering Grandpa and his pipe, remembering high school, remembering going to law school. When we go to Actor Brain to look for our next line, we want to have immediate answers there so we can quickly dive back into Character Brain. Does that make sense?
Yeah.

We have the more organic, which is the video and the Character Brain but then we have to have some technical answers too. Repetition and memorization are part of Actor Brain. That's where we have memorization tools that are more technical. When I have the question "What's my next line?" I need my technical side, my Actor Brain.

I got an email from a young student I've been working with for a few years. He said "I'm auditioning to play an elderly person. 60." *(laugh)* He's about 18.

"Do you have any hints about playing someone older?" He sent me the scene and the character is recounting going to school in the seventies and the AIDS epidemic. And seeing great jazz musicians playing in their era.

At first when he sent me the email I was thinking, "Maybe slouch a little bit and move slowly?" But then he sent me the scene and I thought, no. If you have the video of the AIDS epidemic, then you were old enough to have been there. If you have the video of going to high school in 1975, then you're in your sixties. Have a video of going to high school in the 70s. And then have a video of all the stuff that has happened since. Have a video of when Reagan got elected. Have a video of when Clinton got elected.

Shooting all those videos is what you have to do to play a 60 year old person. Not hunch over and walk with a cane. But know what all of that looks like from a first-person perspective.

I feel like that might be sort of a curt answer. "Well, know what you're talking about!" Have the video of the AIDS epidemic from a first-person perspective. That's what makes you old enough to have been there.

I can't tell if this approach is philosophical or practical or both. But it seems like a great answer to me. Have a video of when the Bee Gees album came out and Saturday Night Fever ruled the day. If you know what that looks like, you're in your sixties. There may be a bit of an affectation with your physicality or your voice, there may be a tiny bit of that. But it is the video and knowing what it was to have been there, that is the truth of playing an older person.

MADISON / MONICA / WALTER Scene
MADISON
Don't say anything. Let me do all the talking.

MONICA
Why should I let you do all the talking?

MADISON
I'm his favorite. I know how to make him do anything.

MONICA
You only think you do. He wouldn't help you on your credit application two years ago.

MADISON
I wasn't his favorite then.

MONICA
And now you are? How did you pull that off?

MADISON
You'll see.

MONICA
Hello Grampa!!

WALTER
My little Choochie! How are you?

MONICA
No one calls me Choochie anymore Grampa.

WALTER
And Madison too!

MONICA
Why am I still Choochie and she's Madison?

MADISON
Good to see you, Grampa.

WALTER
You picked a nice place. They have escargot here. I haven't had escargot before. I've heard of it but tonight I'm actually going to try it.

MADISON
Cool.

WALTER
Gotta try new things. Have you ever had escargot, Chooch?

MONICA
Yes. I've had escargot, Grandpa.

MADISON
When did you have escargot?

MONICA
Well, maybe I haven't had escargot recently, but I'm sure I've had it somewhere.

MADISON
South of France?

MONICA
It's snails, right Grampa?

WALTER
It is? I don't want snails.

MONICA
Well, that's what it is.

WALTER
That sounds terrible.

MADISON
When did you have escargot?

MONICA
Maybe I haven't actually had escargot but at least I know what it is. Have you had escargot?

MADISON
No, I have not. But at least I'm willing to admit it.

WALTER
Escargot for everybody!

MONICA
I don't feel like snails tonight, Grampa. Maybe another night I would want snails. I can't imagine that happening but...

MADISON
I'll try some snails, Grampa.

WALTER
I knew I could count on you Madison.

MONICA
You can count on me too, you know.

WALTER
I know, Chooch.

MONICA
Just because I don't want to eat snails doesn't mean you can't count on me.

WALTER
I know that sweetie. Let's order. I'm starved.

MADISON
What else are you having, Grandpa?

WALTER
I'm having the snails!

MADISON
I think those are an appetizer. It's not a whole meal.

WALTER
Oh.
(They all look at their menus)

MONICA
What made you pick this place, Madison?

MADISON
It looked good. What do you mean?

MONICA
Squid? Steak tartare? I wonder if they have those poisonous blowfish. That would be great.

MADISON
I was just feeling adventurous.

MONICA
Maybe with a side of monkey brains.

MADISON
And I know Grampa likes to try new things. Grampa, you're such an inspiration.

WALTER
Gotta try new things!

MADISON
Exactly.

How's it going?
Good. At first it was difficult to come up with a video as to why we're there. But once I created that, why I wanted my grandfather's attention, It was easier to engage.
I saw, Sarah, that you had filled in that part of the puzzle. I can't read your mind. I don't know what you decided, but I knew that you knew. You had a reason to be there. That worked well from my perspective.
You're right, it's not in the script. We don't know. But you made something up and you knew in your brain why you were there. I was really appreciative of that.
You did several things really well. Technically. With the eyeline and the menu, I was glad to see your eyeline there and breaking the rules of eyeline. That all worked very well.

And you decided at times to say your line just to yourself. That worked well in those moments as well.

Joe, in your Actor Brain, what do you think is up here? They're going to hit you up for money or what?

We talked about that. They have an agenda.

I agree. But in Character Brain, you don't know that.

Right. Character Brain is totally innocent. "This is great. I have the best grandkids in the world." I don't see it coming.

Great. So now turn to Actor Brain. I'm playing a role where my grandkids are going to take advantage of me. Who can I be so that that becomes its most powerful?

Oh.

Perhaps we should decide that you're someone who is easily taken advantage of. Like you're too trusting, you dote on your granddaughter too much, your head is easily turned by flattery. In this scene, it's like you're a kitten and they're a shark. *(Laugh)* I think I'm mixing metaphors but you get it.

Right.

So we can diagram the role as "I'm a kitten. These two are going to eat me." Then when you turn the tables on them, if that's what happens later, it's a bigger event. The dynamic of the scene is much greater if we see clearly who you are in relation to the topic of the scene, who you are in relation to the story.

Joe, I really appreciated your approach to the scene. I felt like you were treating it with integrity, which I will take, but if we change the video a bit of who you are and what's up, we can still have integrity but tell a bolder story.

Talia, you were pretty cold and chilly to your sister. Was that part of your diagramming?

Yes.

Yes, that makes sense and I agree with that. But can we find a way that is still appealing to the audience's eye? That chilly, cold approach can also shut down the audience. Can you find a way to navigate the scene but still be a winning personality? You see the quandary I have here?

Yes.

Even though you're kind of mean to your brother and manipulative and maybe going to take advantage of your grandpa, the audience still needs to like you. Even though you're very flawed it appears to me. But flaws are fascinating and interesting. I need you to find a way to execute the scene but still be appealing to the audience. Only your brother can not like you. Out here in the audience, we still need to like you.

Okay.

Does that feel actionable?

Yeah.

Terrific. Talia, early in the scene, you say "Now I'm his favorite. I wasn't before but now I am." You did something to gain his favor. I don't have to know but I want you to fill in the blanks there. How come you're now his favorite? What makes you so sure? Did you do something for him, say something to him? Did you buy him his favorite pair of slippers? I want you to know why you're so sure.

I liked that scene so much, let's try it again.

Talia, how was that adjustment?

Umm. Good. I played it not so cold and manipulative. We have a good relationship. We're just trying to do something.

Sarah, any thoughts?

I was in Actor Brain a bit.

I think all three of us were more in Actor Brain that time. And that makes perfect sense. I really liked the way you diagrammed the poisonous blowfish line and the monkey brains line. That you didn't hit the punchlines but kind of threw them away.

Sarah, I advise that you really, really hate the nickname Choochie. I'm thinking when you guys were five years old, you were Choochie and she was Chatchie.

Oh, that's hilarious.

So now why is she Madison and I'm still Choochie? *(laugh)* How does that work?

Listen, I liked the moments when you were speaking to yourself but add articulation in those moments.

Yeah. When the line was over, I thought "what the heck?"

(laugh) Awesome. "When the line was over, I thought 'what the heck?'" That could be the title of my next book.

LISA / LOUIS / CHERYL Scene

LISA
Grandpa!

LOUIS
Hello sweetie! How's tricks?

LISA
Trix are for kids Grampa. What's the big surprise?

LOUIS
Hang on. Let me say hello to your Mom first. Hello Cheryl.

CHERYL
Hello Dad.

LOUIS
It's been a while.

CHERYL
Uh-huh. (pause) So did you want me to come inside or stand in the doorway?

LOUIS
Of course! Forgive me. Come in. Come in.

CHERYL
Cause I can stand outside if that's what you want...

LOUIS
No, no. I'm glad to see you.

CHERYL
Let you and Lisa have alone time...

LOUIS
Cheryl, will you please come in? Let me have your coat.

CHERYL
Lisa, take your coat off so you don't get sweaty.

LISA
I already took my coat off Mom.

CHERYL
Good.

LISA
I've been taking off my coat by myself for a long time. Since I was like twelve.

CHERYL
Okay now.

LISA
All by myself.

CHERYL
Enough now. Shhh. Take a seat.

LISA
I've been deciding when to sit down pretty good too. I don't always need instructions.

LOUIS
Did you say twelve? How old are you?

LISA
I'm nearly fourteen.

LOUIS
Whoa.

LISA
Yeah. I'm entering my mid-teens.

LOUIS
That's big.

CHERYL
Why did you call us here Dad? What's the big announcement?

LOUIS
Can I get anyone a drink?

(at the same time)
CHERYL No.   LISA Sprite.

LOUIS
I haven't got any Sprite, sweetie. How about a Coke?

LISA
No thanks.

CHERYL
Can we please get to the point of our visit?

LOUIS
I think I have a Fanta in the fridge somewhere.

LISA
What's a Fanta?

LOUIS
It was popular during the 2nd World War. I have no idea where I got it from but it's been in the back of the fridge since... well since...

CHERYL
Dad!

LOUIS
Cheryl, I'll be right back. Let me get the girl a Fanta. (to Lisa) You want it in a glass with ice, or straight outta the can?

LISA
A glass with ice, please.

CHERYL
Gahhh!!!

LOUIS
See Cheryl? This is part of your problem. You don't want any Fanta. (he exits)

LISA
What is up with you Mom?

CHERYL
I'm just nervous about Grandpa's big announcement.

LISA
Why are you nervous?

CHERYL
Well, announcements make people nervous.

LISA
Excited. Announcements make people excited. Not nervous.

CHERYL
Same thing.

LISA
Not really.

LOUIS (entering with 3 drinks)
Turns out there were three in there. The last three Fantas. The end of an era. So I thought I'd splurge. Fantas all around.

CHERYL
Oh my god, can we stop talking about Fanta!

LISA (looking at her phone)
Says here, it was invented in 1940.

LOUIS
Long time ago.

LISA
They still make it.

LOUIS
Really?

LISA
It comes in grapefruit, orange, citrus burst...

CHERYL
Okay, I'm really going to scream now...

LOUIS
Okay Cheryl.

CHERYL
I mean for real.

LOUIS
No need. We're done talking about Fanta.

LISA *(one more)*
...pineapple...

LOUIS
Okay ladies. Here it is. The big announcement. Drum roll, please.

LISA (imitating a drum roll)
Bdddddddddddddddddddd (breath) Bdddddddddddddddd

LOUIS
I'm moving to Florida!

LISA
What?

CHERYL
Dad, when?

LOUIS
Next month. I put in an offer on a condo and it went through and I'm heading south.

CHERYL
What about Mom?

LOUIS
She's staying here.

CHERYL
Really?

LOUIS
Yeah, see Lisa? You get the best of both. Grandma stays here and you get to visit me over Christmas. It's a win-win.

CHERYL
You're splitting up?

LOUIS
Don't be so dramatic. Think of it as a vacation.

CHERYL
But you're moving there.

LOUIS
Okay then. An extended vacation.

Talia, I feel like there is a similarity between the two characters you're playing today. I don't want to sound mean but I feel you're doing the least you can do instead of the most you can do. You're covering the bases but you're not being adventurous.
I agree. I definitely felt that with this scene.
I want you to have more fun. And that might be the whole note. Have more fun as Talia being an actor and have more fun as the character in the kitchen talking to her dad and daughter. See if you can have more at stake. Your characters are a little bit too together. Like "whatever happens I won't be too thrown by it." But if you're excitable or scattered, you'll be more invested which means the consequences are greater and equals a more powerful scene. Do you see what I'm suggesting?
Yeah.
Find a way to have more fun. Take chances with who this woman is. Be wrong and explore. She might be a bit petulant or she might be "over" her family. Have a bit more fun with that. Does that feel actionable?
Yes.

I've said this a few times in class and I'm not sure I've said it well yet. Stereotyping can be very effective in drama and comedy. You're a parent who is controlling, too much in your daughter's business. We can make fun of that person. What does a dad who is too much into his daughter's business behave like? I hate to say that about stereotypes because obviously that can be a terrible thing in real life. But in drama and comedy, that's kind of what it's about.
I had those instincts a little bit but it seems like it gets back to "selling."
Joe, I think what's going on with you sometimes is that you understand what is needed in the moment, but then you don't get there with your belly. You get there with your brain or your mouth or your ears. So when you decide in your Actor Brain the way a line should go, you've got to shoot the video for the person who does that. If you don't have the video, if you don't have the truth to back it up, you start selling.

What you and I are seeing for the role may be similar, but how you're getting there may be artificially instead of shooting the video so you can be truthful. An excellent distinction, Joe, between over-acting and having longer arrows.

Think of selling as the exterior of the person. What we're talking about here is the interior of the person. That's where we want to be working from. Right now, when you go to sales, it's the exterior.

That made me giggle, which is always a good sign. Alejandro, how's it going for you?

I remember doing this scene before. This time I prioritized video. I've been doing that the last couple of weeks in class. I had more layers of video.

Good. Good, Alejandro. I'm glad you were prioritizing video. I think it paid off. I'll have some thoughts for you but first let me check in with Al. Al, how's it going?

This was a meaty scene and I had a good actor to work off of. It gave me a lot to work with. It's so much easier when you have someone to bounce off of.

Let's talk about your video, Al. That's where my note would lie. It would be in your memories of why you weren't home to look after your son. What you prioritized over your grandchildren. I also think the video should include why you are finally willing to get back in touch with your son. Why now?

Okay.

I thought you did a pretty good job with the scene - you always do, you're a pretty good actor - but I didn't really see the truth behind your language. Is that fair?

Umm.

By truth, I mean the video. The hope or the regret. The memory of "why I didn't call when you turned twenty-one. I meant to call you. I really did. But I was catching a plane to Beijing and they were boarding. I thought you would understand." Those kinds of memories. Those memories and thoughts that don't get uttered. They're not spoken. Those are the things that give our character depth. The memory of your life since you've been a dad. Even the memory of the day your son was born. Those kinds of video are not found on the pages. They're not in the lines of dialogue but they're the things that give our language texture and complexity.

For you to have the thought of the day your son was born. It doesn't make it to language but it's a very appropriate thought for the scene. And the audience won't know that that's what you're thinking but they'll know that you're thinking. And you're living within the truth of being his dad. That's what we bring in. All that nuance and complexity that is not in the script. It comes from our specific memories. The texture that comes from having truthful thoughts that are outside of the language. It's not in the words. The juicy part, the interesting part, the complex part, it's somewhere outside the language.

You've said that before but I didn't remember that.

You know how I'm always talking about video. By definition the video is always interesting. Like just now we created a video - you can use it or not - where you were flying to Beijing and that's why you didn't call on his twenty-first birthday. Because I've created a video, it's already interesting. The words aren't, but the video is. The words are the words, but what we place outside of the words, around the words, all of the things we don't say but are still true. The video is all our memories and hopes and regrets and dreams and fears. Our video is where all those things live.
Of course.
We're always looking for the truth because the truth is interesting because it's true. Okay?
Yeah.

Alejandro, we had talked about emotional range and I asked you to play around more in the nines and tens. Was that part of your exploration here?
Yeah. I just thought I would go for it. Let it rip.
Cool. I'm glad to see that because I wanted to be sure you found those upper ranges and they were accessible to you and that you find them in the right ways.
I would be careful diagramming scenes. Be sure to align with the writer's intention. It may seem to you that it would be great if your character laughs all the way through the scene. But if it doesn't say "he laughs," I'm probably not going to do that. If it doesn't say "he's overcome with emotion," I might not get overcome with emotion. I might want to get right to that line, the precipice of these things, but I don't necessarily want to fall in.
Okay. Yeah.
If it says "he loses his temper," I'm going to give myself permission. But remember, the writer could be there in the casting room. I'm not going to give myself permission to drastically change anything that's intended by the writer. If I am auditioning for this part, I wouldn't start there. I would skirt a little more median, and see if I get notes leading me in one direction or another.
Okay. I definitely blew the roof.
We had talked about that. But remember, once you've blown the roof, there's nowhere to go. That's fine. Some scenes, that may be what's required but I don't think this is one. I think if both of you wished you could reconcile, both wish it could work, it's a bit more tragic when it doesn't. As opposed to you totally don't want it to work, you hate him now. That closes doors. It's more tragic if you desperately wish it could work than someone who's completely shut off. It's more interesting to see the puzzle pieces don't work, they don't fit together. The hurt is too deep. As opposed to, he wants it to work and you don't.
Yeah. I see.
I don't think your character thinks it can work. But somewhere underneath he wishes and dreams that it could work. Then, the tragedy is greater if it doesn't.
Yeah. I was thinking about that earlier.

There's a yin and a yang to it. That felt very much like yang only.

Talia, when I "Sherlock Holmes" this scene, I think that the contractor you're playing is not very good at their job. You were playing her as competent, smart, in charge.

In comedy especially, it's a good idea to consider the worst person for the job. That's often comic gold. For those of us that are a bit older, I'll sometimes use the example of Gilligan's Island. The worst guy to ever tie a knot, let's put him in charge of tying knots, right? He couldn't tie his shoes but let's put him in charge of tying knots. More recently, Michael Scott in The Office. The most immature person available? Let's put him in charge and see what happens.

In this case, we might think of someone who's maddeningly slow, not that bright or unable to pick up on social clues, not quite getting it. I think there's something there we can exploit.

I do like your tendency, Talia, - I've seen this over several classes - to fight hard for your characters. To treat them with respect. I think that's a great tendency. But in this case it might be more fun to follow that comic path of incompetence.

That does sound fun.

I think I'd like everyone to go back into rehearsal and we'll try those scenes with the adjustments.

Let me check in with you, Al. How was that adjustment for you?

Trying to run a video. Parts of a video. I didn't have the whole thing obviously. There were moments that I felt it. It felt real.

Yep.

And you can see that, right?

Yes, I can see that. Well, more importantly, I can see the absence of that.

I know you can. (Laugh)

Alejandro, how was that for you?

I wanted to make it work with my father.

I thought you made great adjustments. Listen, the last line of almost every scene is an opportunity. In this case, I would have you pause before you say it.

I wasn't sure if I wanted to let him or I don't want to let him.

When he is like "Please can I see them?" - and then you take a pause there - think about the tension of the audience waiting to see what you're going to say. That's really juicy. Give the audience a chance to wonder. So a big question is asked of you, that's a great opportunity to build tension in that moment as we wait for the answer. Which is going to be the release of tension. Good adjustments from both of you.

Talia, how was that adjustment for you?

It was definitely more fun.

Good. And for now that may be the whole point. I don't know the whole script and I don't know the character outside of this scene but I like seeing you have fun with the part. And once you do that you start stepping outside of the box and when you do that, you're uniquely Talia. That's how you are outside the box. Inside the box we're all the same but outside we're all unique.

Al, how's it going for you?

Okay. I tried to do a bit more video for this one.

Yeah, you did.

Of course it enriches the experience for the actor and the audience, I think.

Without doubt. Good. There were places where the video wasn't there but there were places where it was. And in those moments, it was very effective. Sometimes the way I put this is - it might sound a little pat but - if we have the video we don't have to act. We can stop acting. We have truth now. We no longer have to pretend it's true because it is. If you really have that memory, you no longer have to pretend you have that memory because you do. We don't have to fake it. I felt like that was happening in places. And now, I no longer have to worry about doing it the good way. The good way to say this line. Actors do that. I'm not an actor, I'm a person. I really had this experience. How I say it is the right way to say it. Because it's the truth.

May I stop you Debra?

Yes.

I think you're doing it just fine. I think your acting is good. What I'd like to see more of… I think right now you're fitting into the room. You're fitting into the theatre. And what you need to do is to dominate the room. Dominate the theatre.

I'm not doing that.

No. You're fitting in. You're likable and believable and all that stuff and it's all very nice. It's like you're a part of the community of people. But it's not a community of people, or a democracy. You are in charge. Think of the audience as unruly second-graders.

(laugh) And there I get a little confused. I was doing a little of that in the beginning of rehearsals and the director said "I want people to love you."

Being in control doesn't mean being unlikable.

Right.

We love someone being in control of a good experience.

Right.

It's not mean to be dominant. This dominance is simply your willingness to lead us on this journey. You're willingness to take us. Even if we don't want to go. Take us.

Okay. Yeah, yeah, I am fitting in.

Well, you're fitting in nicely! *(laugh)* At a party there might be ten conversations and yours is one. But we need your conversation to be the only one at this party.
Alright.
Want to try it again with that in mind?
Yes.
You're in charge of everyone in this room. Unruly second-graders. "Sit down and shut up." And I know that sounds mean but it will be good for them. We're going to learn about something and it's important. You might not want to eat broccoli but it's good for you. You'll thank me later.
Okay.
Once more from the top. Have fun.

May I stop you?
Yes.
How's it going?
Better. It feels better.
Good. It feels better for me also. Debra, your video on this isn't great. In this monologue, you talk about taking a test in college when you were high on diet pills. And that you wrote an essay in a one eighth inch line. I don't think you know what that looks like.
I want you to actually do that. Write the most profound statements from the viewpoint of a blazed 19 year old college student. Keep writing these thoughts over top of your writing, so that it becomes a mess of ink. In my video of this it's in red ink. And then shoot the video of getting your paper back with an "F" on it. You can look at it and go "I can't believe I wrote two thousand words or whatever in a one eighth inch space because I was baked on those pills."
Okay. I can already see it now.
Yes! You've been describing it but not seeing it.
Not like that, no. I just saw scribbles and that's all. I didn't go that far.
That's what she says. That she wrote it in a one eighth inch space.
That's true. If you write that over and over again and in red pen…
It's ink. It's just bleeding ink with a few swirls. Maybe you've even almost torn through the paper because of the pressure of the pen. When you really shoot the video, when you look at the video, the video is fascinating.
It's true! I get lazy. I don't get that specific with the video.
You have to. It's really the only way. Video is very specific.
It's very, very specific. You can't just go "Okay, I see it. Blah, blah, blah. I've got to move on because I need to memorize…"
It only took us a minute here to talk about that test you took.
Right.

A YEAR IN ACTING CLASS

Once we really look at it, really confront it, it's very specific. You spell it out in the dialogue. If you really take what she says literally, shoot the video and confront it, now it's something fascinating and hilarious.

Yeah. Okay.

Right now that's a big problem with this part of the monologue. As I'll sometimes say - rather pithily - "you don't know what you're talking about." Having that "Capital K" knowledge. The knowledge of everything you say. Certainly experiences like this one. Memories are videos.

Just using this video for this little section - making it so much more specific - it helps so much. It's comical. You can see it so well.

It's hilarious.

If you take the example here of writing that essay, and you shoot the video in that detail for everything you say throughout the play, you're done. It will all work.

You sent me an email reminding me of that a couple weeks ago. But I didn't get that specific because I'm worried about the lines. This is a really quick rehearsal period, I thought.

I want to be careful that we don't give power to "This sure is a fast rehearsal period." Or "I've never done a role like this before" or "I've never played a role this large before." None of that matters. Shoot the video.

The thing that makes you look unconfident is when you don't know, with a "Capital K," what you're talking about. That looks unconfident. That looks tentative. Because you're not trying to tell people what you've experienced, you're trying to remember your lines. You need the video to fill in the Character Brain or else it becomes an Actor Brain task of trying to remember what to say next. It comes off as unconfident.

It's true. That's what I'm doing in some of the lines. It's because I didn't have the lines. So I dropped the video and just started memorizing the old fashioned way.

Shoot the video. The specificity of the video will give you the specificity of the language.

Okay.

Take a moment and then try it again please.

       May I stop you?

Yes.

That little pill. You say it's magic.

It's a drug.

Shoot the video of it being magic. Right now it's just something you say. Make it magic! "Ooooh, magic! Oooh!" Now magic means something. As I've been saying recently, there are two ways to shoot a video of magic. One is Magic! Pouf! The other "M-A-G-I-C." Not "M-A-G-I-C." Let's not go that route. It's "Magic! Oooh, aaah!" When you shoot the video on magic and give value to it, it becomes fascinating. It's not just another couple syllables.

And it becomes interesting to watch.

Yeah, because you find it interesting. Now that you have a video, it is.

Right now you're letting the writer choose the words for you. You've got to take over and choose those words yourself. You chose that word "magic." So you've got to see magic before you can say "magic." And that's true of every word in our script. Because if we don't see it first, then the writer chose that word for us. But if we see it and that's what drives our language, then I chose that word. I choose the word magic because I know what it looks like. Otherwise it's "M-A-G-I-C."

Huh.

That's the specificity of the video in direct relation to the specificity of the language. You have to confront why you choose that word, whatever the word is.

Okay. Alright.

Right now in learning lines, you're doing it without the specific video. Shoot the video and now it's a magic little pill. I don't need to go "What's my line? Do I say magic here?" No! I don't need to remember a line. It's a magic little pill. I know it is because I held it in my hand!

Okay. Alright. Thank you so much Duane. It's so inspirational.

Shoot that video. I think you're ready to do that right now. And do that in detail. Everything you say, you have to choose those words.

They're mine.

Without the video, you could have never chosen those words. The writer chose them for you. We've got to get the writer out of here so those are your words. And the video is how you'll do it.

Well, thank you, Duane.

I'm honored to help.

I think your approach to the work right now is really healthy. The thing to consider is how can I make this material as impactful on the audience as possible? With this story, with these words? Yes, do it truthfully, But ultimately, how do I hit the audience in the belly? How do I make this into a belly punch? So when it comes time to create expectation in one direction and surprise in the other, there are ways to create greater expectation therefore creating a larger event. For the audience that's a more fulfilling experience. Greater surprise is a larger event.

And I hate to appear rude toward the audience in our thinking. Different things I say like, "Eff these people" and "belly punch" and "impolite story." I don't want any of this to make it appear that I don't like audiences. Of course we need them. They are wonderful people and sometimes I'm in the audience. I'm one of those wonderful people. But in order to be powerful, we have to be impolite to the audience. That's what powerful is. Otherwise it's "I'm a little teapot, short and stout."

What is being impolite to the audience? Well, it's making them feel tension and nervousness. Isn't that a great action film? A great suspense moment? We love that. Give us goosebumps. Make us cry. You see what you're trying to do to us out here in the audience? None of it is polite.

I'm coming after you.

"I'm not here to be liked" is one thing that I often say. I'm here to make your belly go. It's not polite to make the audience get nervous or even contemplative or introspective or nostalgic. None of that is polite. So the question becomes "how do I get you in a way you're not ready to get got?"

I don't do that in real life. I don't do that at the grocery store. I don't do that in traffic. But when I'm onstage or in front of an audience, I'm coming after your belly.

This is a great conversation but does it feel actionable moving forward?

Yes.

July/August

Alejandro, what's rattling for you?

I was thinking about getting an agent.

Here's something you might think about, Alejandro. Get a manager. And your manager will help you get an agent.

A manager.

Yep. In the L.A. market, it's much easier to get interviews and auditions with managers than it is with agents.

Managers. What do they do?

If you have an audition and your car breaks down, your agent won't help you. Your manager will.

Hmm.

If you don't know if you should wear your blue shirt or your green shirt to an audition, your agent won't help you, your manager will. "Should I say yes to this job or no to this job?" Your manager will help you make those decisions. Your manager will cover you more holistically. They'll say "I really like that brown jacket of yours. Wear that to the audition." Your agent will never tell you that. Your manager will.

Your manager will meet with you for coffee or a drink once in a while. Keep in touch. Be caught up on you and your life. Agents won't do any of that.

A good manager will only have twenty to forty clients. An agency may have hundreds of actors that they represent. So a manager is much more in your corner as far as your career goes. Your agent cares about gigs, your manager cares about career.

Okay. I see that now.

Here's a thing. Your manager will take 15%. Your agent will take 10%. So when you start working, 25% of what you're making is gone. But you've got two offices in Los Angeles with secretaries and people answering phones and returning emails and looking for jobs for you. So it's completely worth it.

It's hard to walk in and get an interview with an agent. Managers are looking for someone to take a chance on. Managers are like "Where's that diamond in the rough that no one knows about yet.?" And that could easily be you.

Lisa, I want to applaud your approach to the scene. As I'll sometimes say, it's like surfing. We don't control the ocean, we respond to the ocean. And I felt like you were surfing effectively and powerfully at times. Some actors will say "Hey, ocean. Hold it a minute. I've gotta act!"

(laugh) Guilty sometimes.

I thought that was really well done.

Do you have any notes for yourself?
Fluidity. Always, fluidity.
Well, let's talk about that. One thing I liked, especially early in the scene, was the way you were using rhythm in surprising ways. The way I will sometimes say this - and I ask actors to emulate - is to "establish a rhythm and upset it." And "establish a rhythm and upset it." Whether you were aware of it or not, you were doing that early on. It kept me unable to predict the rhythm. It keeps my ear awake and ready for anything. It was sort of halted here and then it became fluid and then halted again. You were talking about fluidity but it was the exceptions to the fluidity that made the rhythms work. The interruptions to the fluidity was what makes it powerful. It also upsets the rhythm. The pauses build tension in a beautiful way for us out here in the audience. It's the unexpected in the audience's ear that becomes powerful. Sometimes fluid can put me to sleep, lull me off.
Good point.
Unexpected rhythms are what puts me on the edge of my seat.

I could see that you understood the moral quandary. Great art is about moral quandaries. If there's not a quandary, there's not a question. There's nothing to investigate. You helped guide me to that tightrope you're trying to walk and we might fall in either direction. That is a central vein of a powerful experience for the audience. To walk the tightrope but never fall to one side. You might fall, you might fall, but then you don't. If you fall, it's over. To keep that balancing act and that yin and yang. I'll go left but I'd better go right as well. When you're doing that balancing act, anything might happen.

We know the concept of "1, 2, Pineapple," right? One, two is to build expectation and pineapple is the surprise. One and two create the expectation of three and then pineapple is the surprise instead of three. That's how 1, 2, Pineapple works.
Early in the scene, you're challenging him to a duel. We can create an expectation that he is going to be afraid of you. The more we can create a juicy expectation that he's going to be afraid of you, the greater the surprise when you become afraid of him.
Okay.
A lot of the fun of the first third of the scene is to create the expectation that he is going to be afraid of you. See how juicy you can make that so that when he turns the tables on you, it's a bigger event.
I see.
Usually the way we diagram 1, 2, Pineapple is we'll see the thing that's funny. That's pineapple. Then why is it funny? Because it's a surprise. Now we look at one, two and create a greater expectation that is as opposite the surprise as possible. Creating the expectation of three and then giving them pineapple instead. One, two is the

expectation that he's going to be afraid of you and then giving them a greater surprise when you become afraid of him.

Yeah. I can definitely see that now.

We can juice that up, can't we? You walk in there like a badass. You're Clint Eastwood on a badass day. You're here to lay down the law to this guy. You're young, you're strong. You've got it all figured out. And then "What? You're not afraid of me? This is real?" Okay?

Yeah.

I just want to look at juicing up the expectation so the surprise is greater. Does that make sense to you as far as a dramatic diagram?

I think so, yes. I already see some places where it could be juicier.

I liked a lot of what you did. It was fun to see your sense of comedy when you lose your confidence when he turns the tables on you. But we can juice up the expectation so that there's a greater surprise.

Joe, that reading was verging on sales. What might help is "don't say the threatening line threateningly." Think about how threatening you can be without being threatening. I don't think this guy is a superhero or a gunslinger or has a vendetta. I think he's just a businessman.

What I'd like to do is give everyone sixty seconds of reflection and then try the scenes again. Think about your notes. Work on your video. We'll start at the top.

Can we go back, please? Joe, I want you to simplify. There are still sales happening. I want to see you play the scene with the absence of acting.

Good adjustment Joe. What are you discovering when I ask you to do that? It's okay if you don't know.

It was more real.

On that reading the only things that were happening just now, were what had to happen. Not "Oh. I could do this! I can try that! I can sell this moment in this way!" The things that had to happen were happening. What I like is that you're not painting... painting a second coat with high gloss paint. It was simply what had to happen.

Joe, each time you strip it all away, I think to myself "Joe is a powerful actor." But sometimes you cover your performance in plastic and tie it with a bow. When you strip all that away, you are a powerful actor. Each time.

Wow.

Something I've been saying a lot recently is "Great dramatic or comedic moments are filled with awkwardness. Awkwardness is dramatic gold." We should swim around in that murky, lovely, warm cesspool of awkwardness. *(Laugh)* That's dramatic coin. That's currency. Right now, it was awkward but you moved on pretty quickly. Some of those awkward moments can really sit there. If we're sensing that it's awkward, that means it's filled with tension. That means it has dramatic value.

Okay. That makes sense.

Alejandro, let us see you stewing in that realization. The more uncomfortable, the more value it has, dramatically.

Alejandro, one clue I see when I Sherlock Holmes this is that you say the word "shan't." That's an odd word to say in a contemporary scene. One thing I haven't said in a long time is "If the language is broken, don't fix it. Highlight how it's broken." Right now I think you're trying to fix "shan't." Don't. Highlight how it's broken. Does that feel actionable?

Yes.

Good. So that's what I'll say about broken language. "Don't fix it. Highlight how it's broken." Okay?

Yeah.

Really fun.

Polly, how's it going for you?

I think it was better this time. I think I had better video.

Me too. I think your video is going very nicely.

I might remind you of the concept of throwing some lines away. We've talked about that a few times?

We have.

We can't let everything we say be equally important.

I struggle with that. I don't know why.

It's okay. An instinct that you can try to build in is, "Don't let yourself stay at the same place in terms of your investment in what you're saying." I want alarm bells to happen when we've gotten repetitive. In anything. Rhythmically, musically, dramatically. If it's too repetitive I want an alarm bell to go off. It's okay if we are repetitive for a moment, because we're establishing a pattern. But then upset that pattern. And then perhaps we can go back to it because it works well and then upset it. So we're not doing anything predictably, including our investment in our language. Right now I think each line is getting the same level of investment but sometimes you've just got to throw a line away.

Lisa, there's a phrase I use called "Impolite story." That was a very impolite story. We can do our work politely or impolitely and impolite is better. Impolite is more powerful storytelling and that was impolite and therefore powerful.

Joe, how's it going?

I had some questions and hopefully that created questions for the audience.

Great. I'll take that. I like that thinking. I'll take that reading. There were even moments in there that I thought were viable. Think about that feeling when you're not being so expressive, where you're not letting things bubble to the surface so easily. Instead, contain those impulses and let that fire burn hotter.

I like when I can do that.

Each time you do that, you become a really interesting and compelling actor. Get used to that feeling. It probably doesn't feel good. It would feel good to be very expressive. That would feel good. Change what feels good to the tension, not the release of tension. You can do it good by not doing it good.

Very good scene for both of you. I liked the simplicity. When you played the scene so matter-of-fact, just two men sitting down having a negotiation, without having to say "I'm the funny one." Or "I'm the mean one." It highlighted the scene, the situation was the star. You weren't, the situation was. And that's just fine. Make the situation the star.

Alejandro, what's rattling?

I organized a variety of monologues so I could shoot them, edit them nicely and put them up on various platforms. That's one of my main goals.

Cool. How many of these monologues are you thinking of putting up? I think maybe two or three and you're good.

Two or three?

At the most.

I was thinking about six.

Maybe. But they'd have to be really diverse. Here's a thing: Casting Directors and Agents and all those people, they look at about the first ten seconds and decide if they're interested or not. That's about all. You might grab them, you might get them to hang in there for 30 seconds or a minute at most, but then they're moving on. Keep in mind, regular people watch movies and TV to see a story. Professionals watch reels to see an actor.

We talked about managers the other day and managers might watch the whole thing. Or a person who is looking at you specifically because they know you and are considering you, they might watch the whole thing. But overall, they click on your video, they check you out, you say a couple of lines and they've decided already. "I like him." Or "He's not right for this." But they don't really watch the whole thing.

I know how ambitious you are but I don't think this is the right place for your ambition. To get five or six different audition reels. These are just designed to get you in the room to audition with their material. Not to see a selection of your material.

Okay. That makes sense.

I know how ambitious you are. I don't want you to overwork on these. It's just a business card. It's just you doing you and from there we go for a job. Just a couple different flavors. A comedic and a dramatic. They might go "I like him in this. Is he

A YEAR IN ACTING CLASS

funny?" and then you get a call. But just those two and you're covered. You can check that off your list and move on to other things.

Is that good with you?

Yes.

Anything else brewing for you? Anything else on your burner?

No. I know there's always this little voice in your head going "oh crap. Here we go." But there's excitement there too. Just that little voice of fear but…

I'll just articulate this. I sometimes say "actor cake," It's one of my little phrases, "actor cake." I'll go ahead and give you the whole thing. "Confidence is to the actor what flour is to the cake." Cake has got icing and food coloring but it's made of flour. The fiber itself is made of flour. It's really important for actors to embrace the concept that confidence is the most important ingredient I can have in my cake. *(Laugh)* My cake being me.

Whatever I have to do to get confidence, I'm going to do to get confidence. Confidence can't be given to you. I can't give you confidence. No one can give you confidence but you can take it. You can take confidence. You can seize confidence.

Of course that doesn't mean suddenly we're a jerk and we demand heart-shaped ice cubes in our drinks or whatever. Here we're just talking about meeting the challenge that's in front of us, which can be very intimidating. The camera, an audience, a casting situation. It's one of the most intimidating experiences a human being can face. Of course, other circumstances may be more dire, but you see what I mean. Firefighters do something that's scarier than what we do but only a little. *(Laugh)* We're under a microscope, literally. And, like firefighters, we have a heroic reason to do it. So we don't have to doubt why we're doing it.

That's true. That's very true.

So it's okay for us to adopt confidence in all the ways we can. Adopt it. Even if you have to fake it at first. If you have to fake it at first, go ahead. Because lack of confidence will find its way into everything. It's one of the most insidious things you can bring to a situation. Certainly in the acting world, in the microscope world.

You mentioned you're sometimes a bit nervous. That's okay. It's fun to be a bit nervous. It's certainly fun to be excited and that's all good. Ultimately, just know that you belong there. You belong there. And if you don't get this one, that's fine, you'll get the next one.

Yes. I've been seeing it like "You know what? Let's just battle. Let's go."

Good. Things are falling into place quite nicely for you Alejandro.

Joe, I've asked Alejandro to read opposite you for your show. Are you trying this off book?

Yes.

Okay, Whenever you're ready.

Let me jump in. We got almost all of the way through the scene. Joe, it's going pretty well, don't you think? You had to refer to your script a couple times.

Twice, I think.

It was more than that. A few times you had to refer.

Joe, it's going pretty well. Pretty well. Right now the first line, you're not walking in wondering if Leo is in yet, you're walking in saying "Did Leo get in yet?" It's like "Walk in and say this. Now say this."

Well, I'm rushing in to find out is he in yet? He called me last night and something's wrong.

Okay.

So I come in the door and I look around.

You say "I walk in and I look around." but instead I want your thinking to be "Where the hell is Leo?" Just think that. Don't think about looking around, step, step, talk. Think about "Where the hell is Leo?" If you want to know where Leo is you'll walk in and look around. We've got to replace that.

No wonder it's hard to memorize if you're memorizing lines like that.

I am.

It's pretty difficult to make this transition to using video to memorize lines. But why do you say "Did Leo get in yet?" You want to know where he is. So walk in wanting to know where Leo is. Urgently. Where's Leo? Where the hell is he? Now you don't have to walk in, step, step, look, talk.

We have to take memorization from an Actor Brain task and turn it into a Character Brain experience. The task of memorization from Actor Brain lines to Character Brain behavior.

Don't beat yourself up because I'm giving you this note but I want you to really take this on. Why do I say "Where's Leo?" Not because it's my line but because I want to know where the heck he is. The first-person character experience.

Right now, even though you're getting the lines pretty well, I could tell you didn't have a memory of the phone call last night at midnight.

You're right.

You talk about it for four or five lines. When the phone rang, were you sleeping? Did it wake you up? Where's your phone? Was your wife next to you in bed? The video. "Who's calling at midnight? This is crazy. Leo? What's going on?" Not the lines about the phone call but the experience. If you make that transition, lines will be easier to memorize, I promise. The experience will give you your language. If you really want to know if Leo is in yet, your line "Did Leo get in yet?" will come to you. Because that will be your experience. Not "D-I-D space, Capital L-E-O, step, step, look."

I'll sympathize that it's one thing to theorize this and another to put it into practice in the way I'm asking of you. But when you make that transition, everything will be simpler and more powerful. And you're not out on stage going "I hope I don't forget my line." A lot of actors are out there going "I hope I don't forget my line." And that's deadly. We can't let that be what's going on. Okay?

Yeah.

I want you to rethink the way you're memorizing. Because you're memorizing "What do I say? What do I say?" and not "Where the hell is Leo?" The lines have to become the lines from my perspective. Not the writer typing my words and handing them to me on a piece of paper. That's what's saying the lines now. Once you do that, you're going to see how much easier this becomes.

Okay.

You rock, sir. All that said, it's coming along. He's cute and fun and I think your accent is appropriately… appropriate. *(Laugh)*

Sarah, nice to meet you. Thanks for trying out our class. How was your monologue?

Pretty good.

Do you have any notes for yourself?

I remember the feedback I got in my other class was not to steamroll it. It's hard because you don't actually have a partner for an audition monologue. My biggest goal is to have it be believable. Like I'm actually having those feelings. In my head, like during the pauses, I have to think about "what would she be thinking about?" And what an actual conversation sounds like as opposed to the words just written in the text.

Here's how I would try to move your thinking. And just to let you know, I don't like to give too many notes on someone's first effort…

No. Do it.

This is your dad you're talking to, right?

Yes.

I'd like you to create a stronger video of him and your memories that now give you these opinions about him.

Right.

I'd like you to be thinking about that time when you were fourteen and he embarrassed the hell out of you. And be seeing that video when you say this line and how tough it's been for you when you say that line. Does that feel actionable?

I think the substitution for my dad is going to be the hardest. Especially because he doesn't give a shit. That's hard because my real dad isn't necessarily the right dad for this.

I'm glad you bring that up. Substitution wouldn't be the word I would use. What I suggest is that you shoot the video. The video is really a memory and the memory is a video. I want you to create the memory. It doesn't have to be your real dad, just a video of a dad who is neglecting you in those ways.

Instead of recalling something from your real life, you can shoot the movie, shoot the video. Then you can remember what it felt like. You don't have to use anything from your real life. That's a certain school of acting but it's not one that I ask you to use.
Okay.
Now does that feel actionable?
Do you mean as in able to do it?
As in something to try to implement.
I think so. Trying to have that memory while you're speaking? Yeah, I think so.
Great. One of the things you said was that you wanted it to be truthful.
Yeah.
Another way to put this is "my words are this, *(gesture for speaking)* but what's really happening is this." *(gesture for thinking)*
Right.
So this is what we need *(gesture for thinking)* while we're saying this. *(gesture for speaking)* Say this but bring this in. Now we've got something that is really sizzling.
Sure.
Even though I'm saying this, I'm still thinking about Grandma… that time last week… that time five minutes ago… what I've always hoped… what I've always wanted. That's all your video. And that's rolling over here, even though I'm saying this. And that will give our language texture and nuance and depth.
Right.
Terrific. It seems like you're understanding this well and rather quickly.
Yeah. You're explaining it well, so thank you.
I'm glad you feel that way, thank you.

Joe, I sometimes give a note called "Too much scene." which is where it appears that this scene is the only thing that happens in this man's life. As opposed to throwing the scene aside and asking "who is this guy? what's going on?" and now put that guy into the scene. Not a person who lives within the scene but someone who lives outside the scene. Then we put him into the scene. I don't know if I'm explaining that well.
I don't get that…
The idea being, I don't want our characters to exist for only two and a half minutes. They have to have a life away from the scene. They had breakfast this morning at their kitchen table. They have to pick up their kids from school later today. So it's not only about these two and a half minutes. That dichotomy that isn't the scene is what we want to also be present in the scene and that will make the scene relevant.
(Pause) Good times.

More time creates more tension, more tension creates greater expectation, more expectation creates greater surprise.

Joe, how's it going?

Better.

I think so too. It's the tension of what might happen, not what is happening. For you to keep restraint on those moments is the tension of what might happen. That's greater than the tension of what is happening.

Earlier today, we talked about tension and creating tension and release. In a question like the one Joe has; "And in exchange?" That's a question. Pretty much anytime I'm asked a question, I understand it's also an opportunity to build tension. Because, after a question, what's expected? Well, an answer is expected. If I wait to give the answer, I can create more tension. That pause after the question will build more tension toward the answer, therefore creating a larger event when the answer is given. Does that hold together as a theory?

Yeah. But not all questions need a pause before the answer...

I agree. Another thing I wanted to mention was to "Drop a bomb on the scene." We haven't talked about that in a long time.

No, we haven't.

Alejandro's response, "Nothing," needs to "drop a bomb" on the scene, become a large event. When I diagram the scene, that "nothing" can become a large event. It's not another line in the scene, it's a bomb dropped right in the middle of it. And then everybody's got to react to a bomb just went off.

A bomb is a large event. Most often in scenes there's at least one bomb and often there's two or three. So drop a bomb on the scene. That pause beforehand can help create a bomb instead of a small event or even just another line.

The story of a bomb is partly in the anticipation of it, then in its execution and then in its aftermath. In our reaction to the dust clearing. So we can diagram bombs in that way. I haven't talked about bombs in a long time but it was on the tip of my tongue during the whole scene. Does all of that hold together conceptually?

I think so, yeah.

We can say a line so that it's not a bomb, it's just a tidbit of information, or we can drop a bomb on the scene.

So who are you speaking to on that, aside from generally?

Most of the execution of that would be with Alejandro's pause after your question. But you can help, too Joe, by creating greater expectation with the question.

I got it. Both sides.

That moment of tension can create a lot of juice in the scene and the audience's interest in the events of the scene. Does all that hold together conceptually?

I think so, yes.

Great. Also in terms of a question creating tension and the answer as release... With a question, we anticipate something's coming. And that's that juicy tension we can exploit.

Questions give us the anticipation of an answer. There's other ways to do that. Not only a question.

A phrase something like "I wanted to talk to you about something." *(Pause)* That line is giving us expectation of what we're going to talk about. That expectation is gold, it's money. We can luxuriate in that expectation. Before I say "I wrecked your car."

"I wanted to talk to you about something." Pause. What? What does he want to say? What does he want to talk about? "I wrecked your car." Oh my god! Event.

See how I might be diagramming that?

Mm'hmm.

If I use expectation as tension and then whatever was expected as release or wasn't expected as surprise, then we're literally causing the scene to have a pulse. Get that expectation heartbeat going. There are so many ways to do that. It's very nuanced.

Like, "My daddy always used to say..." *(pause)*

"You'll never believe what happened." *(pause)*

"In other words..." *(pause)*

"The moral of the story is..." *(pause)*

"I've never seen it fail..." *(pause)*

"You know..." *(pause)*

None of these are questions. But in essence I'm saying "I'm going to tell you something." And then make everybody wait for me to tell it. Expectation and then release or surprise. Does that make sense?

Yes.

Good. So those moments are opportunities. Terrific.

Now it might sound like the scenes are going to go a lot slower because we're adding a bunch of pauses. We have to be smart about that, of course. We can't just add time through all of these pauses. We have to pick and choose. We have to also take time from other places.

I'm glad we understand that opportunity for tension and release, which is fundamentally, a huge building block of drama and the audience's experience.

I know that's a lot of breaking down the scene but it's super important.

As I was watching your scene, I was like "Good job, good job, good job..." Except those moments weren't being taken advantage of. The events in the scene weren't large enough. We need to navigate that tension and release so that the audience is breathless for a second and then "Ahhh." And then "What's going to happen??" and then "Ahh... that happened." We're trying to create that experience for our audience and this is one way we can diagram it.

I see. That makes sense.

Super fun.

The thing that's been rattling for me? I want to build my craft. My skill. Like a really good musician. That's what I've been thinking about.

Good. I'm so glad. Somebody's got to be Stradivarius. Somebody's gotta be Jose' Feliciano. Somebody's got to be the expert.

I'll just comment if you don't mind - at the risk of giving you advice, which is not really my job here but... - You're good! You don't have to be the best musician to get a pop hit. You don't have to be the best musician to somehow break through with a song. Or get cast in a quirky show that takes off. You don't have to be the best musician or the most highly skilled. That will serve you in the long run but there's also the short run. You're talented enough and castable enough that you should be going out there against all the other guys and something will pop that is uniquely you.

And it won't only happen because you rehearsed it and did it in class, it will be because you're good at this. "That? I can do that!" And then you do it and they say "I like him." and it catches someone's attention and you're cast or not and then it gets canceled, whatever. Then it's on your resume and you try it again. But I don't think you have to be a virtuoso.

I applaud, my friend... I have so much understanding - I think I have understanding, certainly admiration - for you and your approach.

If you'll allow me, I think there might be a bit too much humility. That you want to get so good, almost craft for the sake of craft. But we want to be rewarded for our craft. We want to be good enough that people will pay us for our craft.

So it isn't only, "I'm going to be a woodcarver forever because I love carving wood." At some point I have to go "Hey. Wanna buy this?" *(Laugh)* "Really? Only two hundred bucks? He's giving me three hundred bucks." Now we have something going. But of course you can carve wood forever just because you love it if that's what you want to do. If you just want to get really good at it. But the other side is "What if I made a living doing this?" And that's the path that you're envisioning.

Yes.

So you're not carving wood just to carve wood. You're carving wood because you want to become good enough that people will pay for what you carve. And then ultimately, that people will pay consistently for it and perhaps at a high rate.

I see so many ways you could spark. You could spark in so many different directions. But you can't spark if you don't flint, okay?

Yes. That's very motivating.

Good, good. I adore, with a capital A, adore the fact that you want to focus on craft and I don't want you to stop. But let's not lay every egg, let's see if this one hatches. We don't have to lay a hundred eggs, this one might hatch.

Often when I'm working with actors I'm like "Hey. Slow down a little bit. Casting directors are tricky and you've got to be careful..." Often I'm slowing actors down. I don't want to slow you down.

They won't cast you the first time. They won't cast you the fourth time. That's okay. They'll keep seeing you. That's the key. Or maybe they'll cast you the fourth time. But they can't see you the fourth time until they've seen you the first time.

Right.

I know how much you care about this and how much you demand of yourself. I think that's all great. I want all the benefits of that. But the drawback might be that you're not relaxed enough to take in and welcome the environment and opportunities around you. Be reciprocal. Outside of that, "I'm a really good, strong actor." Maintain flow outside of that.

I see. I'm going to take that with me.

Working hard isn't the only thing. We can have fun, too. And we can be rewarded for our hard work, also.

Yes. Yes.

Good, my friend. And thank you for giving me this space to give you some unasked for advice.

I'll take all of the advice. (laugh) I'll take it. Anything that comes up. Please.

And I know 99% of our relationship has been in acting class but I've also hung out with you and I'm not really worried about any of this stuff. I just want to make you aware. And thank you, Alejandro. I know sometimes our conversations veer into career and real life and not only scenes and acting. It's a lot to manage but again I think you're on the right path.

And thanks to you. I didn't have much direction before but I'm glad we met.

Me too.

      I got cast in a TV show one time and I was supposed to have an argument with the star of the show then walk out to the end of this pier. Then say a line, get in a rowboat, row out to the middle of the lake and get killed by some kind of underwater monster.

So they're like "Action!" and I argue with the star and walk down to the end of the pier. Scene's going great. I say my line and step into the rowboat... and it completely flips over, tossing me into the water.

I'm wearing a microphone with a pack, full costume and makeup, boots, and a toolbelt. They're like "Cut!" and the whole production was shut down while they dried me off and started over with wardrobe and makeup and everything. I heard someone say "Would someone please show Duane how to get into a rowboat?"

And this was a big production. Cameras up on cranes and cameras on boats.

Anyway, after the crew had all been waiting around for me to get new underwear and a dry toolbelt and everything else,- probably took an hour - we were ready to try it again.

It had been decided that I would say my line from the end of the pier and they would cut. So we could avoid a repeat. We did that.

After I had been assisted into the boat, we were going to film me rowing out to the center of the lake. They call "Action!" and I start rowing. But I had never rowed a boat before. I had no idea how to use oars. The paddles were flying around and splashing but I wasn't getting anywhere. The director yells "Cut!" I heard someone say "Can someone please show Duane how to use oars?"

So they got a couple scuba gear, crew people in the water. And I'm in the boat and these scuba divers pulled my boat along. And they decided to zoom the camera in close so you couldn't see my arms. It was just my shoulders moving up and down. They even had to put in the sound of rowing later.

I'm thinking "I'm never going to work again."

So I'm having the worst day of my career and the only thing left to shoot is my death scene. The monster takes the other end of an oar, we struggle a bit and I get pulled into the lake and drown and get eaten.

"I am going to make this the best damn death scene in the history of television. Years from now, people will still marvel at this drowning/getting eaten scene!"

So they go "Action!" and the monster grabs my oar and we struggle a bit and I dive over the side of the rowboat and into the water.

I begin getting eaten. I'm screaming and gasping for air and going under and the water is splashing around so I couldn't hear if they said "Cut." So I keep drowning and I'm getting pretty tired and my clothes were getting heavy and I was even wearing boots but I was determined to stay in character.

Eventually, I figured they must have said "Cut" by now and I was exhausted so I started treading water and I look... And the boat with the camera on it is waaaay over there. They followed my hat floating across the lake, moved along by the waves I was creating. The camera wasn't even on me.

So look, I could've gone to oar school first, or... get on set, screw it up, keep going. *Okay. (laugh) Yeah.*

By the way, I have a couple of friends who work at that studio and they tell me they enjoy watching the tape of me falling into the lake. They watch it when they're having a tough day.

DAVID / ELISSA Scene

ELISSA
How did you hear about this place?

DAVID
There was a review on Yelp. 4 stars.

ELISSA (wryly)
So of course we have to try it.

DAVID
Aren't you hungry?

ELISSA
Of course I'm hungry. We've been at the beach since noon. There wasn't anything to eat at the beach.

DAVID
Good point.

ELISSA
You can't eat the sun.

DAVID
Nope.

ELISSA
You can't eat sand, unless you have that weird disorder like that Brazilian lady.

DAVID
Right again.

ELISSA
You can't eat the young ladies in their two-piece bathing suits... Much as you might like to.

DAVID
I'm sorry. To whom are you referring?

ELISSA
Those jiggly coeds to our left.

DAVID
What jiggly coeds?

ELISSA
We were about to leave. You said "Well, I guess it's time to..." and you stopped mid-sentence.

DAVID
I don't remember...

ELISSA
And I looked where you were looking and saw three gorgeous girls arriving on our section of the beach. And you stretched, flexed, sucked in your gut... and never even finished what you were saying.

DAVID
I am not sure this ever happened.

ELISSA
And then we sat there another two hours until the girls left.

DAVID
Uh-huh.

ELISSA
Even though I had just - before they arrived - said that I was hungry. You don't remember?

DAVID
Okay. I get it. You would have preferred I not pay attention to those women. Got it. What're you having? The scampi looks good.

ELISSA
David?

DAVID
I remember you love scampi.

ELISSA
David?

DAVID
Or the filet mignon. I remember we had filet mignon at our wedding, remember? I remember that.

ELISSA
David?

DAVID
Yes?

ELISSA
I'm leaving for a while.

When we talk about juxtaposition of ideas, what that means is I say this line but this thought, which is away from my line, is also present.
So, anybody, give me a short line of dialogue to say. Just make it up.
"Where am I going to put my laundry?"
So the line is about where I'm going to put my laundry. I want to focus on the "Juxtaposed idea." So the line is "Where am I going to put my laundry?" The juxtaposed idea could be "My house is an absolute mess." I'm seeing dishes on every counter, there's no place to put my laundry. Even though my line is "Where am I going to put my laundry?" the juxtaposed idea is "My house is filthy."
So this is a different way of seeing video?
I'm taking this opportunity in this class to take the concept and put it under a microscope and look at it. See how these juxtaposed ideas are constructed. Delving into the sort of mathematics of drama.
This is the way we are going to measure the distance between two points. Laundry and a messy house. I might take that juxtaposed idea a bit further, be more impolite in my thinking. So when I see my messy house I think "I'm disgusting." as I say my laundry line.
So my juxtaposed idea is "I'm disgusting." while I say "Where am I going to put my laundry?" So for this exercise, it's as if my lips are saying "I'm disgusting." While I'm actually speaking "Where am I going to put my laundry?"
I have clean laundry. There's nowhere to put my things. And I'm thinking to myself the juxtaposed line, "I'm disgusting," while I say "Where am I going to put my laundry?" As if my lips were forming the words "I'm disgusting."
Okay.
So I might say, "Where am I going to put my laundry?" like this: *(demonstrates a line reading)* That's a logical reading. How would I say "I'm disgusting"? I might say it like this. *(demonstrates a line reading)* Now say "Where am I going to put my laundry" as if I'm saying "I'm disgusting." It might go like this. *(demonstrates)*
I'm taking the opportunity in this class to put this under a microscope. I went so far as to say "Where am I going to put my laundry?" in the same way I would say "I'm disgusting."

The line is about laundry but the moment becomes something more, something complex.

How is that different from video? I walk in and see a messy house…

First, the juxtaposed idea I choose will change my video. I took my juxtaposed idea to an impolite place. Not, "What a nice day. Where am I going to put my laundry?" But instead, I see a pigsty of a place and I'm disgusting.

Keep in mind the inner, private video of "I'm disgusting," probably includes years of being sloppy and maybe failed relationships and loneliness because of it. That's impolite thinking. And that video is your personal video, your memories. Not the external video, your environment.

We can see now, it's the relationship between the line and what I'm thinking.

Right.

I could be saying "Where am I going to put my laundry?" with the juxtaposed idea "Today I'm going to go play racquetball," but that juxtaposed idea doesn't seem as interesting.

Right.

I could be saying "Where am I going to put my laundry," and be thinking "I'm hungry." But that juxtaposition of ideas doesn't do anything for me, either. But with the juxtaposed idea "I'm disgusting." Suddenly there's a spark between those two ideas. Something is happening.

Yeah.

Now, we've been breaking down the concept of juxtaposition of ideas. Now I'd like to go to the Dylan and Paul scene and go line by line through it and consider the juxtaposed idea. I say this line but what can my juxtaposed idea be? We can talk it through as we go. I want you to get specific and I want you to write down your juxtaposed line of dialogue. Just like we did with the laundry line.

Then as we go through the scene, as you say the lines, I want you to use the juxtaposed idea of this new script you're writing. I'll invite you to take it as far as I did with saying the laundry line, with the reading of "I'm disgusting." It wasn't really subtle at all.

No.

That juxtaposed idea makes the audience go "What's happening? Something is happening." Who cares about laundry? It's never about laundry. It's about the juxtaposed idea. And now, laundry becomes relevant because of that juxtaposed idea. The one that we choose that sparks.

Certain juxtaposed ideas have electricity and lightning that flies between them. Sometimes it's because they're further away and sometimes they're too far away and that doesn't work so we've got to move closer because that doesn't spark. We've got to find that place where the spark happens and we go "Ooooh. This juxtaposed idea with that line of dialogue gives off sparks."

Sure.

A lot of the techniques we talk about are included here like "Don't do it good. Do it wrong, Eff it up, Impolite story," they're all tied up in this idea. Because it's a way to not do what I'm saying but make that thing I'm saying come alive.

In any good acting moment, that's happening. You're already doing that. I've seen you all do it at various points. Saying a line but having a contrasted thought.

That's very helpful.

When you first gave me the laundry line, I thought "I'm not sure how to work with that" but as we investigated I became excited about the line. Now it feels juicy. I want to investigate this moment. I want to find out about this person.

Again, it looks like it's about laundry. It's not. It's about the juxtaposed idea.

Sometimes I'll put it like this. Do 51% of this *(indicating idea)* and 49% of this. *(indicating speaking)* More of this *(idea)* than this *(speech)* And in this exercise I might go to 99% to 1%. The juxtaposed idea is how I say the line.

Take a moment and look at your first couple of lines and we'll come back and discuss. We'll discuss what that juxtaposed idea might be and what might be a powerful choice or a less powerful choice. Okay?

Yeah.

Great. Do you feel like a scientist? I feel like a scientist. *(laugh)* Take a minute.

Alejandro, I think you have the first line, right?

Yes.

What is it?

Mrs. Dillon.

With a question mark, yes?

Yes.

Let's just theorize a juxtaposed idea.

I was a little stuck on that…

Let me give you an option. How about the juxtaposed idea of "Here we go?"

Okay.

How would you say the line "Here we go?"

"Here we go."

Now instead say, Mrs. Dillon.

Mrs. Dillon. (laugh) Ah. Okay.

Interesting, right?

Yes.

Now let's try the juxtaposed idea of "Is anybody here?" You're entering a building. How would you say that line?

Is anybody here?

Now, instead, say Mrs. Dillon.

Mrs Dillon? (laugh)

Ooooh. Wasn't it risky and fun?

(laugh) Yeah.

I didn't know what we were going to get with those two readings but both of them intrigue me. I'm intrigued and excited at a line that never intrigued me before. You said "Mrs Dillon" but something else tangible was happening and that made "Mrs. Dillon" electric. It sparked with the juxtaposed idea.

I see.

Let's go to Polly's first line. What's your first line Polly?

"Yes."

Great. What do you think the juxtaposed idea could be?

I was thinking "We're closed."

Okay, how would you say "We're closed."?

"We're closed."

Good, now use that reading and instead say "Yes?"

"Yes?"

Good. Now remember, it's not the answer of that. It's the opportunity of that. Now try the juxtaposed idea "Is that you, Steve?" Let's assume Steve is a coworker. How would you say that line?

"Is that you Steve?"

Now say "yes" instead.

"Yes?" Okay. I see.

Alejandro, your next line.

"I have the 2:15 appointment."

What could be the juxtaposed idea here?

Ummm.

How about "You're younger than I thought you'd be." Try that line.

"You're younger than I thought you'd be."

Good. Now say "I have the 2:15 appointment."

"I have the 2:15 appointment." (laugh) Interesting.

These are not all necessarily home runs. But I hope we're discovering how to play the game. When I say "Don't do it good," the juxtaposed idea is how I don't do it good. That's where the game is played. The words can be said by anybody but the game that we're playing is what makes the words powerful. Outside of the language, that's where the game is played. What the actor does to make the words powerful. Anybody can say them. It's what you do to make the words their most powerful and the experience it's most powerful. That goes directly to juxtaposition of ideas.

How is this diagramming sitting with you, Polly?

I think it really helps. It helps me to diagram it.

Good. Now, when we ask "How do I make the line more powerful?" it's not just a roll of the dice and we hope to get lucky. No, there is strategy to this. So when we examine dramatic diagramming, we're starting to take advantage of the opportunities of the material. Often, we'll figure out the juxtaposed idea and shoot the video that gets us there. Maybe later in the scene when you say "I don't think we have anything for you," the juxtaposed idea is "Where's Hank, the security guy?"

Yeah. I was thinking during that line, I might think "You're wasting my time."

That works well. This diagramming isn't always for the most opposing idea. The most opposing idea for "I don't think we have anything for you" might be "I'm secretly in love with you so I hope you work here." That doesn't work. For this process we might start out with the most opposing idea and then work our way back towards the line. The first one to spark is the one I'll use. As I work my way back, the first one to give me goosebumps.

Okay, yeah.

On the line "I'm a Mom." I might think "My son has that same jacket."

Right.

Again, this is opening us up from the very limiting approach of what makes sense, to what's out there that doesn't make sense, that we can bring into the line until it does make sense. We're playing the game of the line instead of answering the line.

You just clarified the difference between a video and the juxtaposed idea.

I'll reshoot my video to support my juxtaposed idea. If I decide "I'm disgusting" is the right idea, I'll shoot the video that I haven't showered in a month to support it. In this inquiry we can say "Yes, video," but then the question becomes "Which video?"

Right. We're looking at the spark now.

We can shoot a video about laundry and it can be nice and even believable but no one cares about laundry. They care about emotional stress and self worth. They care about how hard it is to be a person.

This is where I need help, I think. More than anywhere else, so this is good.

Thanks, Polly. Working with you this evening is one of the things that inspired this exercise. And Alejandro, also because we talked about juxtaposition of ideas recently.

Yeah. This is great. This is really great.

The line isn't interesting. Something in contrast to - and in juxtaposition with - the line makes it interesting.

Okay. This is very helpful.

These aren't answers of course. We're not finished but we are juxtaposing these ideas well. And you'll see that it's keeping us away from the good line reading. You see what we're avoiding here? The good reading. The one that makes perfect sense. Here, we're embracing not making sense.

Great. Let's continue with this exercise. Polly, what's your next line?

"How did you get in here?"

What's your juxtaposed idea? *(pause)* What were you just thinking when you said it that time?

"Someone should have stopped you."

Great! Now the video is interesting. "Where the hell is Frank, the security guy?" We haven't even met him and probably won't, but I'm interested. The video is "Why isn't Frank at his post?" The truth is always interesting. Now that line sizzles. You see how we're working this out?

Yep.

Good. Alejandro, what's your next line?

"There was no one out front." The way I put it to myself was "I know it's lunchtime."

I think that works. I got scared and suspicious of you when I saw you have that thought. I liked seeing that evil thought escape you on that line, "There was no one out front." That says to me that you are here with her alone on purpose. Scary.

Using the juxtaposition of ideas, there are so many ways to say the line.

Yes. Good. What's the next line?

"Ahh, it's lunchtime." my thought is "that's why no one is out there."

Fun. I'm getting the feeling Polly, that you work with a bunch of under-achievers. You're the only one here, eating lunch at your desk. You have to hold down the fort. Everybody else is out having Taco Bell. *(laugh)*

Here I am at my desk again.

Yes! Once we have this type of video and look to see what blossoms, each of these moments become interesting. Each moment in these people's lives are interesting when we investigate it in this way.

Now that moment, "it's lunchtime," becomes about you being the only one who's keeping this business alive.

Again.

Good, good, good. Alejandro, your line?

"Yeah. Sorry about that, I'm having an unusual day. I'm usually quite responsible. It's just that today, my daughter…"

Okay, there will be several juxtaposed images. Probably three or even five or more. But somewhere in there when you talk about your daughter the thought could be "Here comes the lie." Remember, we decided you don't have a daughter?

Yeah.

So the thought could be "Do what I rehearsed." as you make your excuse about being a dad. Your thinking could be "She's a Mom. She'll be sympathetic." So these thoughts could be whirling in your head throughout that moment. Sound fun?

Yes.

I'm getting, through this inquiry, that your character doesn't want to see her in a crowded office with a room full of people. You manipulated the situation. Maybe you've been stalking her, casing the office.

In the line "I'm having an unusual day," I've seen you juxtapose the thought that felt like "You have no idea how unusual this day is about to get." I loved that approach on that moment.

I don't want to give you a line reading at all. I've seen this moment played by you very successfully, already. I don't want to change what you're doing in this moment but put a spotlight on it and put it under a microscope.

Okay. That makes a lot of sense. This is all coming together.

What I'm hoping this exercise does is help you become more playful. Look further outside of whatever box that line is in. Understand and get excited about dis-logic. Find that goosebump reading. Almost every line has one. And if you don't get goosebumps, keep looking. Because the actor who got the part, they're the one who got the most goosebumps. The actor who gets cast, wins the award, gets the applause, that's the actor who gave us the most goosebumps. And in this inquiry, we're examining where are the goosebumps and how do I get there?

Now we're not stuck thinking logically, "good acting, how do I sound, how do I look?" We're thinking "my apartment is a pigsty," or "she's a mom, she'll understand."

You're going to find that you're already doing this sometimes, instinctively. And you're going to find sometimes that you need to employ it where you aren't.

I'm really glad we got into this. I like it.

I'm glad. What a pleasure.

Fun.

Okay. Let's put this away. My brain hurts.

Imagine how ours feel. (laugh)

Take five minutes and then we'll move on to monologues.

Good, Alejandro, what do you think?

I have no idea. (laugh) I've been trying it a few different ways this last week or so. This time I didn't push as much. I don't know how it actually came off.

In the last ten days or so, this is about the third time I've seen this monologue and I think they were all three effective. You said you're trying it different ways. What do you mean by that?

I mean, each time I'm doing it lately, something different will come up.

Yes. That's exactly where I think you should be. And if it's a film and I'm the editor of this piece, I have three takes of this and they're all different and they're all good. I might take this section from take one and this section from take three and I would have what I need to piece together a great performance.

Okay.

That's part of the beauty of this. You're still exploring. You haven't settled on answers. From my perspective, they were three somewhat similar takes. Your blocking was the same, it didn't look wildly different at all. They were all good takes. From your perspective, they were all different, but from the stage manager's perspective, from the camera person's perspective, the director's perspective, you're just giving consistently good performances. Those nuances as to how they're different, that's your business. You're just swimming in the waters and the tides are rough and you're fighting for your character. To hell with the line readings and answers. You're just feeling and expressing how you feel. Not how you should feel or what you planned on feeling but how you feel.

Good, Polly. How's it going?

Okay.

Pretty good. I like a lot of what you're doing. Of course, you don't have it memorized yet. The one thing I want you to do is to fight harder throughout in between the lines. If that's a two minute monologue, I feel like a minute-fifteen was purposeful and then some of it was taking breaks in-between. I'd like you to fight harder through those breaks. Don't let ourselves say a line, take a break, say a line, take a break. Stay in character, fight through the whole two minutes and that's even when we have to look at our lines.

I intentionally put pauses in there so maybe I'm not quite understanding…

The pauses aren't really the problem. The problem is making sure those pauses are filled and not empty pauses. Of course, I can't read your mind but the appearance right now is that there is intention when you're speaking and not as much intention when you're not speaking.

Okay. So how do I fix that?

Think the character's thoughts even between lines.

Okay. I see, I do that. I go blank in-between. Waiting. That's what I'm doing.

We have to fight through the whole two minutes. Even though we're not talking, we're still moving forward. Just because you've stopped talking doesn't mean you've stopped living. Move forward even when you're not talking.

Yeah.

When I had you do the exercise "say the line but say it like this," I could see that your belly catches on fire. Because it doesn't make sense. It's not comfortable. That little burn in the belly, that's what we're after. Not comfortable. Comfortable is easy and sleepy. Don't let me be comfortable. You give me comfortable and I'm going to doze off. Now you're finding ways to keep us uncomfortable. Thank you. Good class.

Talia, anything rattling?

Not particularly. I just want to have fun and try different things. Going to try to stay out of Actor Brain, being too much in Actor Brain.

Good. Good goals. I like the way you're thinking. If I may, I'll try to address that a bit. Staying out of Actor Brain sounds kind of difficult unless we can figure out what we're going to try to stay in. Let's go ahead and try to articulate the other half of that equation.

What I'm going to try to stay fully in, is Character Brain. Living as fully as possible there. Right?

Yeah.

And just to articulate again what that is, it's the thoughts that are running through all of our heads. The things we remember and hope and wish and dream. Our fears and regrets. That's really what Character Brain is. I sometimes will use the phrase "Swimming in our character's waters." To get under the surface of the water and really explore what's going on down there. Good. I think you're putting the pieces together very nicely, Talia. I think you are connecting the pieces of the puzzle very nicely into a picture that makes sense, I hope. Very good, well done.

Thank you.

Joe, anything rattling for you?

Yeah. I feel like it's the layers of the onion peeling back. So I'm extra engaged and excited because I'm seeing more aspects of creating and then implementing video. Not that I haven't been using video so far but not to the level that I see I can get to. It's fun to explore that so I'm excited.

I'm excited too, Joe. I'm glad that you're taking what I think is another quantum leap. I can't wait to see us apply exactly what you're talking about.

Sara, nice to see you. Anything rattling?

I want to figure out what the best way to act through Zoom is. You have to figure out where you're looking and you're sitting down, I'm used to being on my feet with another actor. So I guess that's my question today, how do I make a believable character across the screen?

Let me try to address that: you can't. The rules on Zoom are very different from what we're used to, face-to-face acting. Ultimately you may find that you're very often auditioning this way, sometimes rehearsing this way, and then when you get to the shoot you may be face-to-face. So there's no way to cover all of our bases.

Technically, your eyeline in this medium would be the same as your eye line in any other on camera situation. That would be that my eye line is slightly above the camera and off to one side. That's fundamental eyeline for on camera. That way the audience has access to my eyes. If you wanted to, you could hang a picture of someone you care about and place it in that position. That way you have someone's eyes to look into. Slightly above the camera and off to either side.

But sometimes you might get to a film shoot and you're shooting a scene with Paul Rudd but Paul Rudd's not there. He's doing a promo somewhere else. There is a stand-in there. Or there's a script supervisor reading the role and you have to fake that Paul Rudd is there anyway.

Film is a surprisingly artificial environment. On the stage we try to make it feel real. On camera, kind of not. Most of your background is stage, is that right?

No. My background is acting classes. (laugh)

Cool. Something a lot of people don't understand that is kind of fun for me to go into: The artificiality of the environment on set.

Let's say you have a scene with Paul Rudd and the two of you are having lunch at a restaurant. Sitting across the table from each other. There are two ways they're going to shoot that. Behind Paul Rudd looking at you is one way and behind you looking at Paul Rudd is the other way.

Let's imagine that it is your take and that all of the crew and everything is behind Paul Rudd. You're the star of the scene. This is your take.

Behind you it looks like a restaurant. The background performers are silently eating and pretending to have a conversation. Once in a while someone will be told to cross behind you. So the camera and Paul Rudd, everything they see is very realistic. It looks like a lunch room. It's very easy to pretend. But it's your take. What are you seeing?

Sure, Paul Rudd is there. But just over his shoulder is a huge camera. And there's a camera operator. Right next to the camera operator there is probably a crew person with tape hanging off of their belt. And a microphone hanging just over your head. There are a bunch of bright lights aimed at your face. There's a table over there with a bunch of coffee cups on it. Your makeup person is standing to the side. The crew and all the people and the stuff around you. And it's your take! It's not Paul Rudd's take. Paul Rudd is looking at something very realistic. You're not. You're looking at the most artificial environment.

That makes sense.

And here's another thing. Your takes are in the morning and Paul Rudd's are in the afternoon. And then the editor puts it together so it looks like the same conversation. It was a revelation to me when I would watch TV and realize that there's no such thing as an invisible camera. When we're looking at you, there's a camera behind him. So if I talk then you talk then I talk then you talk, that's actually morning, afternoon, morning, afternoon. It's not even the same take. It's never the same take of the two of you actually interacting together. There's not an invisible camera behind one of you.

That's really interesting.

I think it's good for us to recognize that sometimes you're going to just have to fake it. That's what we're doing. We have to get good at faking It. Having it feel real is cool where it works. But it's probably not going to feel real when we do it anyway. There's always a camera in your face and a microphone just out of the shot. Lights and marks and a little piece of spike tape on the table in front of you. There's all those artificial elements we have to deal with anyway and I think that being on Zoom is just another one.

I'm glad to get a chance to articulate this dichotomy. It's your take but what you are seeing is not the least bit realistic. So this is really good practice for us.

I think so too.

On set I've got to pretend it's all real and the set is real. I have to do that here also. I'm glad we had this conversation.

Me too.

I invite you to read scripts. There are places online where you can get scripts. You can go and find the script for a movie you like. See what it looks like when it's in script form.

Maybe you're watching a movie or a TV show that you enjoy. A good moment happens. Pause that for a second and think about the script. What was written on the page? Maybe it's some great moment like "Not without my daughter." What is written on the page is four words. But what did the actor do with that? I like to look at the difference between the typing on the page and what the moment becomes. Understand the relationship between what happens here *(words on the page)* and there *(the movie screen)*.

Because when I'm cast in something, I'm going to be given my script. I need examples of powerful diagrams from here to there and see what the journey is. It's not in the script. It doesn't say "said with anguish and regret but maybe there's some hope and determination." It doesn't say that in parenthesis. That's what the actor brought to it. So how can I similarly take what's written here and create that moment?

Okay. I'm definitely excited by that.

Ann, how's it going?

It's a fun piece to do. I have to admit I coasted on "instant logic" for the most part.

Oh! Okay. I think it worked. I can understand that because your character is referencing all kinds of things that there's no way you could understand. You don't know what any of these things are.

Not a clue.

How could you? Ann, I'm glad you brought that one back. "Instant logic" is an approach I haven't talked about in a long time. "Instant logic" means you don't have to justify it later. In fact, it doesn't have to be justifiable. I have no idea what this means but I'll commit fully to the moment anyway. I'll just make it make sense for me right now. Make it true for me right now, regardless of if I could prove it. I don't have to prove it.

Do you have any notes for yourself?

Well, for a lot of the scene, what was driving me was just "stay with it, stay with it." I liked the character and had a lot of fun but I had to coast for the most part because I have no idea what some of these references are.

From my perspective Ann, I feel what you described there in "keep going," was you got up on your surfboard and you rode the wave. That seemed fine to me. I was glad to see you surfing along, seeing where the wave takes you. You didn't try to say "Hey wave, stop." You got on your board and let the ocean be in control. That's something that I applaud.

As you know, I'm often in favor of slowing down, confronting more video. But here, I like that it's moving along, the pace is rather pithy. That is the style of the scene. If you had another day or two before you shot this scene, this pace wouldn't feel as fast as it does right now. It feels fast because it's new but after you've done it a few times, it won't feel as fast.

I was trying to be the one with the head on their shoulders.
That's a great instinct. You can see in this scene that your Mom is a bit wacky. You can be the opposite of that. If she's gonna be that - I can see very clearly what she is - I'm going to try to be as opposite that as possible. I'll be completely together. That's going to create a dynamic two-person relationship. I call this "Odd Couple" diagramming. If one person is very neat, I'll be a slob. If one person is generous, I'll be greedy. This is creating strong dynamics. If you're kind, I'll be mean. Or even if that is not the dynamic, I'm still looking for the difference. Maybe we're both generous. Then if she's generous in this way, I'll be generous in that way. We're still highlighting the differences between characters. That's just good storytelling. When the audience knows the differences between the two of you, each of you carve a bolder path for your individual stories.

Let's talk about persona. Persona is assumptions people might make about you based on your type or look. I'll speak for myself and my persona. My persona can be that I am an authority figure. For some reason I get cast in a lot of authority figure roles. I walk in and they go "here's a conservative looking guy that might be the boss of a company or a bank manager." They see me as mature and reserved. I get cast in those roles pretty often. So that's what people see me as.

That's great when that aligns with the role I'm trying to get. If I'm up for the bank manager, I'll bring that natural persona. But if I'm up for the wacky neighbor, I may have to overcome my persona. Sometimes my persona is something that will serve me and sometimes it's something that I have to overcome. My persona can help me but it can also hinder me, depending on the role I'm up for.

Alejandro, I wanted to commend you on your articulation. In this scene you have the phrase "Four Seas Hotel." It would be very easy for the audience to hear something like "Forsee's Hotel." But you recognized that that was an "Aunt Enid" moment and you gave the phrase extra articulation. I like that the "Aunt Enid" approach is part of your instincts now. Good work.
Okay, thanks.

Joe, how was the scene for you this time through?

I liked it.

Wasn't that fun?

Yeah, I have to get away from that old sales habit.

Oh yeah. So fun. Now things might happen. I will sometimes say "If it feels good, don't do it." A lot of your tendency is toward what feels good. Don't do what feels good. For you to deny that creates a dynamic, an energy in your belly. That's more interesting than that thing you figured out.

I didn't see it the first time but now I can. Thank you.

Absolutely. And let's make sure that that is where your default setting lies. "If it feels good, don't do it."

Sarah, how's it going from your perspective?

Good. There were a few lines… I couldn't figure out why I say this. I'm like, this is an odd sentence. And then what you were saying about logic, like don't worry about it.

Is there a particular line I can help you figure out?

I don't know why she would say "I don't feel like snails tonight Grampa, maybe another night I would want snails, I can't imagine that." There's that change there, but why?

(laugh)

Gotcha. I can conjecture some reasons she might think that way. I bet you can too. Overall though, I'd just like to go back to the idea that comedy is a spin on logic. It's not logic. It's your logic as opposed to everyone else's logic. That's what makes something funny. That your logic is different from the audiences, not the same. We want to find those spins on logic, embrace what is dis-logical.

I like to use The Office as an example because most people know it. Dwight's spin on logic, Michael's spin on logic. I would never logic it that way. But their spin on logic is different. How it's different, is what we want to highlight.

Sarah, you have good rhythms. That is serving you well. But I want you to take more time to confront your language, confront what you're talking about and force us to confront it too. I think that "monkey brains" section is hilarious and it's over too quickly. Keep in mind that awkward is money in the bank. So we're not going to go past awkward, we're going to wallow in the muddy, juicy, awkward waters. Because that's where the tension and interest and "what's going to happen next?" and laughs happen. Tension is part of all of that. If you move along too fast, you're not really raising the tension.

I hear you. That makes sense.

Let us in the audience think about it. Let us ponder the things you're talking about. I think it's a great and generous instinct for you to want to gallop along like that but here I want to fight against it. If you take more time for the moment, it will force you to confront it more and give us a chance to confront it more also. And keep in mind that, awkward is dramatic currency.

That's a good note.

I love that momentum is part of your rhythm. I don't want you to stop that. But if you give us a moment we'll reflect on that awesome thing you said.

We are getting close to the end of class. Before we wrap it up, Sarah, is there anything you hope happens? *(laugh)*

Most of what I hoped would happen has already happened so that's good. (laugh) I guess I want to get back into auditions but I'm holding myself back. I feel the pressure to present my perfect version.

Here is just a simple observation. The best actors are the best people. *(pause)* I don't know what acting is. Well, I guess I must know what acting is since that's my job. *(laugh)* But what is acting doing but revealing humanity? Showing the struggle inside all of us. Being vulnerable, not covering up.

Right.

Every human being is powerful in their way. And it's about being okay with how I'm powerful rather than wishing I was powerful in this way or that way. Because everyone is powerful. Everyone's got the capacity for all the emotions, all the possibilities. We all have that. In a sense it's more about stripping away than it is trying to acquire.

Right. I'll have to remind myself of that. But it's hard because of what society says. It all seems unattainable. But I'll just have to do it right? You miss 100% of the shots you don't take, isn't that what they say?

I know there may be pressure to try to fulfill the typical Hollywood beauty standard. But more than it's ever been before, it's about real people. The industry got called out on the double standard and things have changed and changed quickly. The studios all feel more of a responsibility to represent - especially women - more fairly. And they're being held accountable. To be more inclusive of people of color. To think outside of that white, male box.

And the old-time beauty standards of Marilyn Monroe and Elizabeth Taylor, the flip side of that coin is happening now. Real people, real representation and more diversity. So the energies are trending in a direction that would be more inclusive than ever before in this industry. And probably going to continue to expand in that way. So I hope you won't be looking at the limitations by that paradigm but the opportunities of that paradigm.

Here's another thing I will say in response to the question "What are they looking for?" Here's the answer: "They're looking for you on a good day." They might think they're looking for this or that or this or that. They're looking for you. Okay?

Okay. That's good advice.

What I want to highlight is my uniqueness, not my similarities. What's different about me is more interesting than what's the same about me.

"Three people we talk to:" The person I'm talking to, God or the universe, and myself. The third of those is the most intimate. This also gives us a variety in our verbal and vocal intention.

Talia, what's rattling for you today?
I just want to challenge myself today. Not let myself be stereotypical in my characters. Find a different path.
Don't let it be too easy. Don't let yourself off the hook and don't let the audience off the hook. So we want to be complex. Keep myself uncomfortable and keep the audience uncomfortable too. After all, what happens with a comfortable audience? They fall asleep.
There's another phrase I like to say: "Powerfully off-balance." I want to be powerful, of course. But I also want to be off-balance. How can I be off-balance? Don't do the thing that makes sense. Don't do the thing that I have figured out. Stay in a state of surprise, a little bit off-balance. To be surprised by what happens in the moment, not try to control what happens in the moment.
That's a cool way to say that. Thank you.
Sure.

Debra, what do you think?
It's going well.
What tools were you using?
I was using video.
Yes, you were. What notes do you have for yourself?
I don't know.
That's fine. I'm so glad to see that the video is your go-to. It's a huge difference, isn't it?
Yes.
That's great. For a piece that you didn't have much time with, I thought you had pretty good video. I don't know how much time you had with it, but you were able to look away from the page for extended phrasing. I would like to suggest that the video is a great memorization aid. Is that correct from your experience?
Yeah.
Great, Debra,. I think you have totally turned a corner over these last few months. Your fundamental technique has become something you can really count on.

I'm not sure I know how to give this note. It's not a note exactly so much as an observation. Do you remember the writer O. Henry?
Yes.

The ending is always a twist or surprise. The ending is the opposite of what was expected. O. Henry gives us a very good example of one way to think about story structure. This is like an O. Henry story to me. You see what I mean?
Yeah.
It's a lot like the technique in this class 1, 2, pineapple. O. Henry is a 1, 2, pineapple writer, right? Create the expectation of this and then pay off with the opposite.
Yeah. I didn't do that.
Well, now we've identified it.
Got it.

Alejandro, how's it going?
One of the best takes yet. There was hardly any Actor Brain.
Yeah.
And that felt good. Not to think.
Good. As you know, we're looking for 90,10, right? 90% Character Brain, 10% Actor Brain. And I think you're suggesting that that's about where you were.
Great take. I could use that piece as an example of "Eff the camera." The experience that your character was having was much more important than acting in any movie or audition. Fighting harder for the character than you are for yourself.
I didn't feel there was any time when you were trying to please the audience or do a good job of acting. You were too busy fighting for the character. I think that worked really, really well. Good work.
When you were talking with Debra about tension, that amped me up.
I'm glad that worked so well for you.
Some actors might go "Tension? Oh, I'm going to yell the whole scene." No. You were finding a way to make it tense because it was brewing and bubbling.
Here's a little fine-tuning: As we know, our video precedes our language. Put your video further in front of your language. In other words, know the end of the thought before you begin to articulate the thought. Have the end of the sentence in mind before you start saying the sentence.
If my line is "the other day I went to the market and they were all out of Cheerios," I need to be thinking about Cheerios before I say "the other day." That's what I mean about putting our video further in front of our language. We have to know the point of what we are saying before we start talking. So the point, that's what's driving our language.
So I already know what I'm thinking about.
Right. You know that before you start talking.
I really liked the Cheerios example. (laugh)
That's great.

Talia, how's the scene going for you? Do you have notes for yourself?

Not necessarily. I didn't know which way to go so I decided that I hate this job and don't want to be here.

We want to be careful of emotional values in our characters that might be sending messages to our audience that aren't helpful. Sending the message that we're bored might send the message that the scene is boring. It makes sense that she is bored at work and kind of hates her life but I don't know if that needs to be the case. It's kind of hard to watch someone who is humorless and hopeless or depressed.

Of course that might be the powerful story, that you're at the low point of your life. If that is the fundamental story then we'll tell that powerfully.

But when we find our characters in those types of situations, if we can somehow also bring hope, humor, love, compassion… Despite that it looks like it's just "I'm bored out of my mind at work," right? Sometimes that will be the powerful story but if we can somehow also bring in attributes that the audience will find pleasing… I realize I'm contradicting myself from earlier in class. *(laugh)* Characteristics like humor and charm, even if it isn't on the page.

Sometimes the powerful story is that my character is terribly depressed. But if that isn't the powerful story, I want to find a way to avoid that trap. We want to find a way to bring in humor and charm if at all possible.

So when I do this scene again, maybe I can play that she does hate it there but she's trying to make the best of it?

Excellent idea. That would be very helpful.

There are certain emotional values that I sometimes call a "wet blanket." Nothing grows under a wet blanket. So a wet blanket can be things like depressed or angry or out of it or bored. Nothing really grows. If we take the wet blanket away things might begin to sprout.

Awesome. Yeah.

So making the best of it? Yes. I would enjoy hanging out with that woman you're describing more than I did the woman in the first take of the scene. I would like her more.

Yeah.

And to some degree at least, part of entertaining the audience is making them want to hang out with you. That's just fundamental. I will often say this: "Humor is always welcome, even in drama."

Okay.

I know that you're working today with some dental issues. You're in a bit of pain.

No excuses.

Well, I thought you had a really good take. This is just a random observation. I remember a few times having the best performance of an entire run, the day I was sick or nauseous. Or the day I was exhausted. Or back in the day, the day I was hungover. *(laugh)* And sometimes that headache or whatever can help us because we don't try to do it good. We're merely trying to survive.

The specificity of the language equals the specificity of the video.
Can you explain that more?
I'll try. *(laugh)* A line might have five details in it. There's a video for each of the details. Even word choices. The reason I chose that word is because of the specificity of my video. It's a win-win because not only do I have more video - which gives me truth - I'm also much further along in the memorization process because of the video. Does that feel actionable?
Yeah.

May I stop you? I'd like to try it again from the top.
Talia, this time it looks as if you have made a decision for her that she is upbeat and optimistic. But I feel like you're stuck in that decision. You've had two very different readings of the scene. Let's try it again with you ping-ponging back and forth between the two readings. Okay?
Yeah.
Have fun. From the beginning please.

Talia, I enjoyed watching you ping-pong. And what I hope you discovered was a freedom for whatever, instead of the decision you made about her, limiting your choices. The freedom to do anything even if it wasn't quite logical. You weren't ruled by logic. You had a wider emotional range. I hope it felt better for you.
It did. And it's so funny because earlier, right when I was thinking I felt so restricted, you stopped the scene. So it was perfect.
I'm glad. And in the second take, it was fun to watch you playing the game and that gave more power to the scene and to your work.

Alejandro, you got some good news recently. Could you share it with everyone?
Yeah, I got cast in a short film.
Gianna, you helped him prepare last week.
Oh that's so exciting!
It is exciting. That rocks. And you've just entered the competitive market right? Wasn't that your first audition?
Umm. Yeah. (laughter and applause)
Have you seen the full script yet?
Not yet.

Congratulations. You're one for one. I advise you to quit now. *(laugh)* No, that's awesome. This is your first gig and it's the leading role. You've been working hard, you deserve it. As always, anything I can do to be helpful, just let me know.
Thanks for your help.

Anybody have something they want to discuss?
The other day, we were talking about seeing the end of the video before we start.
Yeah.
I kind of got a grasp but a quick recap would be helpful.
Thanks to all of you for your patience and commitment because this stuff is difficult to explain and comprehend. We are trying to compartmentalize and understand thoughts and control them and even predict them. So thanks again for hanging in there.
Here is a for instance: Let's say I'm in a scene and I come home from my day at the office. And I'm talking to my significant other and my monologue is something like, "Well, today was interesting. I got to the office and parked in my favorite parking spot and I sat down at my desk and I ate my blueberry yogurt and I was wearing my favorite bow tie..." I say all that stuff. What I haven't said yet is "I quit my job." So I'm talking about bow ties and yogurt and parking spaces and yes, those are all part of my video, part of my truth, but I also know that I quit my job. I haven't said it yet but I know that I did it. That that's what I'm going to say.
So I talk about yogurt but only to tell you I quit my job. The whole time I'm talking I know that I quit my job even though I don't say it until the end. So that's the reason I'm telling you about bow ties and yogurt. The final line is driving my language.
You see how that might hold together?
Yeah.
Not to confuse matters but there's another video. One of the reasons I so rarely bring this up is because it's so hard to explain. This video covers why I'm saying this. The video of you understanding. That's a reason to drive my language. I need you to know that I quit my job. That's the purpose of me saying this. And that video is of my significant other going "I understand."
Not only do we need what we say to be truthful - and I use my video for that - but I also need the reason I'm saying it to be truthful. That's part of what drives my language as well. We can all say things that are truthful. There's a red sweater across that seat over there and some posters on that wall. Sure, that's all true but why am I telling you? We need that video, too.
We can parse this out in what I'm currently calling the "I understand" video. Even now as I'm talking, part of my video is of you nodding and saying, "Got it Duane. I understand now." So part of my video is you understanding and I'll keep talking until you do. *(laugh)*

A YEAR IN ACTING CLASS

So I'm telling you something because I want you to know something about me. I want you to know me better. Or whatever that reason might be, I want you to have sympathy for me, I want you to trust me, I want you to admire me or want you to think I'm smart. My video is an image of you going "Uh-huh. Got it. I understand. I forgive you."
I hate to muddy the waters too much and I usually don't mention this because I've identified like six different videos and it all gets too confusing. So I stick to the main one which is our character's memories and hopes, etc. But another of my videos is you going "I understand" or "I'm not mad at you" or "You're so cool, Duane." *(laugh)*
That makes a lot of sense.

I sometimes like to break things down almost to a molecular level. I think of this class as a science, a dramatic science. Fundamentally, look at this line of dialogue: "Tomorrow I'm going to the library." Okay? If I don't know "library," why am I saying "tomorrow?"
Ahh. (laugh)
So I know "library" before I say "tomorrow." Otherwise tomorrow what? Sure, it's a word but there's no reason to say it.
(laugh) I love that. That registered. That was cool.
Great.

That makes a lot of sense. Would that be what's called… I've heard this before and I didn't understand it but would it be my, like… my...(pause)
Are you going to say motivation?
Yeah. (laugh) I didn't want to say it!
I could tell! You were like "Should I say this bad word?"
It's okay. That's not a bad word. It was on the tip of my tongue also. So sure. But I would use the word video instead. As always, I say the answer is in the video. Even to the question "What's my motivation?" The answer is in the child at home you have to provide for. My video will tell me I have a little girl at home and she needs braces and the refrigerator is empty. My video will give me my motivation, my objective, my subtext. That's why I don't use those words. We don't need them when we have video. But that's the only reason. *(laugh)* They're not bad.

An impolite story is a more impactful story. Other acting schools will say to "raise the stakes." And that makes perfect sense but it can be hard to define. What I'll suggest is to get more impolite.
I don't mean our characters become rude, necessarily. I'm sorry the word is clunky in that way. The impolite story being, what's at stake? What are the consequences? It's the difference between someone who's faced a major illness and someone who's had a cold. A major illness is more impolite. Dramatically, it's more fertile. See what I mean?

That's the best example yet.
Impoliteness will make it more important.
Ah-hah. Thanks.

Polly, Anything rattling?
In my real life, people are saying I'm just a little overdramatic. (Laugh) I think I'm letting too much emotion out. I don't know if that's something I should be concerned about or not.
Fun. Polly. I don't really know you outside of class. Do you think there's anything to be worried about?
No. I have a good time and life is pretty good.
If you're finding that you're more expressive or that emotions are more accessible, if you're finding that you don't mind being the center of attention…
I think it's easier to let emotions go now.
And maybe because you have sort of rehearsed them, haven't you? Various emotional states. That makes them more accessible in real life.
Exactly. I think that's it. And it's all good. When they're saying it, it's in a positive way.
That's great if it's working for you. I have to say that a lot of people have shared with me that learning about acting has helped them in many areas of their life.
Exactly.
It makes perfect sense. What are we doing? We're studying what it is to be a human being. An in-depth study of what it is to be human, with a major in communication. And our study isn't about ourselves, it's about people other than us, from different eras, who think differently, feel differently.
People like people who are active and positive and straight forward. It's positive rather than being quiet, not being able to say anything.
Actors look at life from a very compassionate side. It's very compassionate to represent someone else. And to be in the study of it is to be in the study of compassion.
With using video, we're trying to get inside someone else's head. Who they are, what they're doing, how they're feeling. And then we fight hard for them.
I feel so grateful that I have been able to walk among people who are in that pursuit. Actors tell a loving story and it's loving people who find their way into acting. We're studying communication, understanding, compassion. Every time we do our work, we walk a mile in someone else's shoes.
We're trying to feel what they're feeling. Some of these scripts you give us, I would never do what they do but I can try to understand and feel what they're feeling.
And fight on their behalf. Even though dramatically, characters are more interesting when they're flawed. That's why so often our characters make bad decisions. Sometimes we can't agree with these decisions but we try to make their choices identifiable and understood.

I'm not an expert at all in life but so many people have said they've been helped in different areas of their life. This study, this pursuit is a great path to be on. You've been with me almost two years now.

Not quite. About a year and a half.

Good scene. Hey, Polly. your relatives were right! *(laugh)* Good scene from you. You figured that scene out and executed it in a short time. Have you done this scene before?

No, this was the first time.

You've said in the past that you have a hard time figuring out scenes but you figured that out in a short time, really well.

I remember the last time I was in class, that exercise we did. That helped me out a lot. For this scene, I went through it word for word, line by line. That helped me a lot.

Your video was quite good there. There was video driving your language, right?

Yes. Yes, I felt the video.

And I'll point out, you did it very quickly. You haven't had that scene very long. That was well diagrammed and well executed.

Finally, everything is starting to click.

I'm glad that exercise helped you.

It did.

It was apparent when I observed the scene.

One of the things we're watching out for is when the camera penetrates through the character and sees the actor behind the mask. That's a lot of what the audience is watching for. I know that's what I am looking for as an acting coach. I'm watching for the difference between the character in the scene and Alejandro. Right? I'm looking to see if I can see Alejandro and if I don't see Alejandro, that's what we're after.

You're pulling that off. Instead of auditioning for the camera, you're in defiance of it. You're defying it and that's really powerful. Does that feel inherent to your experience?

Yeah.

Not "I hope you like me." "I hope I look good today." "I hope this makes sense." "Did I say that okay?" You're fighting hard enough for your characters that you don't care about the camera being there. You're playing the scene in defiance of the camera, not trying to cozy up to it. That is so healthy because the actor cares about the camera but the character is trying to extort money from this lady. That's really good. I want you to continue in that vein. You're dominating your environment in a very healthy way.

That's good news.

Polly, I want to commend you on your patience in the scene. And I think you could be patient because you had video. Video helps us be patient because the video is complex.

That's something I've really been struggling with. It seemed so slow to me.

You know what happens in those moments? Tension builds. What are we building tension towards? What you're going to say next. And that makes what you say next have more power.

You always say to do it in a way that makes you uncomfortable. Well, I was very uncomfortable throughout much of it.

Good. It should be uncomfortable. You're hiring a guy to kill your husband. *(laugh)*

Alejandro, in this take, a bit of that cadence I ask you to avoid crept back in. In your earlier scene tonight, it was just fine. Here, especially in the last quarter of the scene, it was back.

Yeah. I think I know why.

I'll bet. I think I know why too. You didn't have your video in as much detail.

Yeah.

That's the wonderful thing about video. When we use it and are in touch with it, our bad habits go away. That's another win for the video.

There's a lot of things that I say. One of them is this: "If it feels good, don't do it." I think the first scene you did today where you got really angry and yelled at your dad would be an example of it felt good and you did it. But in this scene the energy wanted to overflow but you wouldn't let it overflow. So the angst and anxiety were in your belly. It would have "felt good" to attack somebody. To take an emotional value and really let it gush. But you kept a lid on it and it was very effective. If that's what you had in mind, I applaud that.

"If it feels good, don't do it" reminds us to get right to the precipice of indulging ourself in an emotion, but then don't indulge. At the very last second, hold yourself back. Find another avenue. I think that's what your instincts are right now. In my Actor Brain, it would feel really good to indulge myself in this emotion. To emote with a capital E. But instead, you're playing the game. Keeping a lid on the kettle.

Yes. I felt really uncomfortable.

You mean uncomfortable in a good way, right?

Yes.

Awesome.

Regarding... What word was it you chose? Perfectionism?

Over-analyze.

Right... That spurred this thought. I love to analyze. I think it's okay. Because what we want to do is, after we've figured everything out, then we'll be sure to "don't do it good." We're going to bring failure back into the equation. We're going to bring questions back in and uncertainty back in. Through the process of acting.

Instead of more and more perfect, we can embrace being more and more flawed in that pursuit. Because we want to play the game now, we can't play yesterday's game. We have to play today's game.

So as we drill down, we're not finding answers, we're finding more complex questions instead of answers.

I'm always asking us to avoid the good reading, avoid the good performance. So that we can stay textured. So always being a bit off-balance, even though you've over-analyzed, you're still off-balance. I would suggest that perhaps, the more you analyze the more off-balance you might have to embrace.

Yeah. Okay.

I might have made a good point there somewhere. *(laugh)*

It was fantastic. Thanks.

One way to think of the video is to ask yourself this: "How do I know?"

When asking yourself what video to shoot, the answer can often be found in this inquiry. It's a good equation for us to be using when generating the video. Whatever your line of dialogue - "How do I know?" - Now the video will come to you.

For instance, maybe you have the line "Susan, who used to work here, she was so demanding."

How do you know she used to work here? If I force myself to answer that question, I'll find myself shooting a video.

"Well, she came in every morning with her extra large coffee and sat at that desk and did human resources at this company for 5 years." And how do you know she was so demanding? "Well, she always yelled at me for every mistake and berated employees in front of everyone and canceled the Christmas party because we hadn't reached our sales goals."

In this case, as I look at it, I'll change my video. She didn't do Human Resources. I'll reshoot my video and make her the Vice President of the company. Human Resources aren't known for being demanding. So we reshoot the video as we explore further.

Even Susan. How do you know Susan? "Well, I knew her from work and that one time I awkwardly bumped into her at Applebees and she usually wore a blue mid-length skirt and I heard she was a part-time pilates instructor." We have to shoot the videos in this detail in order to create truth.

And it's not so difficult. Any of us can do it. We all do it all the time in real life.

But acting isn't real life and that's what we have to overcome. *(laugh)*

September/October

Okay. I told you that since you got extra rehearsal time, I expected the scene to be extra good and it was!

Joe, how'd it go for you?

Ummm… I think… Alright.

What kind of alright?

I was working on some things and they went… alright.

Good, Joe. Fine. I'd just like to point out that if that was a 2-minute scene, like a minute and a half of that was really good. There may have been a few things, you may have fallen out of it here or there but overall, it was just so solid. I want to point out the dichotomy of when I asked you how it went, you thought it went alright or you didn't really know.

I find that to often be the case. For the actor it didn't feel "good," but I'm out here with my fist in the air going "Yes!"

Yeah, it can feel uncomfortable.

We're on a tightrope. A tightrope is uncomfortable. It doesn't feel good to be on a tightrope. We're scared. We could fall.

There's no net.

There's no net. You're just living your life. It might feel great to walk on concrete with your arms out but that's not what we're doing. We're on a tightrope, way up in the air. It's scary.

We can feel good when we get off the tightrope. But when we're on it, it's frightening. That kind of playing the game; uncertainty of how I'm living my life and "It's happening but I didn't plan for it to happen this way but I'm letting it happen because it's happening this way…" As opposed to sometimes an actor might say "I've got to kick-ass in this moment and I've got to kick-ass in this moment and I've got to kick-ass in this moment." Right?

Instead you were just living his life and, I think, thinking his thoughts.

Mostly yes.

For me, it looked like a minute and a half or so. *(laugh)*

I'll take that.

I know we've touched on this before but this is what feels good now. To not feel good. Now this feels good. Feeling good? No. That's not what we want. We want it to not feel good and that's what feels good. So that's the approach. The tightrope is further off the ground.

Gianna, can I give you a note?

Please.

I have a phrase "Help a buddy out." That would be "That thing you said to me has a lot of impact on me."

So when he drops something on you, be more impacted by it. Kind of go "Wow. That's amazing. I feel that." To help a buddy out, be more impacted by what they say.

There's something I call "Self-direction." To be the director of our own work. We all do this to some degree. That is our job at the audition. To fulfill what the director hoped would happen with the scene. To give them what they're fantasizing they're going to get. To give the director what they're looking for. Sometimes it's about thinking like a director and how that may be different from thinking about it like an actor.

Gianna, anything I can do to be helpful?
It felt authentic to me. Did it feel authentic to you?
Sure. I like that it feels authentic to you more than worrying about how it appears to us. Authenticity is authentic. To worry about being authentic is inauthentic. If you're worried about appearing authentic, you're not authentic. So let's not worry about that. Being authentic is what will appear authentic, okay?
Yeah.

Please understand the usefulness of changing body position. It's a tool that will help us create meal changes. I know you know where the meal changes are. Use a change in body position to help change meals.

Good adjustment. You are able to look at a scene and see why it's a great scene. A lot of actors take a long time figuring out why it's a great scene. You seem to get that right away. Well done.

One thing I've identified regarding auditions is when I do it, I get one chance to do it and I can't beat myself up for all the thousand ways I didn't do it. Those thousand ways I didn't do it? I can't punish myself for that. I only got the chance to do it once.
I like that. That's like a life note.

In this scene, there is a chance to show the relationship building between the two of you. Take the opportunity to show us that trust and admiration growing between you. Moment by moment. In the end, the two of you may become close. Partners in crime or a couple or a mentor relationship. The audience responds to those possibilities. Let us see those developments.

You know how I sometimes say, "contrast tells a powerful story." So in this scene I want to see more contrast between you as a tough guy and someone later in the

scene who needs her help. Drop the facade. And the greater facade you create, the larger the event when it falls away. Greater contrast creates a larger event. Right?
Yes.
Isn't that fun?
Yes.

For both of you, I want to look at opportunities to create tension. If I had the line "You know what they say, a bird in the hand is worth two in the bush." Now I could say it like this: "You know what they say, a bird in the hand is worth two in the bush." Or I could say "You know what they say…" *(long pause) (laugh)* Right? Tension.
Let the audience go "What's next?" Then when what's next happens, it's a larger event because there's more anticipation.
There are phrases that we use that send the message "I'm going to tell you something." Once we've created an expectation, if we take a beat, the expectation will build and that is tension. Then that thing we continue on to say, will be the resolve of that tension. Because there's more tension, the resolve will be a greater one giving whatever we say next more impact. More dramatic weight.
That's one reason I may suggest a slower pace, especially if you are naturally quick. One of the reasons it's so effective is because it creates greater anticipation. Think about this when considering pace and where to take a moment. If we let the language breathe a little bit more, we can create more tension. As you know, tension is dramatic currency.

Polly, good work overall. Whatever you're doing, keep doing it. You're getting good with video.
It only took me a year and a half. (laugh)
And you're using it to generate your language. That's helping you become a powerful storyteller.

I'm thinking about how hard it can be to be on the same page with the other actor. Sometimes I do my work and they do their work and we're not seeing it the same. We're talking to different people or in different cities…
Let me address that if I may?
Often, I'll assign a scene to two actors and say "go off and rehearse," and the actors will feel it's necessary to agree on everything. They'll talk about "Is Susan your sister or your daughter?" and think we both have to think the same things. And the other side of that is that we don't do any of those things.
(long pause) I'm not too sure I have a point here. I thought I did but I suppose I don't. *(laugh)* I guess if I tried to find one, it would be that in the audition or early stages of

rehearsal, it's not important that you agree. I think it's important that you know what you know and it's important that your scene partner knows what your scene partner knows. *Hmmm.*
I don't think it's important that the two of you know the same things.

I see the video in general terms but I don't see it with the specificity I need. Maybe I'm lazy.
Got it.
Like the wonderful examples when you were working with me on that play, the scribbling and the magic little pill. I never took it that far. How specific you got and I was like "wow." That's what I'm talking about. That I didn't go that far. That's what I see as most important.
I'd like to suggest that when you do, it's easier from then on. Once we got that specific, from then on those moments worked for you. So much so that you still remember them vividly now, right? Six months later.
Right.
If we do the hard work right away in the rehearsal process, then it's easy after that. Once you've shot those videos the rest is a breeze. You're just surfing.
So it's the initial effort. You don't have to keep shooting video through the four weeks of rehearsal. You've got your video after the first week and after that you're just tinkering, learning your blocking. Get it out of the way early. It has to be done. And don't do it in week three of a four week rehearsal process. Shoot it in week one.
Look what happens in the rehearsal process. You shoot your video early, in that very specific way, and the rest of the rehearsals are fine-tuning. And because you've done the video work, you'll be memorized sooner and almost automatically.
This really helps a lot.

Alejandro, anything rattling?
Yeah. I'm trying to implement all the things we've been talking about. I've been looking at tension and taking those moments…
By the way, everybody, Alejandro got cast as the lead in another short film. *(applause)*
Yeah. Anyway, I was hoping you could help me figure out arrows.
Sure. Here's what arrows are fundamentally: It's going from here *(gesturing)* to here, creating an event.
Going from calm to upset. That's an arrow. I go from upset to introspective. From introspective to remorseful, from remorseful to hopeful. Those are arrows.
Finding a way to not let a whole paragraph mean one thing. With arrows it can be ten things. Arrows are about contrast between moment A and moment B.
And longer arrows - we sometimes talk about unreasonableness - create larger events. So if I go from love to like, that's a short arrow, if I go from love to hate, that's a long

arrow. Or from love to resentment and resentment to hopeful. They don't all have to be extreme, they just have to be contrasted.

Arrows help us in the audience, delineate one idea from another, therefore making each more powerful. The contrast between them gives each more power. As I say, "Contrast tells a powerful story." To go from despondent to optimistic, from contrite to proud.

Your juxtaposed idea can be your secret thought.

The audience doesn't know you by what you say. The audience knows you by what you're thinking. That's where the intimacy comes in. And here we're identifying what you're thinking and that it's different from what you're saying. Giving what you're saying texture. Now that we have a juxtaposed idea, our language can resonate. There's a lot of different words we can use here. Resonance, texture, nuance, consequence, complexity, subtlety, repercussion.

Don't let the juxtaposed idea become an answer. Keep asking questions. It's just more exploration. We don't want to nail it down. Let it live and breathe and surprise us. Don't go "This is my decision and I'm sticking with it." Explore, play, take chances, make mistakes.

Yes.

Wonderful.

Polly, what I wanted from you was more variety in your rhythms. I saw you picking up your cues, which I support, and moving quickly, which is also good. But it was the same quickness throughout. What I'd like is very fast here, then very slow there. More variety.

I don't do that enough.

We're discovering how to fully occupy your Character Brain. The Actor Brain is going to learn lines and then we'll train our Character Brain to say the lines. But now we're identifying that the lines are not a perfect manifestation of our thoughts. Far from it. Just because I'm saying this doesn't mean that's what I'm thinking. At all.

Yeah, I say this but what am I thinking? Now we're embracing that different idea. Don't try to erase it, embrace it. Embrace the difference between what you're saying and what you're thinking. And when the audience gets not only what you say but what you're thinking, they feel like they know you. They have an intimacy with you because they're reading your minds. We're helping them to read our minds by giving them something to read.

The impoliteness is in what you're subjecting yourself and the audience to. We're going to try to tell the story in a way that's going to hit us in the belly. That's what I mean by impolite story.

A YEAR IN ACTING CLASS

Often, I'll give that note and actors get rude. That's not what we mean by impolite story. Impolite story is getting the audience in the belly. It's not nice to get someone in the belly.

It's not polite to make someone cry, is it? That's what we're doing. It's not polite to make them nostalgic or give them goosebumps or laugh in embarrassment.

How do we shoot video to create a greater emotional impact? That's impoliteness.

Alejandro, that scene felt a bit safe to me.

Yeah, maybe a bit too comfortable.

Right. You were like "This makes sense."

Yeah. That's what I was doing.

Nobody wants to see you walk a tightrope on your driveway. You have to get way up in the air before it's interesting.

Okay.

My previous acting coaches have suggested I write down the character's backstory. Questions and details of the past and writing them down and I feel like all of that is basically video. So instead of trying to forge a summary on pen and paper, I'm just using the video that I create.

I am 100% with you. That's the way I was hoping you would see it.

Here's the thing about video versus pen and paper. With video, it remains fluid. When you write it down, it becomes canon. With video, you can change what you're seeing. You can change how you felt about what you saw. You can change how you feel about what you've seen. The video leaves everything open to us instead of putting everything in a box and that box just gets smaller and smaller the more we write.

Your character wouldn't know the name of the elementary school they went to because they had memorized it or because they had written it down. They went there. The character would know because they remembered going there. Much the way you're creating the memory now, by shooting video.

It becomes a movie and our language is a result of the images I'm seeing. That's where gestures come from too. It's the movie.

I think that's about 85% of our work as actors. The other 15% is just doing that powerfully. 85% is video and deciding which video to shoot and the rest is powerful performance in that. We can change the video when we learn more about the character but having a video itself is fundamental. Maybe I was thinking I was not popular in school but I discover that I was popular. I reshoot the video and everyone is giving me high fives and valentines. That's easy. Just reshoot the video. If I had written it down, I'd have to erase and rewrite and re-memorize.

I might say "let's reinterpret the scene" but I can't say "you aren't being truthful." The two of you are already doing that. You have video and video is truth.
I'm still learning but I definitely feel like the video has helped me.

I've given a similar note to you before. Sometimes you're beginning your language but you don't have the video to start the line. By the end of the sentence you have it but - I think in the interests of rhythm - you're starting your next line without video. I'll take video over rhythm anytime.
Sometimes when I'm watching an actor, it seems the video is trying to catch up. We can't let that happen. The video has always got to be first. In fact, I'll often say to "Put your video further in front of your language."
If you're really using that video in the way we're describing, you'll have to confront those images. And by confronting those images, it will help you avoid that sing-song musicality. You won't have to use artificial rhythms. The lines will land because you're confronting the images and letting those images drive your language.
But overall, that was a really good scene.

There's a phrase I sometimes use - at the risk of sounding rude - called "yapping." You know how a little dog yaps but there's no point? That's when we are making sounds with our mouth but it's not driven by the images. We're talking because we have lines to say. It's not driven by anything real. Well no, it's driven by our script, our memorization. But not by truth.

I think the word you're searching for is "typecast."
Yes.
The second half of that word is "cast."
Ahh. (laugh)
So it's not necessarily a bad thing.

I've just been using video. Like, I used to think "I'll say the line like this." Right now I'm just going, "this is what I remember, this is what I'm thinking, this is what I feel." and not worrying about how I say the line.
What you're describing is another thing I say: "Let the video say the line." That's what you just described to me, that the video is talking. Not the script, not the actor, not what you figured out or what it should be. The video is talking.
What I'm saying right now, I didn't plan how I was going to say this. I don't have a rehearsal to figure out the most powerful way to convey this line to you. I just have a video that is racing ahead and I am using my language to try to keep up. That's truthful when we do that. And truthful is better than good.
Yeah.

A YEAR IN ACTING CLASS

With a little finesse. Because truth isn't necessarily powerful. We could go to a laundromat and look in the window and see people truthfully doing their laundry. It's truthful but I wouldn't pay to see it. It's as truthful as it gets but I wouldn't pay to watch.

You don't have to be interesting. Tell the story powerfully and that will be interesting.

What you had been doing is memorizing, memorizing, memorizing. Now you're shooting the video. Have the video. Don't worry about getting it memorized. The lines will come because of the video. The lines will happen if the video's there.
With a slight assist from the Actor Brain going "this is the awkward line" or "don't forget to repeat myself here." Little stuff like that happens in Actor Brain but for the most part when we have the video in Character Brain, we have the lines in Character Brain.
You were using your Actor Brain to memorize before but now you're using your Character Brain and shooting the video that will give you your lines. Well done.
That's definitely a new level of understanding.
That's a result of having your first gig. It's all theory until someone casts you. *(Laugh)*

Let's try an exercise. Talia, tell me about your favorite teacher. From your real life.
Ummm. Let me think…. There's one that comes to mind. Her name was Mrs. Williams. She was also my track coach. She always believed in me. She would push me hard and sometimes I would get frustrated. But she would always come around. She just believed so much in me. She was fantastic.
Okay. End of exercise. Talia, did you see a movie in your brain?
(pause) Yes. I could see her.
You saw her taking you aside, caring about you, there when you needed her, making you mad sometimes. There was a whole movie happening in your brain. Your word choices were a result of the video which is your truthful experience.
If what Talia just said was a monologue and we gave it to Debra, Debra would have to shoot Talia's movie. Talia was telling the truth. How can we also tell the truth, saying the same lines? What do we need? We have to have her video.
You see how the video is working for you, Talia? That you see the video and the words are a response to the video, rather like a narration. Does that feel germane to your experience?
That's a good way of putting it. That kind of clicked something in my brain. Taking the visual of what you see and narrating it. I like that.
Right. What's the video I need and then shoot that video and narrate it.
Not everyone in class ran track in school but what if you got a monologue where you did? Shoot that video. I'm seeing the other kids and people are stretching and it's

outside. Everyone's got numbers on their jerseys. Someone shoots a gun, I guess. *(laugh)* By shooting that video, I'm creating memories of running track.

You know the sound that the track makes when you're wearing cleats? That becomes part of my video as I get more specific. It just takes a few seconds to get a basic video. Then I have the memory to call upon. And the feelings the video gives me are useful and true.

If my line is "and then I went to Zimbabwe for six months," then my job is to shoot the video that gives me that truth. My job is to create a video so that when I say that line, I can say it truthfully. That's my job. Not to say the lines "good" or anything. My job is to create the video so I can say the line truthfully.

So I've got to shoot the video of "I went to Zimbabwe for six months." Okay, I must have bought a ticket. I must have anticipated my trip and had a reason for going there. I must have found my passport and packed bags. I must have landed there and adjusted to the time zone. I must have experienced the culture and food.

Even if I don't know what it's actually like in Zimbabwe, it doesn't matter. I can shoot a video of whatever I think it's like. I can reshoot my video as I gain experience and do my research but fundamentally, it just takes a moment to get a basic video.

In real life, I've never been to Zimbabwe but since I've shot my video, I have a memory of having been there.

I sometimes will say I could pass a lie detector test. I don't know if that's true; it would be an interesting experiment. To see if by shooting the video, creating the memories, we could pass a lie detector test.

If I never bought my ticket, if I never packed my bags, if I never found my passport, then I never got on the plane. I never went to Zimbabwe.

It's that easy. Even now, ten seconds after shooting my video, I have a memory of traveling there. We can add details later.

The coolest thing about all of this is that once we have shot the video, once we have created what we're calling "truth," we no longer have to pretend we have the truth. What a relief that is, to not have to fake it. Because you've made it genuine. And faking it is stressful, and feels terrible compared to telling the truth. But once we do this and tell the truth, then we no longer have to act good, we no longer have to impress anybody, we don't have to do a good job in our scenes, we just are truthful. And that's such a relief. And so empowering.

     My observation, there was less of an answer. We talked about answers and questions earlier. there were more questions this time, don't you think?
Yes.

Leaving room. Leaving room for those questions. The first time was full of answers, this time had more questions. More for us to explore. Good.

So often, comedy is based on misunderstanding. That's so often the case. And misunderstandings are also 1, 2, Pineapple. Right? Because we expect something and get the opposite.

What is a misunderstanding? Well, it's a surprise. A tendency in one direction and then a surprise in the other. Look at the usefulness of that.

Go back to basically any situation comedy. So-and-so is learning to play the flute in the evenings but everyone thinks they're having an affair.

The whole story is a misunderstanding. Comedy includes the misunderstanding. In large ways and in small ways. Look for those opportunities and take advantage of them by creating expectation in one direction and payoff in the other. That's how we highlight misunderstandings.

As a dramatic equation, thinking scientifically, we can think about flow and the interruption of flow. Think of electricity. It flows and then it's interrupted. The flow is like a tendency. A flow has movement and therefore a tendency. "Oh, it's going left to right. It will continue to go left to right." To interrupt that flow is creating a surprise signaling to the audience that there is something unexpected happening. Then it's flowing again. Then it's interrupted again. Tension and release. Tension is expectation and release is surprise or resolve.

How does an actor "own the room?" There's a current. We need that current to be tangible. "I expect it to keep flowing. Wait! It stopped flowing. Why? Oh, it's flowing again. Now I know what to expect. Wait! It stopped flowing again. Why did it stop?"

So that dramatic communication, impactful-ness in our work, has to do with drawing attention in the places where it stops flowing. That moment is worth investigating. There must be something here. We investigate that and get back on the ride again.

That's the yin and yang experience for the audience. With the material, with that scene, with that moment. It's about that zig-zag. That yin-yang. I want to call it "zin-zang" because it's yin-yang but with a spark. Firing, crackling, tangible. Electricity sizzles right? It sizzles and it's dangerous but it's exciting. How we navigate that, on a microscopic level, throughout our work.

Okay.

Dare I ask - and I'm afraid to - does that feel actionable? Maybe I shouldn't have asked that. *(laugh)* Perhaps the introductory question is does that hold together as a concept?

Yes.

So far, so good. Actionable is the next step.

Expectation is a huge part of that. We talked about the "Magic trick" earlier. "Look over here!" but it's really this. Where I persuade you to look at my right hand while I do the trick in my left. Expectation *(right hand)* and surprise *(left hand.)* And in a magic trick, I'm intentionally misleading you. That's okay. We're doing that here as well. We're magicians. I'll use any magic trick I can. "Look over here. Look over here… Gotcha."

Our Actor Brain has diagrammed it that way and then we shoot the video to support it. And we've created a large event.

I hope we can think of that as being actionable. Inviting imperfection is one way to do it because if I'm willing to be imperfect, then I'm willing to have the incorrect thought.

I just had a thought about Mexican food. It's not a scene about Mexican food but it's okay. That imperfect thought. Characters get hungry. *(pause)* That might not have been the best way to summarize this whole speech but it was pretty good up until then. *(laugh)*

Alejandro, anything rattling for you?

Yeah. Thinking about something while the other person is talking.

Good question.

Because that's something the director was talking to me about.

Did she specify what she wanted?

No. I've been thinking it over. What the heck am I going to be thinking about? (laugh)

Let me jump in if I may. A bad habit actors may have when they're not speaking is to be waiting for their next line. That could be something that happens. The actor is thinking "Next I'm going to say this" and waiting for their cue. That's all Actor Brain.

What I want us to understand is that even though they're not speaking, our characters are moving forward. We don't stop moving forward just because we're not talking. By "moving forward," I mean our characters' moving through life.

One thing that can help is to be impacted by what you're being told, what's going on in the scene. We've talked about "Help a buddy out" and to be affected is one way to be moving forward.

While I have a monologue, we can assume we're moving forward. I'm telling my story and I'm moving forward and I'm telling my story and I'm moving forward and then I stop talking. My story keeps happening. Just because I'm not talking doesn't mean my story stops. It doesn't even slow down. Just because we've stopped talking doesn't mean our stories are on pause. Our story is still being told.

That makes a lot of sense.

Does that feel actionable?

Yeah. Most definitely.

Of course, part of that process will still be Actor Brain. You still know your cue. But the 90% that is Character Brain is in a constant state of surprise.

That makes sense.

I've noticed that you treat dialogue differently when you have a paragraph or short monologue. You treat that differently than your single lines of dialogue. Like "This is special because it's a speech." And therefore you have different rules.

Oh. Yeah. That makes sense.

Don't change the rules just because you're making a speech. Your character doesn't know he's making a speech. Your character is just communicating. Keep in mind we never know we're doing monologues and we never know how long our monologues are going to be. I could be interrupted at any point right now. If no one interrupts me, it's a monologue. But it's not different than communication in general.

You tend to get Actor Brain-y when those short or long monologues are happening. Don't change the rules just because you have seven or eight lines in a row.
Gotcha.

The best way to diagram these roles, doctors, lawyers, teachers, police... You have the choice to care or not to care. Choosing to care is dramatically stronger. Secondly, the choice in those types of professions is either "been there, done that," or "this is unusual and fascinating." The best dramatic choice is the second one. The fertile approach is to care and find them *(the other character)* uniquely fascinating.
This helps the audience to care and to find them uniquely fascinating as well.

Jen, one thing I like about your work is that you like to make the audience uncomfortable. Right?
Yeah.
There's a bit of the saboteur there. We want our work to have impact. Politeness just won't do it. I'm here to hit you in the belly. You've been nurturing that approach to your work. It's part of how you do it and that's really helpful. We don't want our audience comfortable. What happens when you're comfortable? You fall asleep right? We want pins and needles. It's the opposite of comfortable.
You have a fun way of approaching that. You're never afraid. You see those opportunities. Am I correct that when you look at a piece, that aspect gets you excited?
Yes. I do prefer the dark side in general.
Me too. I like things with a little consequence. Otherwise it's "I'm a little teapot, short and stout." I certainly want to fan the flames of that. It's powerful and affecting.
We want to have impact on the audience. We don't get to punch them. We have to find another way to hit them in the belly.

I felt like you are having a tendency to want to do it good. As you might have heard me express, I'd prefer you to do it not good. Good is rehearsed and planned. Not good is messy and more interesting and has more surprises and dynamism to it. My feeling is that your Actor Brain was trying to do it good this time. I want you to invite the wrong, interesting way to interpret the line of dialogue, not the perfect one.

Talia, here's a word that might be appropriate in our work: "Unreasonableness." Those things, those choices you're making for your character, they're good choices.

"Unreasonableness" is when we take those impulses further. Fundamentally, being reasonable is not as eventful as being unreasonable. If I see that my character is jealous, I want to follow that to an unreasonable place. That's creating a larger dramatic event.

Okay.

I think you make smart choices but they may be a bit safe. "Unreasonableness" will get you out of your comfort zone and that might be a good thing. Does that feel appropriate?

Yeah.

Characters are carved out more boldly when they get unreasonable. Stories have greater colors as well.

Nice work. Alejandro, I have a technical note for you. In this scene, I thought you were too busy, physically. Especially in a shot like this one, a close-up, your head and eyes were too busy. "Economy of movement" is important. I will sometimes say "Instead of three movements, how about one?" Keep that movement contained. That, in itself, will raise the stakes for your character.

Those movements are releasing tension. Containing that will create greater tension.

Okay.

Only make the necessary movements. Try to contain the unnecessary ones. That will give us access to your eyes which is the only thing we're interested in.

Notice when you're watching a television show or movie, where you're looking. You're never looking for the elbow or shoulder or cheek. I found myself chasing your eyes. It's the eyes we're looking for.

If the lights don't hurt your eyes, you're not well lit.

Alejandro, what's going on with you?

I've been taking more time recently. I used to just reread and reread. Now I spend more time just sitting, creating. Shooting my video. Line by line. Truth is another word I've been thinking about.

(Laugh) I couldn't have put it better myself. At first you said you were taking more time and I thought "doing what?" And then you answered it. You're creating truth. You're shooting video. Hell yeah. Now you're creating intimate knowledge of his world. Not "how am I going to say this?" but "who is this guy and what drives him and what truth is he telling right now?"

I think you're doing that really well, Alejandro and I'm glad that your process has changed.

The first time through, I call the "Sherlock Holmes." We have our magnifying glass out and we're just looking for clues and trying to discover what possibilities lie within those clues. That's the first one or two times through the script.

Then we are going to start shooting video on behalf of our characters. Taking it one line at a time and going "this is my line of dialogue. What video do I need so I can then say this line truthfully?" Which video will prompt this language?

Here's the coolest thing: When you create that video, when you have that truth, you no longer have to pretend you have the truth. Boy is that a weight off our shoulders.

Pretending we have the truth is really hard. But having the truth? Once I know what it is and how to generate it? That's easy.

The video will not let you down. And if you get notes from the director, shoot a different video. You're truthful either way because you know what you're talking about, you know what everything looks like.

If we have truth, we're about 87% finished. The rest is just making it palatable and appropriate and powerful. I applaud your approach. I like the way you're putting your techniques together.

Polly, anything rattling?

The scripts this week, I can relate to. I wonder, are some things just more relatable than others? Because some of them I really struggle with.

So there are some roles that you can identify with.

Yes, and those roles are easier to play.

That's always something that we're going to have to navigate. There are some roles that I might feel are perfect for me and that I understand the character and their circumstances on an intimate level. Or is it a role where I will have to create that kind of a knowledge?

I've never been divorced. If I play the role of someone who's divorced, I have to make that adjustment. There will always be that to navigate.

Our job basically, is to find a way to identify with our characters regardless of what the character is. Maybe I'm playing a killer. Oftentimes, it isn't the specifics of the character but the essence of the character that we can most understand and embody.

I've seen sometimes with these roles that you eventually break through. There's going to be a breakthrough, the only question is how long do you have to wait before you get there? It's going to happen. How can we quicken the pace?

Your musicality was very particular and invested. You were not letting me miss anything. The "kitten" became furrier and cuter. Not because of anything you did physically but because of your musicality.

We can't ask the audience to listen too hard. Because they kind of won't. We do indeed have to make them do some of the work but we have to also be rewarding them. They have to feel rewarded for paying close attention. I don't want them to have to listen too hard. If I'm telling a story, this happened then this happened then this happened, I have to make sure everybody gets it. And if someone misses it, it's not their problem, it's mine. I didn't do my job.

In the fundamentals of telling a story, musicality helps us to use our language to paint a picture. Instead of saying things, I can use my words to paint pictures.

Sometimes I will say "Impose the story on your audience. Don't give them a chance to not get it." Impose the story on them. Confront the audience with the details of your language. That will cause the story to become more boldly colored and textured.

I kind of hate to say this in this way; I'll have to come up with a better way of saying it, that doesn't promote violence. But sometimes it's really fun to play a guy that is "punchable."

Yes.

The audience is like, "I hate that guy." And that is so much fun. You know what's going to happen. In the end your character will get shot in the street and the audience will go "Yay! I hate that guy." It's so much fun to make an audience hate you. This role really calls for it.

Think of the social change we can bring about when we expose how ugly these people can be. People who are manipulative, who take advantage of people who are vulnerable. We get to show how ugly that behavior is. And how much we want to punch that behavior right in the face.

It's fun to make the audience root against you. And if we can make the audience root against you, we're helping them to root harder for Joe's character.

Good, Alejandro. What you're doing is unique. A lot of actors can play nice people but to effectively, compellingly play villains is special.

Talia, that was a particularly emotional scene. Sorry to ruin your Saturday morning. *(laugh)* That's what I do. I just blow into your life on a Saturday morning and bum you out. Sometimes I feel really bad. *(laugh)* I hate to ruin everybody's day. We're just getting started.

I love it.

Thank you for your investment in the scene and the role.

Alejandro, in this take, I think you could have simplified more. I think you're feeling the need to do something and I don't think there's a need to do things. What do you think? Were you feeling the need to do something?

Yeah, I was.

Okay. I want you to understand that you're interesting without having to do anything interesting.

Alejandro, what's up with you?

We had our second table read. There were more people there.

How did it go?

It went well. It went very well.

What I'm trying to do in this class is two-fold. One fold is "What is the mindset of the actor when they are excelling, doing their best work?" What has the actor trained their brain to emphasize and de-emphasize? How do we respond to impetuses and impulses? Do we do that in a healthy way? Are we exploring and allowing or cutting off? The other half is dramatic interpretation. How to make dramatic text or storytelling its most powerful. That's more clinical. That's understanding the opportunities the text is offering.

But the first half of that is the mindset of the actor themselves. How does one excel in our craft in heightened, stressful situations? Such as opening night, such as my big chance in front of a casting director or the first time the cameras roll on my movie.

The stakes are high. Really high. How do we excel regardless of circumstances and impulses? And that is so fluid and ever-changing. It's breezes and currents and winds and your blood flowing.

The actor mindset. How to marry Actor Brain and Character Brain. How to make the material its most powerful and to feel powerful in all the right ways. How to overcome things like "I'm really in San Francisco but my story takes place in Italy." Whatever those things are. There's always a million of them. How do we navigate that? That's really our question.

And I think the approach we have here is practical. Alejandro, you've been here at least a year. And more than once a week. And you now have all the tools to meet high expectations. So congratulations. You've worked really hard. Not only really hard but really well. Nice work. Keep it up.

At your table read the Director of Photography was probably there. And the costume designer and the lighting person. The team met you yesterday. And you kind of blew them away.

Recognize that that's going to be the norm for you. Expect that. Both from you and for you.

Thank you.

Sure. The first of many successes.

Definitely a start.

Character flaws are more interesting than their positive attributes. kindness is nice but selfishness is more dramatically powerful. So yes our characters have flaws. But don't forget to be flawed in your Actor Brain as well. Don't let yourself do it the good way. The good way is the simple way. The easy way. Challenge yourself to avoid the good way.

A phrase I often use is "the only way I cannot say my line is the way I know I'm going to." So as the line is happening we have to re-navigate our moments as they happen. We cannot finish the line the way we intended to when we started it. We want to keep ourselves in the state of surprise. And that's one way we can avoid the practiced, good reading of the lines. The predictable and easy reading.

Keep ourselves a little bit off-balance. Even in that nanosecond by nanosecond frame. A phrase I like to use is "Powerfully off-balance." Powerfully off-balance. So "I'm powerful but I don't know how to be powerful but I'm powerful but I'm not trying to be powerful."

Okay.

If we catch you being powerful that's not going to work. And if you're just off-balance that's not going to work either. So ultimately it's a marriage of powerful and off-balance at the same time.

So it is without that predisposition "say it like this and it will be powerful!" As opposed to making it powerful right now even though we don't know how to make it powerful.

That's a hard concept.

The powerfully off-balance concept is pretty advanced. But I think it is within your grasp. I'm glad you got it well enough to understand its duplexity. The point isn't to win, it's to play.

To take that sports analogy a bit further, It's a game. And if we already know who won, there's no reason to play. So it's about the swing and the miss as much as it's about the home run. We can't just hit home runs. If we hit home run after home run after home run it would become boring. We have to let our characters swing-and-miss. So it's important that we strike out sometimes. That's how we know the game is real.

Alejandro, how was that for you?

There were parts when I didn't have a video at all. It was a good thing. Me realizing "Oh crap, I didn't ask myself a question here."

(laugh) Great.

And for the first time I heard myself using that tone. That tone you have spoken to me about. And I realized it's sort of a… spare tire. And I just now realized when I did that.

(laugh) Your spare tire. You get a flat and stick your spare on there…

Yeah. One of those little skinny ones. (laugh) But I'm glad I noticed it.

There's basically two differences between on camera and on stage. The first being stage actors tend to over project when they're on camera and on camera actors tend to under project when they're on stage. That one is easy to figure out and overcome. The other difference between stage and film is a bit more of a challenge for us to figure out.

Stage is a "succeed" medium and on camera is a "fail" medium. I want to try to break down what I mean.

On stage we have to project ourselves and our thoughts to the back row. So that leads us into wanting to succeed in our communication. Fundamentally we need to succeed in our communication on stage. There's no editor to help you out afterwards. Everybody's got to see, everybody's got to hear you. Everybody's got to have their experience regardless of where they're sitting or how far away they are. We need that. Fundamentally, we have to succeed in our communication.

I get it. On camera, we can't be yelling at our audience.

Yes, but not only yelling in the projection sense of it, the auditory sense of it, but also in the emotional sense of it. It's time for us to bring in more doubt. More unsureness, insecurities and vulnerabilities have to be tangible to the camera. More off-balance. At least for most characters.

But the diagram "what would kick-ass on stage" won't work here. You can't let your audience catch you kicking ass. The camera will catch you at that. That doesn't mean in our Actor Brains we can't kick ass. You can keep kicking ass as long as you're willing to fail at it.

That was beautiful, thank you. That was the best differentiation I've heard.

Tension and release is the building block of dramatic storytelling. We might also use the word expectation for tension and surprise for release. So we're playing that game with the audience. Never predetermined. Never settled. Always pulsing.

I'm getting it, little by little.

Take a movie like Rocky, which most of us have probably seen. Tension is he's getting his butt kicked and release is he comes back and wins and we all stand up and cheer. But it's tense, it's like "aargh!" But at the end the release of tension is so satisfying. In the meta, that's the tension and release in Rocky.

But break it down a bit further, from the whole story to one scene. Perhaps he's having a disagreement with his girlfriend. There's tension and release there too. And in another scene maybe he's having a fight with his trainer. There's tension and release in every scene.

Now break it down a bit further. In the scene just single out one line of dialogue. There's tension and release in that one line of dialogue as well. And if you get microscopic about it, you can find tension and release in between the lines, even in between the words. Tension and release principles apply throughout our storytelling like the atom. It's there in the micro as well as the meta.

Two actors are both playing Hamlet and one is terrific and one is just okay. What's the difference? They're both playing the same role and saying the same lines. The difference is that current, that vibrancy. How to create it, how to nurture it and how to take advantage of it.

Great. That's definitely actionable.

Good job, Polly. As I will sometimes say, "It's not about the line, it's about your point of view toward the line." I thought you did a good job having a point of view about what you said. That really rounded out the character. Instead of merely being the person who says these words. You colored a bit outside of the lines here. Did you feel that was true?

Yes.

She was a lot more than just the things she said. Good. She was unique and powerfully herself.

That's starting to become the way you do things. Well done.

Continue to investigate the flaws in our character. How the character isn't perfect. That can keep us away from trying to perform good. Invite those flaws in.

You're interesting without having to do something interesting. I think it's great and you should be congratulated. A lot of actors think "Oh! I have to do something interesting!" But the best actors are already interesting. Everything they do is interesting.

You're finding a way to bring some of that into your work.

The thing I want us most to avoid is good acting. That on the nose, figured out, makes sense acting. Fearlessness is being on the tightrope of the character who has no idea how to say it, how to be good. No idea they're supposed to say it good because there's no one watching. There was no rehearsal. They are just living their lives.

If I were to talk about your growth - of course I can say many things - It would be that you've begun to display this fearlessness. To regress would be to cling to the safety of the good line reading.

Thank you.

That fearlessness, which is another of our F words, is something we need to cultivate. We can't let the camera be powerful. We can't let the casting team be powerful. We can't let the audience be powerful - even if there's 10,000 of them. You see how fearlessness is a way of seizing your power back?

Yes.

Does that feel actionable?

Yes. I think so.

The audience can't be powerful, you need to be powerful. To do that, you need to be thinking "I don't care what you think. This is what's up. You deal with it." Not "I hope you like me."

To me, as I try to define what is the next step for you, it's when you decide "I don't care about being a good actor at all. I have no interest in being a good actor. Absolutely none." Instead "I'm a guy with a history."

I don't care if you like it. If we're doing drama, I hope you don't. I don't want you to like it. Part of the point of drama is to confront people with what they won't like. If they liked it, it would be comedy. And even comedy is uncomfortable.

So we have to overcome that tendency to please our audience. Our willingness to challenge them is what makes the comic moments funnier and the dramatic moments weightier. The scary moments scarier and the romantic moments romantic-er. *(laugh)* Okay?

Yes.

Excellent.

Debra, I felt like in the beginning and then again at the end, your video was strong and intact and you were using it to generate your language. Is that correct?
Yes.

There was a big chunk in the middle where you didn't have video. During that section you were guilty of yapping. Could that be true?
Yes.

Be careful. Don't let yourself say things you haven't seen. Some of that was quite good. Like I say, the beginning and the end. In the middle you let yourself yap. Is that fair and accurate?
Yes.

That's a really great monologue for you, Debra. When you are employing the technique of video, it's quite good. And when you're not, it's not.
Mm-hmm.

So I think we know what the answer is. *(laugh)*
Yes.

Okay, thank you.

Joe, how's it going for you?
Pretty good. Yeah

How do you feel about that tightrope aspect of things?
Oh. Umm. I think I was walking it a bit.

It felt more safe to me, Joe.
Did it?

It felt a bit more premeditated, a bit perform-y. It looked to me like you went back to fighting for Joe there. Instead of fighting for the character. Remember to fight for him. His marriage is breaking up. He's got to explain things to his family. Don't let us see you acting good. He doesn't care about acting, neither should you.

A YEAR IN ACTING CLASS

Let me check in with you, Talia. How's it going?

Pretty good.

We were working on unreasonableness today. How do you think that's going?

Umm. I feel like I could be more unreasonable. I feel like I'm taking small steps. I think there were small, little arrows. But in this scene and the one earlier today, I think my arrows could have been longer.

Good. I'm with you. That would be my thought as well. I'm glad we see it the same way. Getting more unreasonable is what we call a longer arrow. Right?

Right.

Often I'll give an actor a note that we need longer arrows *(gesturing)* and they 'll be like "ernt" *(moves finger 1 inch)* and I'll be like "No. we need more!" and they're like "ernt." *(moves finger 1 inch)* and I'm like "No. We need more. We need a LOT MORE!" and they're like "ernt." *(1 inch)*

To try to overcome that, I'll sometimes say to the actor "Go there first." Don't worry about how to get there, go there. You can figure out later what the path is. Get there. Go there. Be there.

If we stick to "a little more, a little more, a little more," we may never get where the director wants us to go.

Even if it feels a bit disingenuous at first. Keep in mind that comedy is really a twist on logic. So we can embrace being illogical, even dis-logical in our exploration.

Part of the point of arrows is to go from here *(gesturing)* to here *(gesturing)* to here *(gesturing)* Right now I think part of your diagramming is I'm here and I'm still here and I'm still here.

Okay.

So look for different ways to be unreasonable as well as being unreasonable about different matters. As opposed to the same unreasonableness. Okay?

Yeah.

I really like the way you're putting all this together, Talia. When I give you a note or observation, I see you put it into the exact right place in your brain. *(laugh)* You've only been with us a month or two but you're doing really well.

Thank you.

Thank you as well.

Alejandro, I have to ask. How was your shoot?

It was a… It was a success. They did a lot of shots like you said. There was a lot of standing around like you said. That's what I was thinking a lot of the time. I was like "yeah, he did say there'd be a lot of this." It was cool that I had that insight.

Also what we had talked about regarding the movement. Creating a reason to go here or there or stand up or sit down. So that was helpful.

How did it feel to be in front of the camera? When the quote,"pressure" was on?

I felt good. I had a little piece of paper in my pocket and it said "Fight for the character." Before a scene I would look at it and I'd be like "Okay. The cameras don't exist." I said "Eff the cameras" a lot. (laugh) In my head though, not out loud. (laugh)

That's great. So you got good feedback and vibes?

Oh yeah. It was great.

I'm excited for you and if you'll allow me, I'm proud of you as well. In how you go about your business.

It's not that often that I think being an actor is a good bet. It's not that often. Usually it's a pretty bad gamble. But I think you are a good bet. You get what I mean?

Yeah.

A lot of people, I would have to say "Hey look. Become an architect. Follow your second passion." But for you I'm one hundred percent behind you following passion number one. I'm looking forward to seeing what comes next.

Just before class I got another callback email on my phone. I haven't checked it out yet but I'm very excited.

Awesome.

I thought the scene got argumentative too quickly.

The first line?

No. The first five or six.

Right.

If we start off with an argument we can't build up to an argument. The old adage that a scene has to build is basically true. So leave room at the beginning of the scene.

Got it.

I think your video is trying to catch-up with your language. I want to make sure you put your video first. Be thinking the end of the line before you begin the line. Remember the illustration "Tomorrow I'm going to the library." You have to know "library" before you can say "tomorrow." Sure, tomorrow is a thing but if you're not thinking about the library, why say it?

Right.

The reason to say a sentence is because the thing at the end needs to be said. Not because the thing at the beginning needs to be said.

Okay.

"Next month I'm moving to Florida." If I don't know Florida, why do I say "Next month?" What needs to be said? Florida needs to be said. That's why I begin.

I'm not really moving to Florida, by the way. That's just great acting. *(laugh)*

Make sure you know why you're talking before you begin to talk.

May I interrupt?

Yeah.

You're letting yourself get away with yapping.

Yeah. I felt it.

Don't let yourself yap. I want you to set off an alarm bell in your ear when you're yapping. It's going "ding ding ding. Don't yap." And when you hear that alarm, take a moment. To stop yourself from yapping will probably require a pause. But the pause is worth it. No matter when or how long. Always take a moment to make sure your character's thoughts are driving your language, not your script. When your script is driving your language, that's yapping.

Be sure to have intimate knowledge and purpose for your line. Then you talk. It's always worth taking that pause to go from Actor Brain into Character Brain. Yapping is your Actor Brain pretending it's in Character Brain. We don't need that. We need Character Brain.

Okay. Actionable.

(laugh) How did you know what I was going to ask?

I thought the beginning of the scene had much better video than the end of the scene. That makes perfect sense. We rehearse the beginning of a scene more often than we rehearse the ending of a scene, right? We begin more often than we end. To overcome that, we need to pay more attention to the end. But the beginning of the scene was really good. Don't feel bad. We ask a lot of you in this class. As I often say, "ten minute scene, nine minute rehearsal."

Usually an actor's bad habits are an excuse for the truth. They are not the truth, they're an excuse for the truth. And when we have truth we don't need those excuses. Therefore the bad habits go away. The video will cover those bases for us. That's yet another reason we need video. So we don't have to pretend we know what we're talking about, we really do.

That's great.

Fundamental and easy. But we have to remember to pay attention to it.

The same scene can be diagrammed in different ways. I think in this scene, she's the star of the show and this is your only scene. But what if you were the star of the show and this was her only scene? You see how we might diagram differently?

Yeah.

If she is the star of the show and this is your only scene, your job would be to propel her story. But if you were the star of the show and this was her only scene, her job would be to propel your story.

Just because it's a two-person scene doesn't mean you each get 50% of the story. Good conversation, thank you.

Sometimes, when an actor is trying to catch their video up to their language, they think "what did I just say? Oh yeah, I think I have a video for that." Okay, but too late. The video has to come first. The audience can see the images after you say it. That's their job. You have to see the images before you say it. That's your job.

I want to use the mantra "Of course," instead of "Oh my God." Here's how I do that. "Of course I'm at a call back." "Of course Denzel Washington is in the room. Of course he is." So I can go "Oh my God. Denzel Washington is in the room." or I can go "Of course Denzel Washington is in the room." Of course will serve us better.
"Of course Greta Gerwig is sitting over there." " Of course there's a camera in my face." "Of course I make 20 million a picture." or "Of course I make five hundred a week." "Of course" can replace "Oh my God" in a very healthy way.
Of course I have an audition.
Of course I have a callback.
Of course there's a critic here.
Of course the show is sold out.
Of course my parents are watching. Of course.

There's another mantra I like to use and the more you want the job, the more you may want to use it. Let's say we're up for something big. A Broadway show or a series regular or a recurring guest or co-star... I have a mantra that I like to use and I say this verbatim: "I'm probably going to turn this job down... but it's nice to meet everybody." That can level the playing field and give me back my power.
How's that? Is that fun and actionable?
Oh, definitely.
While we're on the subject I also don't subscribe to the idea of the "big break." "This is my big break." Doesn't exist. There's just the work you do. Do the work. Don't worry about any big breaks. Work will do what work does.
So there's no big breaks, there's no golden opportunity. It's all a break. It's all an opportunity. Today is a break. This class is a break. Rehearsal after class is a break.

Joe, anything rattling?
Yeah. Just wanting to avoid old habits. My last couple of classes have been up and down. And you're holding me to a high standard too, which I appreciate.
You're welcome.
You have my full permission.

Joe, let's try to address it this way. Consider the energy of a moment and whether it is contained or bursts out. Contained energy is more powerful than the energy that sparks out. So it's about keeping a lid on your kettle. I want it to burn hot but don't let it blow the lid. Keep the lid on it. I think that's fundamentally it.

And I like doing it that way.

I know you do...

And things like "don't say the sad line sadly." Or "the angry line angrily." I know that stuff...

Yin and yang. The line looks like yin. How do I bring the yang as well? The words are yin. The words will do the work of the words. What am I going to do the work of? And how is it not the words? Sometimes you fall back into what sounds good or what looks good or makes sense. But when you embrace that "not knowing" approach, you're not manufacturing the energy, you're responding to it. Fun stuff.

In this scene, we're dealing with people who aren't quite with it. Who are clinging to the old ways. I liked the ways both of you embraced their flaws. You were conscious of that, right?

Yes.

It's great to play someone you admire. But I think it's even more fun to play someone you don't admire. Then you get to have fun exposing and showing those people up. That's juicy. Really well done.

Were you thinking about rhythm?

Yes I was aware of it. And I thought in places it might have been too slow.

It was a good scene but rhythmically it could have been better. It wasn't too slow. And it wasn't too fast. But it was too predictable. It wasn't too anything, except that it didn't change much.

I want you to cultivate the instinct to keep things surprising, rhythmically. We don't want the rhythm to become predictable. Be thinking "The rhythm has been the same for a while, something needs to change." And then a moment later "The rhythm has been the same for a while, something needs to change."

Obviously "when?" in the script we change rhythm, will have an effect on the scene. We can refine our thinking on when and how to change rhythms. But for a start, "the rhythm has been the same for a while, something needs to change."

Contrast in rhythm is going to be necessary to keep the scene crisp and exciting.

Joe, I thought your kettle was burning pretty hot during that scene.

I had the lid on.

Yes you did. And it caused everything to burn hotter.

Yeah.

And then the kettle blew at one point which I thought was appropriate. Suddenly everything just boiled over for a second but then the lid went right back on.
Okay.
The dynamics of that was really fun.
In terms of your verbal and vocal approach, there was no "indicating" in your musicality and that was also good. You had the lid on in terms of your verbal and vocal approach as well. And that is very powerful for you, Joe. There's something grounding about that approach. It gives your work more weight and gravitas. All that happens when you keep a lid on the kettle.
I thought the rhythm was pretty good.
I did too. You were yinning and yanging with the tempo. It was never predictable. There was always a surprise in the rhythm. I'm glad you were conscious of that. That keeps the audience's ear awake.

This is more of a philosophy than a tool. I haven't said this in a long time. Anybody know what I'm going to say when I ask for "The answer to every question?" It's from my first book.
I know that.
Go ahead.
Whatever will serve the audience's experience.
Right. Whatever will serve the audience's experience. That's the answer to every question.
It's cool Joe, that you're shooting all this back story and creating all these great images. But I don't want us to do that in order to provide limitations. We do that in order to provide opportunities. The logical answer isn't really the answer we need. Instead, what's the interesting choice, what's the exciting choice?
The story still has to fit together. We can't suddenly go "Oooh, I live on the moooon" just because it's surprising. We have to be responsible to the fundamental story that we are telling. But within that, the unexpected choice can be most powerful. Logic isn't really helpful. The audience can think "Logic? So what? I already know logic."
I don't need it to be logical. I need it to be exciting. I need it to be funny. I need it to be surprising, riveting, profound. Logic really isn't needed.

November/December

Talia, anything rattling?

Not really. Just going to focus on - not with the scene today but with future scenes - I really want to focus on unreasonableness.

Not with the scene today?

I felt like this scene isn't one where I have to be unreasonable.

Oh, you're playing the doctor?

Yes.

I see what you're talking about. Let me clarify a bit about unreasonableness. Your character is together and smart and uses good judgment. She's professional.

The unreasonableness we can find in these types of roles are the consequences of the scene. Unreasonable consequences. Your character may not be particularly unreasonable but the consequences, what's at stake in the scene and the events are unreasonable. You are helping to craft the story in that way.

The character may not be demonstratively unreasonable but we can still get those butterflies and our heartbeat going.

"Unreasonableness" may seem to have a negative connotation but it can be positive too. Love unreasonably. Be unreasonably sympathetic and compassionate. "Unreasonableness" can work any way we wish. What we don't want is mundane, everyday, average. Why is the audience watching? We have to give the audience something they can care about and root for.

It often happens - and maybe I need to change some of this terminology - that when I ask an actor to get unreasonable, they automatically get louder. What about unreasonably vulnerable? Unreasonably unsure?

We are creating events that matter. Giving the audience things they can experience, root for and against. Without "unreasonableness," who cares what happens because nothing's at stake.

Some scenes and some characters can look rather mundane. It can look like "well I just seem to talk for five minutes about astrology." Okay. That's reasonable. What's unreasonable?

What's unreasonable is the need to be accepted perhaps. Or the need to be the smartest one in the room. Or the need to impress everyone with my intelligence or spirituality. Or the need to be my very best at my job. Those things get unreasonable despite the apparent mundanity of the text.

Debra mentioned standing out at the audition. I want to stand out at the audition because I'm the best actor. Not because I'm different. I'm different because the scene is better when I'm in it. Not because I'm the most this or that. But because the scene itself is more powerful when I do it than it is when the other actor does it. That's how I want to stand out. Not because I do it with an accent or a limp. But because "It works better when that actor does it."

For those of you who have studied improv at any point, you're familiar with the concept of "Yes and." In a basic improv scene it might go something like "It's a beautiful day today." And the other actor says "Yes and I can't wait to go to the beach." And the first actor says "Yes and I'm going to wear sunscreen." Right? So we're building and not denying.

In a way, unreasonableness is yes and-ing the opportunities in the scene. It's a way to build upon.

In improv, obviously the bad response would be "no." As in "it's a beautiful day today." "No it's not." Now we don't have anything. It's not a beautiful day, we can't go to the beach, I don't need sunscreen. Nothing can happen when we deny. When we accept and enhance, things happen. That's what matters. So at an audition, when another actor does the scene, it's about one thing but when you do it, it's about five things. Because you're yes and-ing this moment and this moment.

If the best doctor ever is confounded by a medical situation, then it is a confounding situation. If a relatively good doctor is confounded, well… get a better doctor. *(Laugh)* It's the same in roles like psychiatrists, social workers, any professional. Their thinking is "I've seen it all. I've handled it all. But this situation is uniquely interesting and challenging to me."

Mmm. Yeah.

If it's confounding to the best doctor, then it's really confounding. Then when your character fixes it at the end somehow and everything turns out okay, then it's a larger event.

Just some thinking from a diagramming point of view.

Joe, you and I have been talking about a scene in something you're cast in - Joe got cast in another film by the way - the scene in the record store. It's similar here.

In Talia's scene, she's going to look at the x-rays and the minute she does, there's a bomb. It's like Boom. And she thinks "Oh my god. I've seen it all but I've never seen this."

That happens in my scene for sure.

Good. The kid is showing you their favorite record and as soon as you see it "Boom." And you think "I've heard of this record but never thought I'd actually hold it."

If you think about the movie Pulp Fiction, when they open the box and the light comes out, it's like that. We don't know what is happening but we know it's amazing.

Talia, in your scene, it's when you see the x-rays. Joe, in your scene, when you see the record. It's often appropriate for us in our characters to be thinking " I've seen it all, I've seen it all, wait. Boom. This one is particularly fascinating to me, and I'm an expert." Look at TV shows… doctor shows, lawyer shows, cop shows. The stories are all told in that way. "Seen it all but this one is special." Fun.

When a reasonable character becomes unreasonably invested, it tells the story that this is a large event. By reacting unreasonably, we are telling the story that we are in an unreasonable situation. An unreasonable situation carries more dramatic weight. So "Unreasonableness" is not only in the character but also in the stakes of what's happening.
Okay. That makes sense.
I wouldn't want us to assess a role and say that the best way to play this role is safe.
I definitely did that. Thank you.

Jen, I've seen you apply this concept quite well in the past but I think you forgot to apply it here. That is the concept of "It's hard to be a person."
Yeah.
It slipped your mind on this scene?
Yes.
I like to present something so personal and vulnerable, that the audience almost feels guilty for watching me.
If you come across someone you don't know well and they're crying, you don't stare at them, you politely turn away. You give them their space. It's a personal moment. You have no business being up in their business, right?
We want to confront the audience with those moments and make them see us, even when it's uncomfortable. We're almost invading the audience's space by making them invade ours. Does that concept hold together?
Yeah, the impoliteness.
I want the audience to almost feel guilty that they're watching me in such a private moment. That's how we can use our vulnerability as a weapon. *(laugh)*
That's how you move an audience, right? That's how someone leaves a movie and says "Yeah. That hit me."
It's almost as if we're committing emotional assault.
Exactly.
The bottom line in this scene is she misses her dead husband. How can we explore the vulnerability of missing someone? The loss.
Does that feel actionable?
Yes.
A pleasure.

Andre, there was a place about two thirds of the way into the scene where I thought you settled in. And I want to address what I mean by that.

There was a line that you said about change being inevitable. I felt like it was the first line in the scene where you knew what you were going to say before you started talking. Earlier in the scene I felt you knew what you were going to say while you were saying it. Do you see the difference?

Yes.

In that moment you not only said his words, you made his point. In that moment you spoke from the heart instead of from the brain or from the mouth. You understood what he was trying to say and you helped him present his case. It was powerful because you aligned yourself with his intentions.

I'm going to have you both go back and start the scene again. Even if it slows the scene down, be sure to know what you intend to say before you begin talking. Does that feel actionable?

Yes.

Let's take 60 seconds and try this scene again from the top.

Andre, how's it going for you? How did you feel about those adjustments?

Better. I felt that I slowed down a bit and that helped me be in the moment.

Great. I'm glad that was your experience.

I have a lot of little sayings. The one I'll use now is "Capital K." And the K is for knowledge. It's important that you know with a "Capital K," what you're talking about. Does that feel actionable?

Mm-hmm.

I like to caution that without that "Capital K" knowledge, without knowing what you're talking about, "You don't know what you're talking about." That's a great way to insult someone, to say "you don't know what you're talking about." But in this application, it's really important that we know what we're talking about. Don't just talk. Have knowledge. Our job is to have the perspective that causes these words to be said.

Mmm. Okay.

Does that hold together conceptually? This is your first class. Am I doing a good job so far? *(laugh)*

Yeah. I like that.

Alejandro, you went into that monologue and you were focused on the specificity of your video. Is that right?

Yes.

It paid off. Excellent. That specificity of video. That is the new standard I want you to be holding yourself to. Not just video but specificity of video. Not vague.

And I also want to remind you of the cadence I asked you to avoid. And I have suggested that when the video is strong that cadence goes away. It did here. You completely avoided that old habit. Not by avoiding the cadence but by having the video.
Okay.
Very good work regarding your video. And when you hold yourself to that standard, everything else falls into place.

Good scene. Hilarious in places.
Most of the great comedians make themselves look foolish. Not the other person. A comedian who makes the other person look foolish is mean.
A great aspect of comedy is to allow ourselves to be seen behaving foolishly and having foolish perspectives. Alejandro, you're really good at allowing yourself to look foolish. The joke is on you. That is often a very healthy approach to comedy.
You embrace that really well, Alejandro. Well done. You need to have a healthy sense of security to be able to say "This is what I look like when I'm a total idiot." *(laugh)* You're surprisingly good at that kind of comedic take. You're good at making fun of yourself and your characters. Showing us their heart, vulnerability and naivete.

I was thinking to myself " Whoa. Andre's doing really good in this scene." I guess I'm an amazing acting coach because that was a lot of growth from your earlier take. *(laugh)* In one class you've gone from beginner to "Way to go."
Thank you.
It was fun to see your level of playfulness and investment in the character and what's happening. You felt freedom, right?
Yeah.
From your first reading to your second, there was a tremendous amount of growth. If you keep improving like this you'll be better than all of us by next week. *(laugh)* Well done.

Jen and Alejandro, for both of you today, particularly in your monologues, you were feeling powerful. Not the distraction of "Oh my gosh, I'm an actor. Oh my gosh, I messed up that line. I hope they like me. Is this believable?" That wasn't even part of your experience.
The word ownership comes to mind. The level of ownership that you both have when it comes to playing a role. In fighting for someone else, in being in front of a camera, in dealing with judgment in whatever areas pop up for us judgement-wise.
If you can maintain that level of ownership, you're just a good actor. It doesn't matter what the role is. Or any of the details, whether it's comedy or drama. Whatever. You've done the work now to really let your instincts take over. You've built really good instincts.

Now it's about trusting them. I want you to recall what it's like to have that sense of ownership.

If I was a famous director, and we're in a casting office, could you do that here? If it's opening night and you're sold out, can you do that there? Can you do it when someone says action and the camera rolls? That level of assuredness and ownership. I don't care who's watching. It's not about any of that. It's about my character's life and vulnerabilities. There's a big "Capital F" pointed at everything else.

That's something we are chasing. It's kind of like a narcotic. Fighting for someone else.

Talia, I'm going to ask that in terms of your pacing and rhythms, you default towards the quicker choices.

Okay.

In terms of syncopation, and how it impacts the audience's ear. I will often put it this way: "Anything that can be said in a beat and a half, can be said in a half a beat."

Both are impactful. The earlier, quicker choice is probably best. There is more surprise in the early choice.

The early choice has more excitement to it. The same line, the same intention, later, might not have the same excitement to it. It might settle back into something unexciting. Does that feel actionable?

Yeah.

It's not important that we get the details. Who said what, how much things cost, those details are not really what the scene's about. It's what you're saying but not what it's about. It isn't about those details. They're not important to the audience. They're important to you but not to them. What's important to them is who you are, more than the details of the story. You spelled out those details really well. More in detail than the audience actually needs. It's not going to be about the details of your small business. The powerful story is in the big, universal ideas. It's going to be about family. It's about trust and love and beauty and compassion.

Oh, I see. That makes sense.

Alejandro, You are good with patience. As I sometimes say, "patience is advanced acting." But I want to give you a goose toward moving things along. You've got to pick your spots. We can't let the whole thing be ponderous.

The bottom line is I'd like you to use more contrast in your rhythms. It became a bit predictable, rhythmically.

That makes sense.

Don't let the rhythm get predictable.

I don't know if we have talked about syncopation. Syncopation basically means "between the beats."

I was a young actor, maybe in my twenties, when I decided it was important to speak between the beats. It's a way to keep the audience's ear awake as opposed to speaking on the beats. I still use that instinct today. I've been acting my whole life. I've only had about ten quantum leaps, and that was one of them.

In music, they call accents between the beats syncopation. There's a quality of energy and surprise in syncopation.

Jen, another great take. I don't know which I liked better. Thoughts?'

I was thinking about compassion and when you think of all the doctor stories where they should have those boundaries. He shouldn't go home and think about this dying woman but he can't help it.

From my observation, one thing you guys are both doing well is "fighting harder for your characters than you are for yourselves." You're not worried about "How am I doing? I hope Duane likes it. I hope the audience likes me. I hope this makes sense. I hope I'm believable." I see a young woman in a doctor's office and a doctor who is dealing with a prognosis. You're fighting hard. As long as you keep on "fighting harder for your characters than you are for yourself," - i.e. "I hope I'm a good actor." - as long as you keep that up, you're going to keep finding this type of success.

And you guys have done the work. You've gotten rid of all the bad habits, for the most part. Sometimes we have to be reminded. But you've done the work. You've cleared the path for yourselves. Now it's just fighting for your characters. It doesn't matter what the role is. It doesn't matter what the time period is or what style, fight for your characters.

You've cleared the path to do that powerfully and effectively. You've avoided bad habits and enlisted good ones.

So this is about trusting yourselves to fight for your characters. Knowing what that feeling is. Your Actor Brains are quiet. When the scene starts, you're not worried about the scene, you're a young woman with a diagnosis. You're not worried about the scene. Screw the scene, you've got real problems.

Right.

I don't have time to worry about a scene. I'm dying. *(laugh)*

All your headshot is doing is getting you in the door. It then gets crumpled up and thrown away. No one needs it now. You're there. What counts is really you. That's why your headshot has to represent who you really are.

Okay.

On the day, be confident, be rested. All those sorts of things.

Thinking of headshot-ness, it's the same as our theories in on camera classes here: What's most important is the eyes. That's what we want the audience to be drawn towards. We don't need them looking at our cheek. We don't need them looking at our chin or our ear. None of that is you. What's you is in your eyes.

So you want the audience drawn to your eyes.

When you're looking at your best friend, that's where you look. It's the place where the intimate communication happens.

Okay.

An expert headshot photographer - or even a good one - will understand that. We really want to use our eyes to draw the audience in.

There's a phrase used: Smize.

Eyes smiling?

Yes. Smiling with your eyes. It became kind of a Hollywood joke because everyone was saying "Smile with your eyes" and it became "Smize."

Now it's kind of passe and even cliche but it's still true.

When you're watching an actor or actress, that's where you look. There's something in their eyes that makes them seem fun or…

When you're at a movie theatre and you're looking at a 40 foot screen, you could look anywhere. Where do you look?

The DP and the director will help you out here and make sure that the eyes are available. And on set we have awareness of that principal, too.

Ultimately, if you care about somebody, where do you look? When your kid is crying and you say "what's wrong?" you are looking into their eyes as you wait for the answer. The eyes are where the audience gets to know you on a personal, vulnerable level.

Consider this: Our eyes are the only parts of our body that aren't covered by skin.

That's so disturbing, Duane! (laugh)

Sorry if that "icks you out," I can understand that. But we're looking at your organs.

Ewwww. (laugh)

The eyes are the only place the audience can fall in love with you. They can't fall in love with you through your forehead or your cheek.

I think of this approach to acting that I am espousing from us is more a philosophy than a technique. In this approach we might contradict ourselves. We might have to walk a different tightrope. I like to think of it as a philosophy, more than a technique.

I would agree.

I followed the path of Zen thinking and philosophy. Yin and Yang. Equal and opposite reaction. I was able to apply some of those principals into dramatic equations.

I began to see that things like tendency, expectation, flow… those are really dramatic equations. Or maybe dramatic math. Like if there is this much flow in this direction, and I interrupt it in this way, what will be the reaction when I interrupt that flow? What reaction will it create?

We work with the other person to create flow.

Then the interruption of flow and how effective that can be. Because when you come back to flow, flow is special again.

Expectation and surprise. Tension and release. Flow and interruption of flow. All of those things are dramatically relevant.

What if I were to say "there's such a thing as 100% of anger?" Okay. If I can create a world where there's a way to quantify anger and I recognize what 100% of anger would be, in an angry moment, what if I took 26% away? If I recognize the potential and capacity and what that is, what if I take away 31%? Am I creating a vacuum? Am I creating a void? And does a void create movement?

I'll grant you there's no way to quantify that. But theorize that you could.

Then "if this is 100%, what if I did 14%? Or 54%? And what does that create as far as the yin and yang of the moment?"

Nothing is only tails. Heads exists too. Otherwise the coin doesn't have dimension or consequence.

A few of your pauses were too long. Consider the other actor having to wait. They want to say "Get out" but can't because it's not in the script. That long pause before your line makes things awkward for the other actor. You see what I'm suggesting?

Yeah.

I want to create more momentum in your rhythm. Then, when we take the pause, it's the exception to the rule, not the rule.

Okay. I was doing some "Hail Mary's"

(laugh) I like the sports reference.

It's important that we stay ahead of our audience. The audience needs to be moving pretty quickly, trying to stay with us. We can't let them walk or stroll or certainly can't let them stand and wait. We need to be just ahead of them yet not too far ahead. If we're too far ahead, they'll lose interest in our train and wait for the next one.

Then we wait for them and they catch up to us and catch their breath but then we're off again. We can't outrun them and leave them in the dust. We want to go fast enough that the audience is just able to keep up with us.

Polly, I want to commend you. I felt like in that scene, the lines came from your belly.

He did a good job creeping me out.

Yes. That gets your belly going! In a help a buddy out way, he can't be creepy unless you get creeped out. So you were helping him be creepy. That's helping him tell a powerful story. A lot of good things were happening in this scene.

I'm starting to get a feel. I couldn't describe it but it's a belly thing.

I often mention "head, heart and gut." The head is easy. Well, not easy... but it's only the intellectual understanding. The heart is where we find the sympathy, the empathy. But the belly is the hardest to get to. That's where involuntary emotions happen. That's where we get chills and butterflies and tears and goosebumps.
Yep.
When our belly is in the scene, we're really starting to hit it.

Talia, how's the scene feeling for you?
Umm. Okay.
I thought in this scene, you started off in the same place as where the scene ends. It's okay that you're thinking of leaving him and that you're pissed off about the beach, but there are other ways to play the moments. Right now I think, where you're ending up is where you've been the whole scene. How does that ring with you? Am I right?
You mean you could see where it's going?
That's a good way of looking at it. We could see where it was going.
I can see that.
Sometimes acting is a bit of sleight of hand. It's like "look over here!" and then you hit them from here when they're not looking.
Yeah.
Have the fun of the dis-logic of a light playful moment for instance. Then when the heartbreak at the end of the scene happens, there's contrast.
Okay. Yeah.

I'm tempted to talk again of momentum.
The scene has to be over with... Whatever happens in the scene, it has to happen "before we know it."
A phrase I use is "Before you know it." "Before I knew it they broke up." "Before I knew it, she walked out on him."
The alternative is "after I knew it." "Oh, they're gonna break up, they're gonna break up. See, they broke up." *(laugh)* Right?
The momentum aspect of arriving before the audience... We've got to get there before they do. The scene's got to be over before you know it. Otherwise, it's after you know it. Then, it's too late. The audience has already gone home. *(laugh)*

Another phrase I use - and sorry I have so many phrases - is "don't say the sad line sadly."
Yes.
The line is already sad. To say it sadly is redundant.

If you're playing Hamlet, do you do Hamlet in your head doing the video or...

The basic idea is to shoot Hamlet's video and then use the video when you're playing the role. So Hamlet thinks there's something suspicious about his dad's death. So I'm thinking "My dad died and I don't like it. I think someone did him in."
So you're Hamlet?
I'm thinking Hamlet's thoughts. It is pretty simple.
It is.
You were talking about Chekhov and Stanislavsky and other theories... There's nothing exactly wrong with those approaches... except I don't think those approaches use video. To me, any truth, any memory is video.
If I ask you to tell me about your first car, what happens when you answer me truthfully? Your brain goes to videos, opens the file "cars" and looks for the page "first car."
If you're Hamlet, you go to videos and open "Dad." Open the file "death" and then within that open "suspects."

It's really important of course, to take care of yourself, both mentally and physically. So always do that first.
I think you have this mentality already, Alejandro, but I want to put it into words in a way that may be helpful, in case it's a mantra that you might need to call upon. I will say to myself "I am a machine. I don't get tired. I don't get bored. I don't make mistakes. I don't need a day off. I'm never late. I'm always ready. I'm always prepared. There's no such thing as a bad day. I'm a machine."
Most people don't get to do what we do. Follow our dreams, create, actively put art into the world. Confront the status quo. Most people don't get to do that. They don't. We do.
It's not a word that I use often but I feel very blessed to be able to do what I care about. And I don't ever want to take that for granted. There are people doing jobs that they hate. If we're fortunate enough to do this, then we've got to understand the discipline that is required to stay in the game.
Acting is kind of my religion, frankly. When it's time to be in service to my church, I can't be tired today.
Is that helpful?
Yes. Thank you.

I don't mention this often - because some actors might feel left out - but I'm a sports fan as well. I like to adopt a bit of the Kobe Bryant mindset. That killer instinct. I am lucky enough to play this game. If I'm ahead by 30 points, I'm still playing my best game. If I'm down by 30 points, I'm still playing my best game. That's that Mamba Mentality. I'm going to bring my best every time you put a basketball in my hands.
I like to consider the similarities between being an actor and excelling in a high stakes sporting situation. The combination of concentration and relaxation needed. That mindset. In the sports analogy, that free throw with no time on the clock and we're down

by one point. Game 7. You've made a million free throws. How do you make this one? This is the one that counts right now. In that moment we need the right ratio of concentration and relaxation.

A lot of our work is making the audience desperate to find out what happens next. That's a huge part of our work. Do you see how I'm diagramming that? If we can make the audience desperate to find out what happens next, we have a hit show. Well done.

It appeared to me during the scene that you were prioritizing video over performance. I'll take that. Continue to prioritize video over everything else. It appeared to me that in class today that's what you were doing. I really liked the results.

Alejandro, anything I can do for you before we end our class?
Um. Maybe we could do it again?
Oh. Kobe's not ready to end the practice yet. *(laugh)* Sure. Let's try it from the top.

Alejandro, anything rattling for you?
I was thinking about the moment before. Like, the moment before we act.
Nobody's life begins when the camera rolls. The life has been living before the camera catches them. Your character had to walk up the stairs in order to enter the room, perhaps. Or the character has been crying in the hallway and has to walk in and look like everything's fine. And all we see is the character entering the room. So we as the actor will want to know what happened before. What happened five seconds ago, what happened thirty seconds ago. And have those things in mind for us.
I don't think what I just said was particularly inspiring *(laugh)* but was that at least clear?
Yeah.
We have to know where we're coming from. That's part of it. Sure, we're entering a room but why are we entering the room? What do we expect when we enter the room? Those inquiries can begin way before the camera sees us.

Another thing - and this is totally technical - is right before I hear the word "Action" from the director. I'll lightly close my eyes and turn with eyes closed toward the brightest lights. Sometimes the bright lights can be overwhelming. Maybe you're shooting on the beach and you're facing the sun because that's how you're lit best. Close your eyes lightly and look toward the sun. Then they're saying "Standing by… Sound, Speed, Camera, Background aaaaand Action." Right before action, turn away from the light source, back into the scene and open your eyes. Having faced the bright lights with eyes closed, your eyes will have become acclimated to bright light. They will be constricted. This will make you less sensitive to the bright lights.

That makes sense.

This only works for about thirty seconds and then you may begin to get overwhelmed by the bright lights again. Depending on your level of sensitivity. But at least it will get you off to a good start.

But that is all technical and before "action." The most important thing for us to remember - and you already know what I'm going to say - is to fight hard for our characters and F everything else. Including the camera, including the audience, including the director.

I was doing a scene in a film recently, and I was chasing a guy into the room. In the previous scene, my character had been chasing him and this scene started with me entering. In that case, I spent quite a bit of time before the scene began, doing jumping jacks off-camera.

I was doing that to try to raise my heart rate, get my blood pumping, trying to get out of breath genuinely, without having to fake it. The physiological reactions that happen when we're nervous or excited.

That sort of activity can cause physiological changes. The kind of changes that might happen if we're fearful or threatened.

Sometimes we may have been sitting around for three hours, waiting for set and lights. A few jumping jacks is a good idea. To make sure that you are fully engaged physically, that you're not sleepwalking your way through the scene. This will get your body alert and your mind alert as well.

I will also suggest you say "F the camera." Part of the technique of "F the camera" is to make the camera find me. I'm not going to show myself to the camera. Let the camera do its job and let the camera find me. I'm not going to show myself or demonstrate to the camera. I'm going to do my scene and fight for the character and let the camera do what the camera does. It can find and see what it wants to find and see. None of my business. I've got a life to save or a love to rekindle or whatever the scene is.

Sound actionable?

Yes.

Are you memorized on this?

Almost.

The camera will catch you trying to remember your next line. That can't be part of your process. Okay?

I won't let that happen.

Very good.

I don't think your video on this is complete. You may have been thinking that since it's a commercial, you don't need to keep the same standards regarding video, that it's the exception to the rule. But it's not. Video is the one unbreakable rule.

In this piece, you say the product helped your business but I don't think you yet know how it helped your business.

That's true. I honestly didn't think about that.

Shoot the video of how the product helped your business. You say it "streamlined" your business. What does that look like? Shoot the specific video to give you that truth.

Also, I want you to create more intimacy with the camera. You can approach the opening as a secret. "I have a secret and I want to share it with you because I care about you."

I often ask actors in spokesperson work, to cast the camera as someone you care about and want to protect. Maybe your sister or Mom, someone like that. In this scene, it's business related so you can cast the camera as a trusted peer. Think about the intimacy you might feel with such a person and see if you can create that sort of intimacy with the camera.

Okay.

Great.

I'm having trouble with this line. On set, I can ask the writer about that line.

Whenever you ask a writer about a line, you're sending the message that you think it's written badly. If you're asking about a line, you probably do think it's written badly.

Okay. Good point.

"What does this mean?" is sort of code for "You're a bad writer." *(laugh)* "What could you have possibly meant by this?" *(laugh)* "Is this a typo?" "No, it's probably not a typo, it's the best my talent had to offer." *(laugh)* So I rarely ask about a line.

I'll just see what kind of feedback I get about it.

That's a good approach.

One of my favorite words is "viable." That just means you might get the part. Not that you necessarily will get it but that you might. And Talia, I feel your work and your work ethic are viable.

I'm a director as well. When I'm directing, I think of myself as an advocate for the audience. What would make me, in the audience, enthralled, give me goosebumps, butterflies, tears? That's what directors do. One thing I really like to espouse for ourselves as actors is "Self-direction."

If we self-direct well, we're going to give more directors what they want. And if we give more directors what they want, then we'll get cast more often.

So to self-direct is to adopt that point of view. If I was in the audience what would I find fascinating, thrilling, etc. Again, that's what directors do.

I'm not one to pander to the audience. I'd rather challenge you than please you. So I don't coddle the audience. I'd rather find a way to confront them and get to their belly.

It's not fair to get to someone's belly. You've got to do it when they're not looking. You've got to do it against their will, perhaps. I would never get someone in the belly in real life. It's really not fair. But when I'm in front of an audience, that's what I'm doing.

So for me, even when I'm in the audience, I don't want to just be pleased. I want to be taken. And look at the impoliteness of that word. Taken. I would never take something in real life. Certainly not a person. But if you're in my audience, I'm taking you.

And when we finish that sentence, I'm taking you on a ride. I'm taking you on a journey. I'm taking you on an adventure.

I wonder, Lisa - and I applaud you should this be the case - that your focus is on being quote, unquote "believable."

It is.

I think that's fine. You are. You are believable. That's good. I think you're covering a lot of bases very well there.

The flip side of that coin is why I should get excited about the events in the character's life. How I can get excited about that and it's not just another moment that's happening kind of naturally. Right? So take more advantage of the opportunities. And you might have to consider this in your own brain as over-acting. I think that would be okay, perhaps, in search of larger events and more frequent events.

Alright.

A lot of actors fear over-acting but a worse problem is under-acting. Well, not worse but more prevalent. Under-acting is a bigger problem.

Any smart and experienced director knows, it's easier to get an actor to do less from a too-big performance than it is to get an actor to do more from a too-small performance. So if you're going to err, err toward over-acting.

Talia, I think overall, you're really good at playing together, stand and fight type of characters. But in this scene, and perhaps in your work overall, I'd like you to add more vulnerability. Vulnerability really lets the audience in on your secrets. There's a lot of texture there for you to play with. Audiences almost always care about characters who are vulnerable. Vulnerability is almost always welcome. The other character in the scene doesn't know that you're afraid but the audience does. Does that feel actionable?

Yeah. It does.

I'm going to ask you to do this scene again. This time through, I'm going to ask you... whatever your decision is in the moment, go further with it. Don't let anything be generic or average. Make sure there's something happening in each of your moments. Don't let it be just waiting or nothing happening. Look for ways to create more events in the experience of the scene.

Is that actionable as well?

I'm going to try. Yes.

Talia, how's it going for you?

It felt better than the first time. I think anything would have felt better than the first time. It felt fine. I'm still not exactly sure what's going on in the scene, so it's kind of hard to come up with something.

"Instant logic" can help with that.

Alejandro, how's it going?

I've been working on fighting hard for my characters. And using video.

Good instincts. My adjustment would be in raising the stakes on the scene. What's happening and why it's important.

Okay.

It felt to me perhaps genuine, but not necessarily fascinating.

Yes, video is something I'm going to ask that we always have. But now that leads to the question: "Which video?"

Raising the stakes is to make it more important, which helps the story become more important, which helps the audience to feel rewarded for their investment.

Okay.

How do we make the video more eventful? Both in frequency of events and also larger events when they do happen. This will make the stakes higher.

Higher stakes means greater consequences. That usually means more anguish, more pain. Those ideas are dramatically charged.

When I watch acting now, I'm watching for something different. I'm seeing when actors have a video and when they don't. I saw two plays this week and there were two actors that were just wonderful. I could see that they could see their video. I don't think I'm there yet but I want to be that type of actor.

When you were watching these actors, what was your experience? What was happening to you as you observed their performance?

Part of me was thinking about the actor but mostly I found myself awed and into it and... taken.

Yes! I think that's at the core of what you're talking about. Debra, as I was looking forward to having you in class today, I was hoping it would go in this direction.

I think those actors… and let me know if I'm right, Debra… I think those actors are on the attack. As far as the audience's experience.

Yeah. I agree.

And those other actors, the ones that aren't as good, those actors are kind of on the retreat, aren't they? There's a little bit of "I hope you like me." There's a bit of "I'm scared you're going to find out I'm not a good actor." And the most effective actors are like "Eff it. Here it comes. Deal with it."

Those other actors, they did okay. I don't mean to put anyone down.

Of course. But you have to be discerning.

But there's a big difference when you get goosebumps…

Exactly. Because they're on the attack.

And Debra, that's something I really want to foster in your work: the attack. That's something I wanted to address with you and I'm not sure I could have put it better than the way this discussion has put it.

I'll share with you a little anecdote. This happened in rehearsal. There was a young woman on stage and the director kept berating her. And he was doing it in a way that I thought was mean and unnecessary, but he kept berating her and berating her and she took it and she took it. Finally, she burst into tears and ran out of the theater through an exit door into the alley outside. The stage manager said "Take five everybody."

Five minutes later, that actress came back to downstage center and we picked it up right where we had left off. Her eyes were red and her face was wet. And I hate to say it but… she was a lot better. I kind of hate to say it. I hate to think that that kind of technique works but she was better. In fact, she was a lot better. And she stayed better. It was a breakthrough for her. A quantum leap.

Now when I analyze that experience in retrospect, I think that when she came back down stage, looking a mess, all the sheen and veneer had been stripped away. Virtually the worst thing that could have happened, happened. And it happened in front of everybody. And she was pissed off. I don't know if she was pissed off at him or herself. But she came back downstage center and she let us have it. And my observation was that she was a better actor. Not only in that rehearsal but moving forward as well. She took it up a few notches and never looked back.

I want us to take that lesson without anyone having to be abusive to us. But I want to take that lesson.

Now when I think about that young woman's acting up to that point, she had been getting by. She was okay. She was probably as good as most of the rest of the cast. But now she had become a fascinating actor. The kind of actor you can't take your eyes off of.

In a sense, we've got to get pushed to the point where we don't give a fuck anymore. And I can't push you there. It's not in my nature. And I don't want you to push yourself there either. I don't want you to be emotionally abusive to yourself. I don't want you to beat yourself up mentally.

But let's understand what it is to be pushed beyond the point of any reason. Beyond the point of any vanity.

And I'm not going to be mean to you so you can do that and I don't want you to be mean to you so you can do that. I don't support acting coaches or directors behaving that way. But we can still see the equation and make the adjustment. Learn that lesson without having to go through that experience.

Does that feel actionable?

Yeah.

She was trying to bludgeon us with that performance. She was trying to tear down the walls of that theatre with her performance.

There is something subversive happening in a great performance. You in the audience may be laughing and applauding and standing up at the end but I'm trying to hurt you. I'm coming after your belly. That's why you came to the theatre.

It's so powerful to go out on stage and think "I hope you hate it." Not "I hope you like it." "I hope you hate it." If you hate it, that means you're crying at the end. Good. If you hate it, that means you wet yourself with excitement or terror. Good. I'm not trying to make you like it. That's too easy. I'm trying to make you hate it.

Another word that comes to mind is we want to be riveting. Look at the impoliteness of that idea. To rivet someone. That is not polite, is it? It sounds like a horror movie to think of someone being riveted. Again, it's not a thing that can be done politely.

We would like the audience to be awed. We say awesome now and it doesn't mean the same thing. The word "awe" actually comes from the Bible. It was what people felt when they were in the presence of God. You want to awe your audience? You had better be powerful. Get comfortable being uncomfortable and have fun being impolite.

That's very powerful. Thank you.

What fun.

Debra, in your Actor Brain, what were you working on?

I was trying to be assertive. I was trying to do that a lot and it ended up being a little. I dipped my foot out there and was like, nope. Bring it back in. (laugh)

That's what I wondered. You were dipping your toe in the water there. And I could tell that you felt powerful in the moments when you were doing that. You fell back into old habits in a few places - "good" line readings and such - but overall I felt there were only a few moments when you were not on the attack.

Now I want you to get more comfortable when you're on the attack and start relishing in that. Right now you're not really comfortable. When you dipped your toe in, the water felt freezing to you. That's okay for now. Moving forward I want you to really dive into those waters and really confront us. You were on the verge of confronting us with that material. I liked the way that it was heading.

I don't think this has anything to do with anybody's ability or skills. It's got to do with the mindset and being sure that we're on the attack. Making sure that the audience is affected by that thing I just said. If they're not affected by it, then there was no point in saying it.

Just about every character has something that they're unreasonable about. It might not be the thing that most of us would be unreasonable about but they're unreasonable about something.

Be sure to look for the 1, 2, Pineapple. Writers are very good at giving you those opportunities. And the pineapple the writer gives you, but you are responsible for the 1, 2. "How much can you 1, 2?" is really how the joke will land. How much expectation can you create?

A reminder that you don't have to do something interesting to be interesting.
Okay. Yeah.
The first time through I thought you were trying to be interesting. This time you were more interesting because you weren't trying to be interesting.
The scene itself becomes the star if we let it. As opposed to me being the star of the scene, we can let the scene be the star of the scene. The situation. And that time through you let the scene be the star.
Okay, yeah. That makes sense.
Super fun.

Debra, I think I'm beginning to see glimpses of the actor I always hoped you would become. That was more "Here it is, deal with it." than "I hope you like it." That's really coming across well.
I can feel the difference. It's not "how am I doing?" and "Am I getting this character?" It's more "Here it is."
I'm into it. Stay on that track. That unapologetic, take no prisoners approach.

Sometimes we can't see where our character is in the beginning but we can see where they end. Once we know where we end, we can go back and start in a place that is contrasted with where the character ends up. This will help make sure that the journey is a satisfying one. We can make sure that between the beginning and the end, we cover as much ground as possible.

I'm sure you've all heard me say some semblance of this: "All of our thoughts start with video. All of our words start with video. My words are an imperfect result of what I see."

Hmm. That was quotable.

(laugh) I saw Joe writing it down.

Imperfect is what really drives it. That takes me away from the selling and how am I doing and how do I look?

Imperfect is important. Our words are an attempt at communicating our video but they are not my video.

That's what life is, really.

I think so too.

I was in my thirties when I first became a director.

Oh, like 50 years ago.

(laugh) Roughly. So I was a new director and I'm watching actors and I'm watching actors - and I think it was one of my first "Aha moments" in becoming a conceptual artist or whatever the term; I think of myself now as sort of a Dramatic Scientist - One of the first "Aha moments" I had, was in the idea "No matter how hard I try, I can never communicate perfectly."

Dramatically I found a great deal of power - and pathos perhaps - I thought that concept carried a lot of weight dramatically. That no matter how hard I try to communicate, I can never do it perfectly.

There aren't words to describe exactly how I feel. Feelings are feelings and words are words. They're not the same things.

There's this word we use, it's called "love." We can love our parents, our children, our partners. Or we can love spaghetti or a pair of slippers. It's the same word: "love."

So the meaning of the word isn't a real thing. It's just what we use to substitute for something real.

Along the same lines, another dramatic leap was in the discovery that "No matter what I do, I cannot make you feel the love I'm offering."

Dramatically this helped me a lot. The idea that love cannot be given, it can only be accepted. I can't give it to you but you can accept it. And how we miscommunicate and misdiagnose and hit the wrong mark in our attempts at love, that's where a lot of drama and perhaps the human experience really is. How am I trying but not succeeding?

Does that feel actionable? I would be really impressed if you said yes. *(laugh)*

It's thought provoking.

Challenging. Insightful.

I'm glad you find it compelling and, I hope, actionable.

I don't know about actionable. (laugh)

It's hard to be a person. It's hard to be a teacher. It's hard to be an acting student. It's hard to be a Mom. Of course it's hard. It's hard to be a Dad. You might have the most wonderful situation and circumstances but it's still hard.

When the audience sees that we struggle in our characters - at just being a person - they identify. It's hard to work a nine-to-five. It's hard to care about somebody. It's hard to have responsibilities. It's hard to have fears. It's hard.

We all have that stuff. We all overcome it, to whatever degree we can, day by day. There's universality in that. Let the audience see that aspect of our character's lives.

Let's remember the "Intimate glimpse". The audience knows there's something up. Even though your lines are "there's nothing up," the audience can see that there is. So they feel an intimacy with you because they know your secret, they know that you have a secret. You're helping to share with us that you have a secret. You're putting the audience in the position of investigating your thoughts. Giving them something to be curious about. Then they feel rewarded for their inquiry.

Debra, anything rattling for you today?

Yes. Small roles. Is the process the same no matter what the role or style or size of the part?

In some ways, yes. We always will need video. Video is the unbreakable rule. The video changes and the style will change with it.

Okay. That's what I wanted reinforcement on.

As you know, I'm usually asking us to consider both yin and yang in our characters. We're trying to show both sides of every coin. But sometimes, especially in small roles, they're designed to only show one side of the coin.

Maybe we're playing Rude Customer Number 2. We don't need to decide "Oh the only reason I'm rude is because my wife left me and I never became a trombonist..." If you're Rude Customer Number 2, you're rude. We don't need the flipside of that.

Sometimes our job in the script is to represent an emotional value, like greed. I don't have to show both sides of my coin here. I'm just playing greed in this story. Or in our earlier example, I'm just playing rudeness in this story.

Usually, we want to create questions for our audience that are going to get answered. In a one line or one page role, we don't need those questions because we're not going to get a chance to answer them.

Just a reminder to raise your eyeline. Remember that your eyeline should be a bit higher than the camera. When you get to choose where your eyeline is, we want the camera to look up into us rather than down at us. Same thing in theatre. When you are choosing your eyeline, make it a little bit higher than the back row of seats. And usually that would be in moments when our character is thinking or remembering.

On camera, whenever you have a human being you're addressing, use them for your eyeline regardless of where the camera is.
Okay. Thank you.

Debra, how's it going?
Pretty good. I felt good about it.
I'm glad you did. I'm taking note of how much more powerful your work has been lately.
There's a freedom in it.
Right and you're really starting to know what it's like to take advantage of that freedom.
I'm stepping outside of what I'm used to, what's comfortable to me. It's taken me a long time.
Once again, Debra, I feel like we're beginning to see the actor that I hoped you would become.
Thank you, Duane.

I have a friend who is a coach I respect and in his coaching, he wants the first time you say the lines out loud to be when you're in front of the camera.
That would scare the heck out of me.
I think the science behind it is good. We don't want to memorize how we sound. And if we repeat and repeat our dialogue, we might simply start mimicking the sound of our own voice.
It's not necessary to speak out loud in our personal rehearsal process. It may serve us and the overall production but I don't think it's necessary.
When I'm rehearsing at home or even memorizing, it's not an out-loud process for me. When you do it over and over again, you start to build trenches for yourself that can be hard to get out of.
Interesting. That's a whole new concept for me.

Alejandro, anything rattling for you?
I'm trying to develop a roadmap for how to approach scenes.
As usual, something great to talk about. Is there a step a, step b and step c to a scene? The first two or three times through I just read it. I don't make any assumptions about the scene, I just read it. Just "Sherlock Holmes," looking for clues.
One of the clues I'm looking for is, I'm going to start to determine style. Is it a western, where everyone rides horses and herds cattle? If so, there's a certain style. Is it science fiction? Is it a mystery? Is it scary? Light and funny? Is it rude?
Because ultimately, our job is to do the material it's best. Not our best, it's best. So the style inquiry is a big part of it.

After that, I'm going to start shooting my video. The video of the Character Brain. What video drives me to say these words? Not "what video equals these words?" But "what video drives me to say these words?" And then I'll start to shoot that video.

For instance in Actor Brain, we might decide that a pause would be effective. So we shoot a video in Character Brain that will give us a reason to pause such as "this is going to be difficult to say" or "I wonder how I feel about that." Then we're pausing but we're doing it in Character Brain.

That's about it. Another thing I'll say is "I'm not done until I get to the goosebump reading." Just about every scene has got an opportunity for goosebumps.

The goosebumps reading is going to take advantage of the events. Shoot the video that will make sure that the events are large, not small.

I think that each scene, each role, and each project is unique. They're like snowflakes. There are no two that are the same. So my approach can change as well. But this process can give us a guideline for how we can approach our work.

What your friend says about waiting to say it for the first time on camera, that sounds terrifying to me. I don't know what I sound like until I hear it.

But that's what life is like. That sentence you just now said, you didn't know what it was going to sound like until you heard it.

That's one of the things I want us to embrace here. We don't know how we're going to sound until we say something. I'm only going to attempt to communicate.

That's one of the things that becomes so artificial in actors. They communicate perfectly. In real life, there are so many flaws in our communication. Actors seem to think their job is to communicate perfectly, to get rid of all of those flaws. Part of the great human struggle is the inefficiency of communication.

Communication, if it's honest, is inherently imperfect.

If it's perfect I can see your rehearsal. It's the imperfection we're trying to embrace. It's the imperfection that makes it so beautiful. Makes it human. It's in the striving to communicate.

Jen, how's it going?

We had a hard time. We were trying to do something to make the scene interesting.

I'll just share that most of the time, when I look at material and think it's lacking, it's my approach that's lacking. It's not that it's not there, I'm just not seeing it yet. There are so many times when I've read a script and I thought this script is terrible, and I go see it and it blows my mind. I had no idea what it could be.

I think that's why you were thinking "Oh, this isn't working. We have to do something to make it work." I don't think we can fix the material. I'll often say "Don't fix the language." And here "Don't fix the script." It's like what I said earlier, we have to do the material it's best.

By the way, the script you're doing is from a network pilot script. So somebody thinks it's good!

Alejandro, I like that you're comfortable with a slower pace. But here is a key to pauses: Pauses are okay when they are filled with something. Right now, I think your pauses are waiting for something to happen. That's going to sap energy and interest from the scene. Make sure your pauses are filled. They can't be empty.
Okay. That makes sense.
Our character's brains are never pausing. The language may pause but our brains, our video, continue moving forward.

I'll often say "images are extremely specific." Look at a photograph. Yes, it's a picture of Grandma but what is she standing in front of? Where is the sidewalk? What is she wearing? There's a tear in her hem. Where is the grass growing and where is it not growing? Which blade of grass is tallest?
It isn't usually necessary to compare blades of grass but the specificity is there if we do investigate. The closer we look the more we discover. Words are boring and surface. Images are fascinating. Images are automatically worth investigating.

For almost everyone who takes my classes, there seems to be a moment when it's time to act, something in our brain seems to switch over to "Oh boy. Now it really counts. Now it really matters. I was rehearsing on my own and it didn't matter, but now it does."
I'm going to ask us to fight against that. Don't give power to the camera. Don't give power to me. Don't give power to your classmates or the audience or the casting director. You keep that power.
Yep.
When you're playing basketball, and you are taking a shot from the three point line at the end of the game, in that split second between when you catch the ball and when you shoot, you can't be thinking "Oh my gosh. This is it. If I make this shot I'll be the hero. Don't miss it! If I miss it we'll lose." That shot doesn't have a chance to go in.
In that situation, you need to shoot as if you're a kid shooting baskets in his driveway. Shoot like it's a practice. Don't shoot it like it's the biggest moment of your life. Don't give your power away. You're an expert basketball player. Do what you do. You can't shoot it better than you shot it the other times it's gone in.
At an audition, a class, the first take on camera, in rehearsal or on opening night. I want us to stay away from thinking "This is a big moment." We can't move away from what we do fundamentally well because the circumstances are trying to dictate to us that we should. We can't give our power away to our circumstances.

Sometimes I'll see rehearsal and it's going great and then we turn on the cameras and suddenly it has to be something it isn't and the actors have to be something they're not. Because we've allowed the circumstances to get in the way of our technique and our fundamental approach to being an actor.

"Dance like nobody's watching."

Well, almost. This is more assertive. Because people are very much watching. You know they're watching. They know they're watching. Dance like no one's watching feels like I'm trying to get over being self-conscious. This is more "Here it is and I don't care if you like it. In fact, I kinda hope you don't."

Oh really?

Yes. It's not about getting over being self-conscious, it's about dominating your environment.

Talia, anything rattling for you?

Yeah, I wasn't in class last week and I missed it. I was working a couple monologues I've done in the past and I just want to remember to have fun with it. I'm trying to think of ways I can get out of my comfort zone. Sometimes I catch myselfl leaning back into what's comfortable when I feel I do a better job when I feel uncomfortable. So I want to focus on doing that more.

That's great. I'm delighted that that's where your focus is. I think that's exactly where it should be. I identify with what you're saying and reflect it back to you as well. So, really well put.

One thing I might suggest in order to help nudge you a bit, one way you might get to that place you're talking about is to embrace doing it wrong.

The right way is the safe way. So for you to decide "Okay. I'm not going to do it the safe way." The safe way is the way you cannot do it now. You have to do it wrong. Find a wrong way to do it.

Okay.

I think you'll find you're having fun and as you reflected, when you look back on it, it went well but while you're doing it, it doesn't feel good.

One of the analoges is sports. If you're hitting a home run on every swing of the bat, you're playing on a small field where the fence is only ten feet away and someone is pitching underhand.

Or if, everytime you shoot the basketball it goes in, then you're playing with a hoop that is only four feet tall and you're sitting right next to it.

That's not interesting. Get away from the basket. Challenge yourself to miss. Nobody wants to see a game where the players make 100% of their shots.

I know I am mixing metaphors but what we are aiming for here, is a moving target. If it's this close and I'm going "bulls-eye, bulls-eye, bulls-eye," then there's nothing happening.

But to be willing to try to hit the target but know that it's moving and nearly impossible to hit, now we're really playing an interesting game.

I like that.

I'll just take the sports metaphors a bit further. One of my favorite players of all time, Kobe Bryant, one of the best players in the history of the sport, maybe the very best, in his career, when he shot the basketball, it went in 47% of the time.

Wow.

He is, in my opinion, one of the greatest that ever played. 47%. He missed more than he made. Lebron James, 46%. You want to be great? Miss some shots. Miss more than you make. Now we're playing the game.

Thanks for letting me take that analogy a bit too far. Basketball and drama are my two interests and the more I know about each, the more I realize they're the same thing. So I love the analogies I get to use between the two.

It helped.

Well done, thank you.

Alejandro, anything rattling?

Yeah. I was going to ask you about mantras. Something to have with you when going in.

That's a great thing to talk about. There will be several answers. It depends on what the circumstances are and where you're coming from.

Is it an Actor Brain thing we're addressing? Is it a Character Brain thing that we're addressing? That means there are at least two mantras, one to take care of Actor Brain and one to take care of Character Brain. But of course there is more than one way to address each of those.

I'll give you a couple, I see you have a pen there.

I'll start in Actor Brain. Probably my favorite to start off with, helps us get over nerves and being intimidated, you know what I'm going to say. It's "Fuck these people." We can go into detail on that later if we need to.

Another healthy Actor Brain mantra is "I'm going to fight harder for the character than I'm fighting for myself."

Now a mantra in Character Brain might go like this:

"I have to get my daughter back." Or "I hope my boss doesn't find out I'm sleeping with his brother."

Those are Character Brain mantras, all dependent upon the circumstances of the scene. Those would be examples.

"I have to save my farm." "I'm going to ask Juliet to marry me." "I'm secretly in love with you." That's Character Brain stuff.

So, when you're sitting there onstage before the lights come up, or on set waiting for the director to call action, you can self-impose the thought "I'm secretly in love with you."

"Action!" "I'm secretly in love with you. I love you, but you don't know it." Good morning. Yes, it's a beautiful day. "I'm secretly in love with you. I'm secretly in love with you." Does that feel actionable?

Yes.

Keep in mind character mantras - well, any mantras - can change throughout your work. You don't have to pick one and stay with it.

I think other acting schools might call it your "objective." That's probably a good way to think of a Character Brain mantra. "I gotta get out of here." "I gotta quit this job." "I hope I win the lottery." Whatever it is.

The character's first person, private thought, that's a place where we can find our Character Brain mantras.

And then when we slip back into Actor Brain, we go "fight harder for the character than I'm fighting for myself." "Eff these people." "Eff the camera." That's a beautiful mantra. Those are Actor Brain thoughts.

I didn't realize there were two kinds of mantra we could use. Actor and character.

Well, we're trying not to spend too much time in Actor Brain. Most of our Actor Brain mantras are there to help you back into Character Brain. So just pick one starting with F and you'll usually be okay. (*laugh*)

And Actor Brain will be quiet because Actor Brain is usually concerned with "Do they like me? Am I acting good?" If we put a big capital F in front of all of that we can keep Actor Brain quiet.

Yes. That's what I want to do.

Actor Brain mantras can pretty much be summed up in the F word in whatever context we want to use it. I even go "Eff the line. Eff the scene. Eff the moment. Eff the pause." I might be pausing but I'm also "Eff this pause." If I'm in Actor Brain, it almost always starts with F. Get back into Character Brain.

Of course sometimes we need to be in Actor Brain in order to properly execute the task of being an actor.

In a fight scene for example, that doesn't start with F. We have to pull the punch. If we're a dancer, we can't go "F the choreography." We have to do our job.

But most of the time, Actor Brain is concerned with judging ourselves and that is where we need the mantras that start with F. A big capital F in front of all of that.

Character Brain mantras are what we're after. Actor Brain mantras are just there to help us overcome obstacles, the Character Brain ones are where we want to be living.

Okay?

Yeah.

Great discussion.

I would almost go so far as to say "1, 2, Pineapple" is the foundation of everything funny.

Hmm. Okay.

Expectation and surprise. Make the audience expect something and then don't give them that, give them the surprise. That's what a joke is 90% of the time.

And it's prevalent. In cases like this, the whole monologue is a "1, 2, Pineapple" but a line of dialogue can be a "1, 2, Pineapple," also.

I see a bit of a quizzical look on your face,

I was going to ask if you could give an example of one in just a sentence.

I have one.

Okay Joe.

From Mel Brooks, he's talking about how he won't go on an airplane, he says "If God had wanted us to fly, he would have given us tickets."

Good one.

That's a great example, Joe. And there are millions of them because it's every single joke. Every one liner, every joke is setting you up to think it's this but then it isn't, it's that.

And I'm manipulating your expectations as I tell the joke and I'm having fun doing it. Creating expectation is the key, the smart part. Anybody can see pineapple but how strong can your 1, 2 be, leading the audience toward 3? That's the fun part.

And it works dramatically, too. In the "tickets" example, we might diagram "serious, serious, funny." The inverse is also true: "funny, funny, serious."

Okay.

Super great. I'm glad we had this discussion about 1, 2, Pineapple. It's been a minute.

It has, yeah.

When you took my note "don't do it good," it seemed like it was a little bit uncomfortable for you. And I was like "Yes!"

I want us to get comfortable being uncomfortable. Lots more questions than answers. For both of you. The first time through seemed like just answers. This time through was questions. Now we're getting juicy.

Well done.

Alejandro, one thing that works very well in your technique is that you hang in there. You don't stop and go, "Sorry, I messed up." You hang in there. And the director and producer and editor are going to thank you for it.

Talia, anything rattling for you?

Yeah, actually. My sister and I went to see Everything, Everywhere, All at Once. And we were talking about our favorite movies. My top five are movies that brought out a lot of emotion. It's uncomfortable and gets you in the gut. I'm usually bawling my eyes out or the movie makes you think about something.

It got me thinking about what you're always saying.
What is the word you use? Impolite? It brings out a lot of emotion in the audience.
I left that movie thinking I want to be the type of actor that does that. I want to make the audience uncomfortable. I want to be able to evoke those emotions.
I appreciate your pushing me to be uncomfortable and not be safe in certain roles.
When it's safe, you don't remember those performances. The ones you remember are the ones that hit you in the gut. You're uncomfortable. So that's what I've been thinking about since yesterday.

Great. That's really well put.

You mentioned impoliteness, the impolite story being the one that hits the audience in the belly. I don't go around hitting people in the belly all day long but when you're in a darkened theatre watching my performance, that's exactly what I'm trying to do.

And there's an opportunity to do that in almost every scene. That's what we have to recognize.

I haven't seen that movie yet. I hope to soon. When you watch actors that are having that kind of impact, what qualities do you think they possess that impacts you so much?

It's the gut thing that you talk about. It feels real and it just hits you.

     A word I had in mind was vulnerability.

Mmhmm. Yes.

You are seeing people's bellies. That's vulnerable. When we see involuntary emotions, that's the magic of that.

And consider the bravery of the actors to show themselves so - pardon the word - nakedly, openly. To bare all, emotionally.

People don't do that. We hide stuff. Of course we do, that's how we get by. (*laugh*)

The audience is reading your mind and that's a very intimate thing to do.

That vulnerability, that willingness to show ourselves. That's brave. And I think it's available in almost every scene. Fabulous.

     Debra, anything rattling for you?

Good conversations already today in class.

I just want to thank you, Duane. You have such a positive, frank, inspirational way about you. You're so patient, giving and economical. I just really love these classes.

Thank you so much for that perspective, Debra. It is my pleasure.

     You can think about your five favorite movies. You'll find that they all hit you in the belly in an impolite way. E.T., look how impolitely you're hit in the belly. "E.T. go home" is designed to make you yearn, make you desperate to want to help this poor creature that is slowly dying. It's designed to make you weep. Nothing polite happening there.

Wizard of Oz? Impolite. Hurricanes, wicked witches, flying monkeys, setting a scarecrow on fire… look how impolite it is. A young girl is lost and someone's trying to kill her. Despite how impolite it is, we show it to five-year olds.
Impoliteness is fundamental to greatness in our work.
Impolite storytelling creates greater events. If the story is polite, the events are small. If it's polite, it's forgettable. Impoliteness makes the events greater. More is at stake.
You should call this class dramatic science.
Nice.

Even when we're not speaking, I want us to be moving forward.
Right.
And I feel right now, you're waiting, you're not moving forward.
Okay. Yeah.

Where I have a note for you is in video. You're not prioritizing your video enough. Your video was chasing after your words. Don't let that happen, make sure the video is first.
It's okay if you take a moment to make sure you have the video that is going to say the line for you, instead of "what did I just say? Oh yeah…" and then using your video for that line. Video first.
If you don't have the video, you have to say it "good," you have to try to convince us you have video. That is so much work. Don't try to convince us you have video, have video.
I get nervous about the delay.
That's going to happen. I'll point out that it takes some time to shoot the video, but once you've shot it, it doesn't take much time to recall it.
Out of all the stuff we talk about, video is the unbreakable rule. I always want us to have video, regardless of style. I know it may sound a bit rude but when you don't have your video, then you're yapping.
It takes just a moment to identify the video and then to shoot it.
Can you spell out how I shoot the video?"
The answer to the question "What is the video?" is often the phrase, "How do I know?" You've got that line inviting him to Pilates. And then you've got the line "I know you're busy." Ask yourself, "How do I know he could join me at Pilates?" In that line, the video is of him on a mat next to you, sweating and smiling. And then going for lunch and having a salad. And him saying "Thanks Mom. I had a great time." Now you have the video for him joining you at Pilates.
And "I know you're busy." Okay. Ask yourself, "How do I know he's busy?" Well, in your video, "The last couple times I called he said 'Can't talk now Mom, I'm in a meeting.' And maybe he took a part-time job to make ends meet." Now you've got a video for him being busy.

Now, I don't have to convince people I know he's busy. I don't have to say it like I mean it that I know he's busy. I no longer have to do any of that. I actually do know he's busy. Simply.

How do I know you're busy? Extra job, two kids, car broke down. Boom. You've got your video.

And incidentally, as a bonus, now that I've done the work on "busy," I see it's related to "Pilates." He needs some "me time." A Pilates class would be good for him.

The details are always interesting once we shoot the video in great detail.

I know it sounds daunting. But we just shot the video of him joining you and him being busy, and it really didn't take much time at all.

No.

It's not like it's going to take me an hour to shoot the video for this line. It's just a few moments and then I have the video. To recall it takes almost no time. Once I've shot it, I've got it and now I have a reason to say this.

Talia, How's it going for you?

I don't know. I feel like I'm not connecting with it yet.

I thought, physiologically, you were too calm. The physiological aspects of being excited will help.

In a scene like this one, I might suggest you step off-camera and do a hundred jumping jacks and then come back and do the scene.

What happens when we're scared or excited? Our heart races, we get a bit out of breath. In order to induce that, we can do some jumping jacks or run around the parking lot or whatever to get our body excited. Get our belly involved.

You see how that might help if your heart races and you're out of breath?

Yeah. I think that's where the disconnect came from.

That's a good way to address where you're coming from.

That's a really good idea. Cool.

There were a few places in the scene where I wanted you to take a pause. When the tension is at its highest, don't just let it fritter away. When the tension is at its highest, take a moment so you can exploit that tension by making us wait for the resolution. That's creating a larger event. Look for those opportunities. Does that feel actionable?

Yes.

It's applicable in almost every scene. Make the audience anticipate.

Maybe I have the line "Here's what we're going to do." And then I pause. I have communicated that I'm going to say something. And then I pause. And then "here's the thing I'm going to tell you." That pause builds tension toward what I say next, creating a larger event.

Of course we can't pause after every line, we have to pick and choose.

When we shoot the video, we have an experience, we don't have lines.
When we don't have the experience, we can fall back into old habits. Our voice gets artificially high or we stress personal pronouns, for instance. Those are the habits. The video will take care of that.
You've gotten pretty good at covering up for the fact that you don't have video. So it's hard to break that habit. If you're a good yapper, it's pretty hard not to yap.
One solution is for you to stop trying to do it "good." Get rid of "good."
We don't want "good." We don't want or need "good." It's just not useful.
"True" is what we need. And "true" is inherently flawed. So embrace the flaws.

Instead of trying to look good, confront the audience with your unwillingness to look good. "I'm going to be onstage for an hour and a half and I'm not going to look good. Deal with it."
If you're trying to look good, you're giving the audience your power.
I'm not here to be liked. I'm not here to look good. I'm not here to sound good, I'm not here to convince you. I'm here to drop something on you. You deal with it.

If they see one hundred actors for the role, be one of the ten best or one of the ten worst. Don't be the middle eighty.
And I'm afraid that "good" approach might get you as high as eleventh but not top ten.
Eleven is as high as the "good" approach will get you. You've got to be willing to be one of the ten worst in order to be one of the ten best.
Perhaps up to now in your career, you've gotten away with it but here we're striving for something different.
Thank you.
You are welcome.

I feel like you're touching all the bases. To use a baseball analogy. You're touching first base, second, third and then home. But after touching first, go out to the bleachers and get a hot dog. Then after second, go into the stands and dance with the mascot. Then after third, go to the organ and play Take Me Out to the Ballgame. Then touch home. Don't just do the minimum.

Debra, anything rattling?
A while back you talked about an exercise where you asked actors to shoot the video of a piece word by word. Even little words like "the." Can you talk about that again?
Okay. You mentioned the word "The." Think of a video for "The."
It's just a little word.

No, a little word is "T.H.E." That's not the video for "The."

When you're saying "The... car." What does "The" mean? It means this specific car. Not any car but this specific one.

When you say "A," like "A car." What does "A" mean? It means "one of these" or "one of many."

People often think those little words are just there to connect the other words and that they don't need video. Not so. "The car" is different from "A car." What's the difference? It's in the video.

I'd like to suggest that when we learned words - when we were one and two and five and twenty-five years old - what we learned was actually the video of that word. There are usually arrows and action.

I used to enjoy the challenge of trying to draw a word. I don't have a chalkboard but anyway, someone give me a word and I'll try to describe a drawing.

The.

I might draw five x's and then circle one of them. That's "the."

Somebody else give me a word.

That.

Two x's, an arrow toward one of them.

Huh.

Two options and I choose one. That's what "that" means.

It's also what "this" means but in my video the arrow would go left if it's "this" and go right if it's "that." Same drawing, different arrows. That's just my video, yours could be different.

Again, that's what we learned the word meant when we were two years old. Now, we don't go "Gosh, what does 'That' mean again? Hmm." But when your brain chooses the word "That," it's choosing that image.

Your brain doesn't think "T.H.A.T." It thinks "two things with an arrow to one," and we say "That."

I wouldn't claim to be an expert in brains, by the way, or childhood development or cognition... but I would suggest that when our brain is functioning and we're choosing our own words as opposed to a writer giving us our words, that is what is happening.

When I do this exercise with actors, I ask that they go word by word. If the line is "I grew up in Iowa," we just go "I. I. I." What does "I" mean?

For me it's a circle with lots of arrows, surrounding and pointing to it. That's "I."

"Me" is slightly different. It's a circle with arrows surrounding it, pointing away.

"I" is pointing towards and "Me" is pointing away. That's just my video.

What about "Us?"

A cluster of circles with arrows pointing at them. "Us."

What about "Them?"

Circles over here, circles over here with a line dividing them and an arrow pointing in one direction. "Them."
Yeah. (Laugh) Wow.
Anytime we understand what a word means, it's a picture. Even words that are not an object.

I have often said that in your video, you cannot get too specific. And you can see by this conversation that I mean that.
If we're doing the work to this specificity - How does my character phrase this line? What are the specific words in between? What grammatical choices does he make? - the answers to all of that can truthfully be found within your video.
When we shoot the video to that specificity, I dare say we will find we can be truthful as well as memorized.

I'm just trying to illustrate how the brain works, when the words are mine. rather than when I've been given them and told to memorize. The truth is only when the words are mine.
I really like having these conversations. I'm just glad there is anybody who is interested enough to participate. (*Laugh*) I love actor geeks. Thanks for being an actor geek with me.

I saw a minute of rehearsal and the video was way better there than what's happening now. Your character says he has phone calls to make, you didn't see phone calls. You said "I've warned you about this." You didn't see yourself warning her.
Yeah, you're right.
I think as soon as the camera rolls, you start thinking Actor Brain thoughts like "Okay. Here's money time." That's where the big F has to come in. The more our instincts are "this is important," the bigger F we have to put in front of it.
Maybe you're seeing images after you've said something but certainly not before. If you don't see it first, you give a yappy reading.
I want you to trade "how good do I sound, how good do I look, do I make sense? Do they believe me?" Trade all of that in favor of video.

Joe, I liked your approach in general that you didn't overplay.
No, I didn't.
I was watching some footage of you today and I was taken with the fact that each time you strip that exterior stuff away, you're fascinating. All your drama stuff, all the heartbreaking stuff… the more we get rid of your exterior the more beautiful your interior becomes. You let us in in a way you otherwise can't let us in. When you overplay, we don't investigate as much because we don't need to.

Underplay. Keep your secrets.

I'm very encouraged in a number of ways.
I remember Polly, when we first started working together… To see you now not being in your own way. To not be in your head about acting but to really fight for her. You're seeing what she saw. You're fighting for her. And that outside influence of "How should I look?" or "How should I sound?" "Am I doing a good job?" That stuff is being very quiet. You're fighting… you're raging for your character. And I just want to fan that flame. When you fight for her, you make all that other stuff go away. Good work.

I say this a lot to stage actors, not as much to camera actors. It's the concept of "At and away."
In your scene with Debra, it feels as if your energy is going at Debra, at Debra, at Debra. Embrace away. You're getting stuck in an "at" energy. Embrace "away." Does that feel actionable?
Yes.
Good. That's with eyeline, body language and intention.
"At and away" is physical, it's mental, it's emotional. But also, energy-wise. Your energy feels like "at" right now. Embrace "away" as a contrast.

Your character has gotten too self-expressed. Too efficient at self-expression. I want to bring up more inefficiency in your expression. F it up. Don't be too good in your communicating.
Okay.
Okay?
I think I understand that.

Talia, anything rattling?
Yeah. When I'm doing comedy in this class… Like in your head, you're like "I can do comedy." I thought I was funny but then I find out I'm not hitting the moments. When you point out the moment, it's so obvious in the script. It was so clear in the script but I didn't catch that. But I want to get better at discovering that on my own.
Well put, Talia. I'm with you as far as how you're navigating that.
When I am chilling, Netflix and chilling, I watch lots of comedies. A favorite is Modern Family. I invite you guys, when you're watching comedy, look for examples of "1, 2, Pineapple" and they're everywhere.
In an episode I watched recently, one character said "I'm sure he's forgotten all about it." And another character enters and says "I can't stop thinking about it." I'm paraphrasing but that's the diagram.

One line is creating expectation and the next line is surprise. The humor works because of the expectation of "I'm sure it's this" and then surprise of "It's the opposite of what you just said."

That joke is told five times per episode of any good comedy ever. Whether it's The Office or Parks and Rec, Cheers... doesn't matter which ones, The Good Place... Look for that diagram. In an old classic comedy we'll see a character say "There's no way I'm going camping this weekend! There's no way I'm going camping this weekend!" Cut to: Camping.

Expectation: 1, 2, and surprise: pineapple. It's kind of every joke.

So Talia, when you say you do comedy and you're missing something, it's probably the opportunity to create greater tension and therefore greater surprise in our 1, 2, Pineapple. In comedy if it isn't happening, it's probably because the expectation isn't great enough and/or pineapple isn't opposite enough.

If we create greater expectation and then a larger surprise, we'll be diagramming comedy more correctly.

Well, that's about as much fun as I can have in three minutes. *(laugh)* Good. I hope that feels actionable.

Yes.

Keep in mind, sometimes you have the 1, 2 and your scene partner has the pineapple. Or vice-versa.

We're focussed on acting but dramatic theory is true across the board. Not only in acting but writing, performance, direction.

So even though it may not be a "big laugh" pineapple, there's still value in expectation and surprise, even if it's not hysterical.

You're absolutely right, Joe. I'm glad for that perspective.

In a way, I want that expectation and surprise to be part of our synapse. It's built into things like "don't do it good, arrows, unreasonableness." There's expectation and surprise involved in all of that diagramming.

That's how an actor is scintillating, fascinating. Everyone can say the same lines. The actor who is scintillating and fascinating is the one who has that synapse. Expectation and surprise is huge.

Look for opportunities to create expectation towards what's going to be said. Everytime a question is asked, there is the expectation of an answer. Therefore it's an opportunity to heighten tension towards that answer which is going to be the release of tension.

Alejandro, what's rattling?

Using more of myself, instead of trying to become… especially in an audition situation where you don't have a lot of time, using more of myself.

Great. Thanks for sharing your process with us.

You may be moving toward revealing yourself rather than covering up or packaging yourself somehow. Not putting a shine or a sheen on yourself. You're stripping all that away.

I now see you willing to just be you. I don't think it's a limitation. I think it's a revealing.

That makes a lot of sense.

What I want you to be comfortable with is your own self "in the role," not your own self "as the role," necessarily. I think that's part of what's happening now.

Do you have to put something on to be the character or do you have to take something off? In this conversation you're leaning toward taking something off. I'm all for that.

That makes sense.

To fine tune a bit and get a bit semantic, I'd rather we start with "I'm comfortable with myself" rather than "I'm comfortable as myself." If I'm comfortable with myself I can do anything but if I have to "be myself," that's going to limit what I can do.

It's a very fine distinction but you don't have to limit the choices for your character to just whatever comes naturally.

Perhaps your character is silly or has a quick temper and those things don't come naturally to you. But you can do those things and be powerful. Because you're doing those things doesn't have to make you feel disempowered.

To take it back to what we were talking about, being on the precipice of putting your armor on or taking it off… Our armor was me not being comfortable with myself. That's why I armored up with this character, these choices. As opposed to I can take the armor off and take chances and find I don't need the armor after all. *(laugh)* I love to take these analogies as far as they'll go.

I think I understood 99% of that.

If you did, I'm impressed. *(laugh)*

Polly, anything rattling?

A scene I'm doing tonight seems to be ethnic. How should I approach that?

In this case, I would advise you not to put any particular ethnicity on it. I agree, your son is Giovanni and his cousin is Izzio, it sounds like it could be an Italian family.

If you are just okay with an accent, I like to suggest a 10% rule. Just a flavoring of what the accent might be. Just a flavoring, a hint.

For the purposes of our acting class, I'd like to focus on what's similar between us and our characters, rather than what's different.

Does that feel actionable?

It feels easier.

Overall, don't do any accent unless you're good at it.

Let's take away from this that the universal story is the one we want to tell, not the specific story.

In this scene, make it a scene that every Mom can understand, every son, every parent, every child.

One thing I haven't said in a while is to choose love. The audience will care more about each of you when each of you care more about each other.

We talked about the "Intimate glimpse." One practical way is to be preoccupied. When our character is preoccupied, we are helping the audience see in to our secret. As they read our minds, we are giving them something to read. The more preoccupied you are with what you're not saying, the bigger the thing is that you're not saying, the bigger the secret. That's what the "Intimate glimpse" is.
Preoccupation is one way. Taken further, it can lead to obsession.
Obsession is dramatically powerful as well.

The more difficult it is to say something, the bigger that thing is that you're trying to say. If it's harder to unearth the secret, that means it's buried deeper. It's got more power, it's got to come out.
That makes a lot of sense.
Coming along nicely.

Something we've talked about before, which crept back in here, is your tendency to say all of your lines with equal importance.
I did it again?
Be sure to throw some lines away. Some lines are not as important as others.
You got it.

Shawn, I saw something I enjoyed there. What I usually call a "false ending."
That's useful comedically.
We talked about that.
It's fun to send the message that "I'm done talking," and then decide to add something. You had a couple of those. I'm glad you took that note and you did it well.

I noticed something tonight that happened with a few of you. It's what I usually call the "Actor motor." It's that "keep going, keep going, keep going..." motor that actors have. That's artificial.
Actors have that "keep going" motor because there's a camera in their face and they have a scene to do and lines they have to say before they forget them. *(laugh)*

So they've got that actor motor and I'd really like to dial that thing back. Sometimes let's not keep going. We can just stop. Later, we can go again.

There were moments tonight that were lovely but it was "Oh, I have to talk, I've got more lines..." Let that lovely moment sit there and be lovely. Let's just enjoy it. Watch out for the "keep going" motor.

In real life, we don't know we have more lines or we always have more lines so there's no rush.

The artificiality of doing a scene and having lines of dialogue and a camera watching you, those artificial things - the pressures of that - make us feel uncomfortable taking time. Fight against that.

Does that feel actionable?

Yeah.

Raise your hand if you think that applies to you.

(All raise hands except Polly)

Polly, is your hand up?

It is now. (laugh)

Those lovely moments? We've earned that.

We lie awake at night dreaming of those beautiful moments in acting, beautiful moments of drama and comedy, affecting the world, changing the world, creating more love, beauty and understanding in the world... When we've done that, just take a second and really be in that love.

Good class tonight. I'm so grateful. Thank you.

Debra, anything rattling?

I always have a plan coming into class and today I want to actually achieve it.

Great conversation to be having.

I'm sure we all identify with that. Perhaps we have an audition or opening night or the first day of shooting. There's that expectation we place upon ourselves.

When you rehearse it... you know how it's sometimes better in your living room?

Got it.

The diagram you're talking about... It's great in your bedroom but then you get in the lights or in front of people and it's not as good somehow. I think we can definitely all identify with that.

Here is perhaps the antidote for that poison. It's worth it to look for a cure for that disease.

You know what I'm going to say. Here's the antidote: Don't do it good.

I know.

You knew I was going to say that, right?

I did.

The idea that the one you did in your living room doesn't count but this one does? No, it doesn't. Don't let yourself think this one matters. The only difference we're finding between doing it by yourself and doing it in front of people, is you're trying to do it good now. Somehow we've decided - and it makes perfect sense - that this is the one that counts.

What happens when we think "this one counts?" We try to look good right? We try to impress. That's when we need to be reminded, don't do it good.

Avoiding the good way will give you ten possible avenues to flourish and surprise us and surprise yourself. The un-good way. The un-good way gives us opportunities, the good way gives us answers.

It's like you've jumped out of an airplane in a parachute, there's an X on the ground and you have to avoid it. Don't land in the X. It looks like a target and where I'm supposed to go but we want to land anywhere but there.

Instead of "this one counts," it's time to not do it good. Give yourself a chance to explore what you didn't think was a possibility.

Remember the phrase "The only way I cannot say my line is the way I know I'm going to." That's how we throw towards the bulls-eye but make sure we miss.

No home runs allowed. *(laugh)* Bunt. Strike out, take a walk, hit the ball but run to third instead of first. No home runs. And if there is a home run in there, it'll be a pleasant surprise, won't it?

As opposed to home run, home run, home run. Which is what we think we're supposed to do. No. Swing and miss., foul it off, take a pitch. Really play the game. If you have the game figured out, that's not a very complex game.

Does that feel actionable?

It does.

You know, the audience could read the script and they'd already get the good way. They could read it and go "I get this. That means exactly that and that means exactly that and that means exactly that..."

Actors aren't even needed if they are only providing the good way. We don't need an actor if we assume what the page already tells us. We could all just read the script. *(laugh)*

The line isn't complex. The line is the line. The actor is providing the complexity. Avoiding the good way gives the line complexity and something for the audience to be curious about beyond what we say. Even in contrast to what we say.

Debra, my fantasy version of you as an actor includes exactly what we're talking about. It will be when you don't give an F about how good you are. How good we think you are. When you successfully and actually in your fiber don't give an F.

I know that's against your nature. Of course you care. We're compassionate, caring, open... Actors are the most wonderful people in the world because of the inquiry they're on. So, of course it's not in our nature to throw a big capital F in front of everything. It feels wrong, it feels bad. It's something we've been told our whole lives not to do.

Embrace the freedom to do it wrong. Embrace the opportunity to do it wrong. The piece of paper and the typing on the piece of paper is obvious. It's easy. Embrace the discomfort, the uncertainty. That line reading I prepared is safe. That line reading that happens naturally is dangerous. Embrace the danger.

I wouldn't want to watch a wire-walker walk on the sidewalk but I'll watch when he's up on the wire.

Sounds fun?

Very fun.

I appreciate this conversation.

Me too.

The human being doesn't know how to say the line. They just care about their daughter or their neighbor or winning the election. I want to see you caring about winning the election, not caring about being a good actor.

I haven't mentioned this in a while but here's a reminder: Don't say the sad line sadly. It's redundant. The audience could read the sad line in the script and get the sad reading. We have to divert from that. What we're doing is in defiance of that. Find something else to bring along with that sad line. In contrast to the sad line.

We can substitute any emotional value here - don't say the angry line angrily, etc - bring a contrasting thought to the angry line.

Of course, we might say the sad line sadly if it's the exception to the rule, but look for opportunities to bring the contrasting idea.

Talia, it looked to me like, in your actor brain, you were feeling pretty powerful with that equation.

It looked like "I'm having fun manipulating the scene and putting my spin on it and doing it wrong." Did that feel powerful?

Umm. Yeah. Yes.

I hope you felt more electricity in your belly.

Definitely.

Great, great, great.

Sometimes we can "Fall victim" to the scene or "Fall victim" to the character description. "She's only this or she's only that."

Keep in mind, if you say it, you're responsible for the video. Not after you've said it, before.

What does it look like? Now I can talk about it. What does it look like? Now I can talk about it. If I say it, I've got to know what it looks like, otherwise I would have never chosen that word. Without the video, how would you know what word to choose? You wouldn't.

Don't let yourself talk first. See it first. Hold yourself to that standard.

It doesn't take much time to shoot the video. And then even less time to recall the video and use it to drive your language. Our brain works faster than our mouth. Much faster.

You can look at your script and go "Okay, I have a three page scene. How many words do I say? Oh, 328 words." Okay, get to work shooting 328 videos.

Your character talks about going to rehab. Get specific in your images. What does rehab look like? We cannot get too specific in our video.

Cannot get too specific?

No. Now I look at the video and get specific and there's a cafeteria, Doris, the lunch lady who's nice to everybody and serves grilled cheese sandwiches. We can continue to get more specific. Pancakes on Sundays.

Just by getting specific, it becomes more interesting. Doris has been working here for 27 years. The more I look at it, the more interesting it becomes.

I can't have a general photograph. There's a photograph or there isn't. If it's a photograph of my uncle when he was in the marines, all I have to do is look at it and it's not general anymore. Really look at it. The picture is specific. I don't have to get specific, it is specific. He's wearing a green uniform and in the desert somewhere. Holding his gun across his body, it's a black and white picture. As soon as I look at the picture the details are there. I just have to examine.

As I look at it, I see there's a medal on his chest. Did he get that for bravery? Now, I'm interested. A vague image of a man won't do. We have to really look at it.

I try to imagine his face and his eyes…

At the risk of contradicting myself, those details don't actually matter. What color hair and how tall? No one cares. Not useful. It's not the specifics of the image that matters. It's how I feel about the images that is useful.

What are my feelings and memories when I am confronted by this picture? That's what we're exploring.

In the example of my uncle in the marines, I look at the picture and I feel proud. Or I feel remorse. Those are things that matter dramatically. His eye color has no dramatic weight.

I sometimes say, "I'm here, my video is there. In the space between us, there is a place to swim. The murky, swirling waters between me and my video."

The video is there to give us the experience. Then we swim in the feelings and reactions that the experience gives us.

We talk a lot about video but the video is not the end of the process. The end of the process is swimming in that pool between me and my video. What are those waters like? Those currents and temperatures of that pool that I swim in.

An exercise I sometimes do is ask you to shoot the video of this line: "I saw him at the counter." When you have a video for that line, raise your hand.

(5 seconds)

Okay, good. Now the color of his hair doesn't matter, what matters is how you feel about him.

When I see him at the counter, he is in a trench coat and facing away from me. He makes me feel intimidated and maybe a little scared and anxious. That's what counts, how I feel in relation to what I see. You can shoot whatever video will give you the desired reaction.

Debra, when you see him at the counter, how does he make you feel?

Intrigued. (laugh) He's a handsome man. In the grocery store.

Good. I'm intrigued. Alejandro, when you see him at the counter, how does he make you feel?

He's got my coat that he stole. I feel frustrated and angry.

Good. As soon as we look at the image, it becomes interesting. The story of the image. As soon as we create an image and then investigate it, confront it, the image becomes fascinating.

Jen, how about you?

I just want to back away, not because he's scary or anything but because he talks a lot and is awkward and I don't really have time…

Good. When we focus on how the image makes us feel, something interesting always happens.

This has been really helpful.

Alejandro, anything rattling?

I've been thinking about… you remember how I used to approach roles with a lot of anger or characters that were hard? I'm thinking about finding a more positive approach.

I'm always grateful for these conversations.

The way I'll phrase it is "Love is the only thing anyone cares about." Choose love whenever you have the opportunity.

You're looking at positive and negative, we might call it loving and non-loving, is that right?

Yeah.

People identify with love and care about love. *(laugh)* They don't care about anything else. Justice is about love. Activism is about love. Medicine is about love. Everything is about love, ultimately, or trying to find it.

So when it comes to making choices in a scene, do you care or do you not care? You care.

Okay, yeah.

Do you love this person or do you not love this person? You love this person. Do you love opera or do you kind of like opera? You love opera. That's our default setting. Within that, wonderfully powerful stories are often told. How difficult it is to love, how hard it is to find love, how difficult it is to keep love. Somewhere along the line, you can look at any great story and it's about that.

So that's not all kissy-kissy, is it? There are a lot of difficulties and challenges and obstacles to love. That is also a part of our powerful storytelling. That love isn't always sappy and sweet, love can be painful and difficult.

All of that hold together?

Yes.

Great. Even those roles without love, our character doesn't love, we're the bad guy, we're the killer, the extortionist... We get to play those roles too. They're a lot of fun. Even those roles are about love. Those stories are the denial of love and the lack of love.

If we can point the audience toward love, illuminate the path towards love, that's going to be a compelling experience for them.

Harry Potter illuminates the path toward love. So does Wizard of Oz and To Kill a Mockingbird. It can be difficult, Schindler's List is about love. If it matters, it's about love. Everything is about love if it's powerful.

That's something I'll lead with in my auditions.

I've already had a great class and we just got started.

Alejandro, how's it going?

I was trying to amp up what we talked about at the beginning of class.

In what way?

That loving approach. I was trying to genuinely be interested in her. To learn what she was teaching me. That mentor, mentee relationship.

Great. I felt that love out here. In the story, you just met. But somehow, you met her and you loved her.

Sometimes in the audition process in Hollywood you may have what is called a "Chemistry read." They want to see your chemistry with the other actors. That's what it is. It's love. Capital L love.

You made the choice for your character, "I want to know this woman," and it gave you great chemistry. And she did as well. Her character was interested in you. That interest from both of you provided the love that drove this scene. And it made us care about you and what happens next.

There are a thousand things to think about. I've got about a hundred and twenty five sayings I use. They're written down somewhere and new ones emerge all the time. You can't do all of them, all the time. Nor do you have to. No one can juggle 125 balls. Pick four or five and juggle those. And then if you need to, put one down and pick up another.

I'm excited for someone besides me and this class to know how good you are. That's starting to happen. You're starting to get out there and people are starting to see that you're viable. You've done the work. They're going to be excited to meet you and excited about what you're offering.

If you don't mind, I'm going to begin wrapping up class. I've had a great time as always.
Anything I can do in closing for you Debra?
No. It's just been fun. It's great to be back. And I learn something every time. I seriously do.
We can study for years and years and still be learning stuff.
And even if it's something I've heard before, it's been a long time since I heard that and the refreshers are helpful in not only understanding, but in incorporating these ideas.
And I am proud of the work you guys are doing as well. Alright, thank you. I enjoy these conversations.

NOTE FROM DUANE:
Thank you for being interested in this book. And apparently getting all the way to the end. I hope you found it actionable!
actorsworkhouse@gmail.com and @NotReallyHamlet on Instagram
Keep Acting!

INDEX
CRITICAL THINKING FOR THE ACTOR